GCSE AQA
Music

There's a lot to get your ears around in AQA GCSE Music, and the
new Grade 9-1 courses are tougher than ever. Luckily, help is at hand...

This brilliant CGP book explains everything you'll need
to do well in your coursework and exams. Musical knowledge,
study pieces, compositions — you name it.

What's more, each section has plenty of warm-up questions and
exam-style practice. And to help you finish the course on a high note,
we've even included a realistic practice exam at the end!

Complete
Revision & Practice
Everything you need to pass the exams!

Contents

Published by CGP

Editors: Cathy Lear, Caley Simpson, Ben Train, Ruth Wilbourne

Contributors: Catherine Baird, John Deane, Elena Delaney, Rob Hall, Angela Major, Peter Maries, Mel McIntyre, Sam Norman, James Reevell.

With thanks to Hannah Totman and Karen Wells for the proofreading.
With thanks to Jan Greenway, Laura Jakubowski and Holly Poynton for the copyright research.

Audio CD edited and mastered by Neil Hastings.

For copyright reasons, this book can only be sold in the UK.

ISBN: 978 1 78294 614 4

Clipart from Corel®

Printed by Elanders Ltd, Newcastle upon Tyne.

Based on the classic CGP style created by Richard Parsons.

What You Have To Do For GCSE Music

Music GCSE doesn't cover every single aspect of music — if it did it would take forever. Instead you focus on four main 'Areas of Study' (AoS for short).

You Learn About **Four Areas of Study**

For each Area of Study you'll learn the basics of that style or period — e.g. the musical structures, the instruments used, the context the music was originally created in, etc.

You have to be able to answer questions on all four Areas of Study, but you only need to look at study pieces for two Areas of Study. One of these has to be AoS1, but you (or your teacher) can choose which of the other pieces you study. The four Areas of Study are:

> **AoS1 — WESTERN CLASSICAL TRADITION 1650-1910** (covered in Section 6)
> Your study piece is the 2nd Movement from Haydn's *Symphony No. 101 in D Major* (*The Clock Symphony*).　*This is the compulsory piece — you have to study it.*

> **AoS2 — POPULAR MUSIC** (covered in Section 7)
> Your study pieces are The Beatles' 'With A Little Help From My Friends', 'Within You Without You' and 'Lucy in the Sky With Diamonds' from the album *Sgt. Pepper's Lonely Hearts Club Band*.

> **AoS3 — TRADITIONAL MUSIC** (covered in Section 8)
> Your study pieces are Santana's 'Smooth', 'Migra' and 'Love of My Life' from the album *Supernatural*.

> **AoS4 — WESTERN CLASSICAL TRADITION SINCE 1910** (covered in Section 9)
> Your study pieces are Aaron Copland's 'Saturday Night Waltz' and 'Hoe-Down' from *Rodeo*.

They Test You With a **Listening Exam...**

worth 40% of the total marks

At the end of Year 11 you do an exam. You listen to excerpts of pieces from all four Areas of Study and answer questions on what you hear. You'll also have questions on your study pieces.

...And With **Coursework**

The coursework is work done during the course. Obviously. It's split into two chunks:

> **PERFORMING**
>
> *worth 30% of the total marks*
> 1) You do two performances.
> 2) One has to be a solo performance. This can be a piece you play or sing, a DJ performance or a realisation using music technology (e.g. sequencing).
> 3) For the other, you have to perform as part of an ensemble. There must be 2 or more players in the ensemble, with distinct and separate parts.

> **COMPOSING**
>
> *worth 30% of the total marks*
> 1) You compose two pieces. One is based on a composition brief. You'll be given a choice of four composition briefs, which might have a stimulus (e.g. a poem, photo or some notation).
> 2) Your second composition can be anything you like — it's a free composition.

Err, Miss... Is it too late to change to Physics?

Welcome to the wonderful world of GCSE Music. Breathe in the cool clear air. Listen to the birds. Relax.

Component 1 — Understanding Music

At the end of the course, you have the joy of a listening exam. All 1 hour and 30 minutes of it.

The Exam Tests All Four Areas of Study

1) The listening and understanding music exam is worth 96 marks (40% of your total mark). It's divided into two sections — Section A and Section B.

2) Section A is the listening section — it's worth 68 marks and lasts for one hour. You have to listen to and answer questions on excerpts of music (played on a CD). You'll be told which Area of Study each excerpt is from and how many times it'll be played. You'll be given writing time for each question.

3) You have to answer all 8 questions in this section — they're on unfamiliar pieces from all four Areas of Study (most only need short answers). One question will probably require musical dictation.

4) Section B is the contextual understanding section — it's worth 28 marks and lasts for 30 minutes. You have to answer the first question, which is on the study piece from AoS1 (Haydn's Clock Symphony).

5) You then have to answer one of the next three questions — on whichever other AoS study pieces that you've looked at. There aren't any excerpts to listen to in this section — it's all based on your own knowledge. One part of each question needs a longer answer (it's worth 8 marks).

Some Questions are Multiple Choice

If you're stuck — guess the answer. There's a chance of getting it right.

Don't mess these up by rushing — read all the options carefully.

What is the texture of this excerpt? Put a cross in the correct box. *[1 mark]*

☐ homophonic   ☐ monophonic   ☐ contrapuntal   ☐ antiphonal

Some Questions Just Need a Short Answer

These questions are only worth a few marks so don't waste time writing your answer out in a nice long sentence — just write down one good word for each mark.

Name two instruments playing the theme in this excerpt. *[2 marks]*

For questions worth 3 or 4 marks, you'll have to write a bit more.

They Sometimes Give You an Outline of the Music

You'll be given an outline of part of the music called a 'skeleton score'. It will just show part of the music — the melody, rhythm or lyrics, say. The skeleton score will help you with answering the question. You might be asked to fill in the pitch, rhythm or chords of a short section of the music.

Fill in the missing notes in bar 4. The rhythm is given above the stave. *[3 marks]*

Some Questions in Section B Need Longer Answers

There are a couple of questions where you have to write a longer answer — a few paragraphs of writing. Make sure you cover all the key points of the question in your answer.

Explain how The Beatles use melody, metre and rhythm in 'With A Little Help From My Friends'. *[8 marks]*

Shiver me timbers — 'tis the skeleton score...

Concentrate on answering just a few of the questions each time the music's played — it's less confusing. Have a go at the Practice Exam on p.167 to give you an idea of what it'll be like.

Component 2 — Performing

Pick your pieces carefully and practise till your neighbours beg for mercy.

You Have To Do **Two Performances**

The combined time of both your performances must be at least four minutes.
Your ensemble performance must be at least one minute long.

SOLO PERFORMANCE

You simply play one solo piece of your own choice. It can be a traditional performance,
a DJ performance or a realisation using music technology (if you're using multi-tracking, you must
have a minimum of three tracks, at least one of which must be performed live). Your solo can be
accompanied (if it was written with an accompaniment, you have to perform it with accompaniment).

ENSEMBLE PERFORMANCE

For your ensemble piece, there must be at least two of you playing or singing, and your part can't
be doubled. Like the solo performance, this can be a traditional performance, a DJ performance
(with other DJs or live musicians) or a realisation using music technology. For a multi-tracked
performance, you must perform at least three tracks (one must be live), and there must be one or
more other parts (one has to be live). You have to play a different piece than your solo piece.

You have to hand in the music you've worked from for each performance. This can be
a score, a lead sheet or a recording of the piece made by someone else — a 'guide recording'.
(For music technology performances, you have to hand in an annotation, giving details of how
you produced your piece.) You also have to hand in digital recordings of your performances.

You Get Marks for the **Difficulty** of the **Piece...**

1) It's obvious really — a very simple piece will get fewer marks for difficulty than a complicated piece.
   But there's no point trying to play something that you're not capable of and then messing it up...

2) Choose your pieces carefully — ideally they should be the hardest level that you can
   play well. If you pick something too easy, you'll be throwing away difficulty marks.
   If you pick something too hard, you won't be able to play your best, and you'll lose marks
   for musicality. Get your music teacher or instrument teacher's advice on what to play.

3) If you choose an easy piece, you won't be able to get as many marks for the areas described below.

...And Marks for the **Quality** of Your **Playing**

*Music technology performances
are also marked on balance,
panning, effects and style.*

You need to show off your 'musicality' and technique (how well you play your
instrument, including techniques specific to your instrument). You get marks for:

1) **ACCURACY:** Learn the notes, play them in time and in tune. Most importantly, keep going
   — your performance needs to be fluent. Lots of stopping and starting or slowing down for
   tricky bits will lose you marks. Don't worry about the odd slip, but start off well prepared.
   For DJ and music technology performances, this includes pitch and balance as well.

2) **EXPRESSION AND INTERPRETATION:** Your performance needs to be expressive — to make
   the audience feel something. Pay attention to stuff like dynamics, tempo, mood, articulation
   and phrasing. It's all about how well you communicate — i.e. how you interpret the music.

When you're playing in an ensemble, there are other things that you'll get marks for. Play in time and
in tune with the other players. Really listen to the other parts, so you know when you should be part of
the background and when you should make your part stand out — the ensemble should be balanced.

Practice makes perfect...

No doubt people have been going on at you about practising since you were knee-high to a piccolo.
It gets boring after a while. I expect you know that you need to do lots of practice. So I'll say no more.

Component 3 — Composing

For one composition, you can write whatever you like — but for the other, you have to follow a brief.

You Have to Write **Two Pieces** for **Coursework**

1) The <u>total</u> time for both pieces has to be <u>at least three minutes</u>
   (you won't get <u>any</u> marks if they're <u>less</u> than three minutes).

2) You <u>don't</u> have to perform your compositions <u>yourself</u> (but you can if you want to).

3) You can compose for <u>any</u> combination of <u>instruments</u>, <u>voices</u> or <u>DJs</u> and
   can use <u>technology</u> (unless the composition brief tells you otherwise).

4) One piece you write has to follow a <u>composition brief</u>:

   - The composition brief will be given to you by the <u>exam board</u>.
   - There will be <u>four different composition briefs</u> to choose from.
   - You can <u>choose</u> which one you do (though your <u>teacher</u> might suggest which one to pick).
   - The brief might include a <u>stimulus</u> — <u>written words</u> (e.g. a <u>poem</u> or some <u>text</u>),
     <u>images</u> (e.g. a <u>photo</u> or <u>film clip</u>) or some <u>notation</u> (e.g. a short <u>melody</u> or <u>rhythm</u>).

5) You should be given the composition brief <u>halfway</u> through your GCSE course — by which
   point, you should have <u>studied</u> the different areas (and looked at the <u>study pieces</u>) in detail.

6) The other piece you write is a <u>free composition</u> — it can be in <u>any style</u> you like.

Each Piece is Marked on **Six** Different **Categories**

Each composition is worth <u>36 marks</u>, based on two different categories (there are up to <u>18 marks</u>
available for each category — you need to use <u>at least two</u> different elements to get all 18 marks).

RHYTHM, METRE, TEXTURE, MELODY, STRUCTURE AND FORM:
To get top marks in this category, think about things like <u>changing time signatures</u>,
using <u>compound metres</u>, <u>syncopated</u> and <u>dotted</u> rhythms, <u>cross-rhythms</u> or <u>tempo changes</u>
(including <u>rubato</u>) — see Section 2. Try using <u>homophonic</u> and <u>polyphonic</u> textures,
<u>imitation</u>, <u>canon</u> or <u>antiphony</u>, <u>ostinatos</u> (or <u>riffs</u>), <u>conjunct</u> or <u>disjunct</u> melodies,
different <u>ornaments</u> or <u>blue notes</u>. Texture is covered in Section 3 and melody is covered
in Section 4. You could use <u>one</u> of the forms covered in Section 4, such as <u>ternary</u>,
<u>rondo</u>, <u>theme and variation</u>, <u>ground bass</u>, <u>popular song form</u>, or <u>12-bar blues</u> (see p.130).

HARMONY, TONALITY, TIMBRE, DYNAMICS, PHRASING AND ARTICULATION:
Think about all four types of <u>cadence</u>, using <u>major</u> and <u>minor keys</u>, <u>modes</u>, different types of
<u>harmony</u>, <u>changing key</u> (<u>modulation</u>), <u>dissonance</u> or <u>pedal notes</u>. This is all covered in Section 3.
You should try and use both <u>solo</u> instruments/voices and <u>groupings</u> of instruments or voices,
<u>synthesized</u> or <u>digitally-produced sounds</u>, <u>tremolo</u>, <u>vibrato</u>, <u>reverb</u> or <u>distortion</u> (for appropriate
instruments or voices). You should also use a variety of <u>dynamics</u> (including <u>crescendos</u> and
<u>diminuendos</u>), as well as a range of phrasing and articulation (e.g. <u>legato</u>, <u>staccato</u>, <u>tenuto</u> or
<u>marcato</u>). See p.19-20 for dynamics and articulation and Section 5 for instruments and timbre.

For each composition, you have to produce a <u>programme note</u> — a <u>written report</u> that covers:
- The <u>purpose</u> or <u>intention</u> of the piece (you should specify the <u>audience</u> or <u>occasion</u> you wrote it for).
- The <u>musical elements</u> you chose (e.g. the texture, structure   *Each programme note should be*
  or rhythms you used — anything from the lists above).   *about 150 words long.*
- Any <u>equipment</u> you used to compose the piece.

You have to hand in a <u>recording</u> of each composition, as well as a <u>written version</u>
and your <u>programme note</u>. There's more information about these on p.7.

Component 3 — Composing

Well, the good news is — the compositions you have to do for GCSE only need to be a total of 3 minutes long. No one's expecting an opera. Something short will do.

Here Are Some **General Things** To Think About...

DEVELOPING YOUR MUSICAL IDEAS

Don't just use a good idea once and then forget about it. Build up and develop the good bits — e.g. by changing the rhythm from short notes to long notes or the key from major to minor. See Section 3 for loads more techniques and devices for developing your ideas.

MAKING THE STYLE CONVINCING

Listen to lots of music from the style you're composing in.
Make your piece sound like 'the real thing' by using similar musical ideas — e.g. in a Baroque gigue, use a lively tempo, regular beat and a harpsichord.

THE POTENTIAL AND LIMITS OF YOUR RESOURCES

Once you've chosen the instruments, think about all the ways they can make interesting and contrasting sounds — e.g. pizzicato bits for strings. But also remember the limitations — e.g. clarinet players need time to breathe. Think about the highest and lowest notes your chosen instruments can play — there's no point composing a brilliant piece if no one can play it.

One of your pieces will have to meet the composition brief, so there'll be extra things you have to bear in mind to match the brief.

STRUCTURE

Organise your music with a clear, definite structure (there's lots of information on different structures throughout this book). Even if your composition doesn't follow a traditional form, you'll need to make sure it doesn't just ramble on aimlessly.

When You're Composing, Make Plans **Before** You Start

1) Making a musical plan helps to organise your ideas — it's a bit like writing an essay plan. It'll also help when it comes to writing your composing log.

2) Music's got to be organised, or it just sounds like a load of random notes. The most basic bit of organisation is the timing (beats in a bar). The next biggest chunk is the phrasing.

3) The overall shape is called the structure or form. The structure could be the verses and chorus in a pop song, or the movements of a symphony. Composers usually decide on the structure of a piece of music before they get into the detail.

4) It's OK to design your own musical plan, but a lot of people use 'tried and tested' structures like the ones described throughout this book — because they know they'll work.

5) 'Tried and tested' structures are like templates. The general organisation of your ideas is decided for you — you just need to add the details.

6) For the piece that follows the composition brief, it's probably a good idea to use a 'tried and tested' structure as your composition will need to be in a particular style or form.

7) Your plan should include ways to vary the different sections — have a look on the next page for some ideas.

Clarinet players need time to breathe? Amateurs...

So the main thing to take away from this page is 'be organised'. I'm not expecting you to be organised in all aspects of your life, just in your compositions — and planning really helps.

Component 3 — Composing

There are lots of things you need to think about when composing. This is not a complete list (just a few general ideas), but it'll give you a few things to bear in mind.

Most Music Uses **Repetition** Repetition Repetition...

1) <u>Repetition</u> means using a <u>musical idea</u> — a chunk of tune — <u>more than once</u>.
2) Repeating bits is a really good way of giving music <u>shape</u>. A recognisable tune works like a <u>landmark</u> — the audience recognises that tune <u>later</u> in the piece. That's how <u>choruses</u> work.
3) If you're planning <u>your own</u> piece of music, try repeating the best part of the tune.
4) You can even repeat <u>whole sections</u> — in <u>rondo form</u> (see p.93), one section is repeated lots of times.

...and **Contrast**

Repetition is really important — but <u>constant repetition</u> is <u>boring</u>. Good compositions balance repetition with <u>contrast</u>. The aim is to do something <u>different</u> from the repeated bits to add <u>variety</u>. Here are some ways you can <u>vary</u> your compositions:

These changes will get you extra marks for your compositions.

PITCH AND TONALITY

You can create contrast by changing the <u>organisation of pitch</u> — e.g. changing the melody from a <u>high register</u> to a <u>low register</u>, and swapping between <u>conjunct</u> and <u>disjunct</u> tunes (see p.54). You can also change the tonality by <u>modulating</u> between <u>major</u> and <u>minor keys</u>.

TEMPO AND RHYTHM

Changing <u>speed</u> from <u>fast</u> to <u>slow</u> (or vice versa) is a good way of creating contrast. You can also change the rhythms — try a mix of <u>dotted</u> and <u>straight rhythms</u>, or <u>long</u> and <u>short notes</u>. You can change the <u>articulation</u> too — try <u>legato</u>, <u>staccato</u>, <u>slurs</u> and <u>accents</u> to vary your piece.

DYNAMICS

Changes in <u>dynamics</u> (<u>loud</u> to <u>soft</u> and vice versa, and <u>crescendos</u> and <u>diminuendos</u>) will instantly create contrast.

TEXTURE

Changing between a thin, <u>monophonic</u> texture to a thicker <u>homophonic</u> or <u>polyphonic</u> texture (see p.45) will create contrast.

Decide How To **Hand In** Your Work

For each piece, you give in three things — a <u>written version</u>, a <u>recording</u> (though you won't be marked on the <u>quality</u> of the recording, just the composition) and a <u>programme note</u>. There are a few <u>options</u> for how you present your written version.

1) The **WRITTEN VERSION** can be either a <u>score</u> (either <u>handwritten</u> or <u>computer generated</u>), a <u>lead sheet</u> (e.g. a <u>vocal line</u> with <u>accompanying chords</u>) or a <u>written account</u> (a <u>guide</u> to what the listener should <u>hear</u> in the piece).
2) Give as much <u>information</u> as possible. <u>Dynamics</u>, <u>tempo</u>, <u>expression</u> and <u>articulation</u> will all improve your mark. There should be <u>enough detail</u> for someone else to be able to <u>recreate</u> your piece.

The **RECORDING** must be <u>saved digitally</u>.

Even though you don't get marks for the quality of the recording, good recordings are easier to mark. It's also in your best interests to produce an accurate one.

The **PROGRAMME NOTE** is a <u>written report</u>. It should be about <u>150 words</u> long.

The Basics

These two pages give the <u>essential basics</u> you'll need to get through Music GCSE.
Make sure you know everything here before you go on into the rest of the book.

3 | TWO LINES OF MUSIC |
The top line of music has got a tune
— it's the <u>melody</u>. The bottom line
is the <u>accompaniment</u>.

1 | CLEF |
These symbols at the start of a
line tell you how <u>high</u> or <u>low</u> to
play the notes. All the different
clefs are covered on <u>page 10</u>.

2 | NOTE |
Each note is shown by a separate <u>oval</u>.
The symbol also tells you how <u>long</u> or <u>short</u> the note is.
The symbols are shown on <u>page 16</u>.

7 | TIME SIGNATURE |
The numbers tell you about the <u>beats</u> in a <u>bar</u>.
Time signatures are covered on <u>page 12</u>.

9 | KEY SIGNATURE |
There are no flats or sharps, so this
piece is in the <u>key</u> of C. Keys and
scales are covered in <u>Section Three</u>.

8 | BEATS |
Each bar has the <u>same</u> number of <u>beats</u>. Beats,
bars and rhythm are covered on <u>pages 13, 16 & 17</u>.

THE PIANO KEYBOARD

Some of the diagrams in this book make more sense if you know what's what on a piano keyboard.
The white keys play <u>natural notes</u>.

*Note: The white
notes from C
to C make the
scale of C major
(p.24).*

The black keys play <u>SHARPS</u> and <u>FLATS</u>. Sharps and flats are covered on <u>page 11</u>.
The C in the middle of a piano keyboard is known as <u>MIDDLE C</u>.

The Basics

⑤ STAVE
The five lines are called a stave. Notes can go on or between the lines, or on separate short lines above or below.

④ BAR
The vertical bar lines split the music into bars.

bar line

⑥ TRIPLETS
The '3' and the curved line show these notes are triplets. They're explained on page 17.

3

⑪ PITCH
Notes higher up the stave have a higher pitch. Notes lower down have a lower pitch. Look at page 16 to see where the different notes go.

⑫ CHORD
More than one note played together makes a chord. See Section Three for more about chords.

⑬ DOUBLE BAR LINE
You get a double bar line at the end of a piece (or section of a piece).

⑩ STRUCTURE
The melody's built out of two different tunes — phrases and structures are covered in Sections Three and Four.

TONES AND SEMITONES

Tones and semitones are the gaps between notes.

On a piano, a semitone is the gap between any key, black or white, and its immediate neighbour.

The gap from any key to a key two semitone steps above or below is called a tone.

semitone   semitone

C#
C   B   C

G   A

tone

Clefs

Clefs are the <u>curly symbols</u> that you find right at the <u>start</u> of most written music. The treble clef is used for high-pitched music. The bass and alto clefs are used for lower-pitched music.

The **Treble** Clef is the **Most Common** Clef

1) The treble clef is used for <u>higher-pitched</u> <u>melody instruments</u>, e.g. flute, oboe, clarinet, violin, trumpet and horn.

2) Music for <u>soprano</u> and <u>alto</u> voices is written on the treble clef, too.

3) The sign always goes in the same place on the stave, with the curly bit wrapped around the line for the <u>G above middle C</u>.

MIDDLE C

The **Bass** Clef is used for **Low-pitched Instruments**

1) The bass clef is used for <u>lower-pitched instruments</u> like the tuba, trombone, bassoon, cello and double bass.

2) It's also used for <u>bass voices</u>.

3) The big blob always goes on the line for the <u>F below middle C</u>, and the two little dots go either side of the line.

MIDDLE C

The **Vocal Tenor** Clef is for **Tenor** Voices and **Lead Guitar**

MIDDLE C

Here's the 8.

1) Each line and gap in the vocal tenor clef stands for exactly the same note as it does in the <u>treble clef</u>, BUT that little '<u>8</u>' underneath means that the notes are played <u>one octave lower</u>.

2) It's used by <u>tenor voices</u> and <u>lead guitar</u> parts.

The **C** Clef can **Move** Up and Down on the Stave

The C clef always has its <u>middle point</u> on <u>middle C</u>. It can be used as two different clefs, depending on its <u>position</u> on the stave.

1) When its middle point is on the <u>middle line</u>, it's the <u>alto clef</u> and is used for <u>viola</u> parts.

MIDDLE C

2) When the middle point is on the <u>fourth line up</u>, it's called the <u>tenor clef</u>, which is used for the <u>higher notes</u> in <u>bass instruments</u> like trombones, bassoons and cellos.

MIDDLE C

Make sure you know your clefs...

You don't see the vocal tenor or C clefs very often, but you've got to know what they are when they <u>do</u> turn up. The treble and bass clefs are used all the time — aim to get so good at reading and writing them that it's easier than English. The only way is to practise. The notes are written in full on page 16.

Sharps, Flats and Naturals

On a piano, <u>natural</u> notes are the <u>white</u> ones. <u>Sharps</u> are the <u>black</u> notes to the <u>right</u> of the white notes. <u>Flats</u> are the blacks to the <u>left</u> of the whites. So each black is both sharp <u>and</u> flat.

♯ A **Sharp** Makes a Note One Step **Higher**

1) A sharp sign next to a note tells you to play it <u>one semitone higher</u>.

When you're writing on the stave, put sharps, flats and naturals before the note they affect. If you're writing text, put them afterwards — F♯.

2) A <u>double sharp</u> — **𝄪** — makes a note <u>two semitones higher</u>. If you see C𝄪 you play <u>D</u> — it's the <u>same note</u> going by a different name. The fancy name for notes that sound the same but have different names is <u>enharmonic equivalents</u>.

♭ A **Flat** Makes a Note One Step **Lower**

1) A flat symbol next to a note means you have to play it <u>one semitone lower</u>.

2) A <u>double flat</u> — 𝄫 — makes a note two semitones (a tone) lower.

The **Key Signature** is Shown with Sharps or Flats

KEY SIGNATURE

This key signature's got one sharp — on the F line. You have to play every F in the piece as an F♯.

1) Sharps or flats written at the <u>start</u> of a piece, straight after the clef, tell you the <u>key signature</u>.

2) The key signature makes notes sharp or flat <u>all the way through</u> a piece of music.

3) Sharps and flats that you see by individual notes — but not in the key signature — are called <u>accidentals</u>. Once an accidental has appeared in a bar, it applies to all notes of the same pitch for the rest of the bar, unless it's cancelled out by a <u>natural sign</u>...

There's more about key signatures on p.24-26.

♮ A **Natural** Sign **Cancels** a Sharp or Flat

A <u>natural</u> sign before a note <u>cancels</u> the <u>effect of a sharp or flat</u> sign from earlier in the bar or from a key signature. You <u>never</u> see natural signs in the key signature, only in the music, as accidentals.

This stuff should all come naturally in no time...

Double sharps and flats are uncommon and quite peculiar — it doesn't seem that <u>logical</u> to write C𝄪 when you could write D, but sometimes you just have to, I'm afraid. It all depends what key you're in.

Time Signatures

Those two numbers at the beginning of a piece of music tell you how many beats there are in a bar and how long they are. Whatever you're playing, don't ignore them.

Music has a **Regular Beat**

1) You can tap your foot along to the beat of any piece of music, as long as it hasn't got a horribly complicated rhythm. The beat is also called the pulse.

2) If you listen a bit harder, you can hear that some beats are stronger than others.

3) The strong beats come at regular intervals — usually every 2, 3 or 4 beats.

4) The strong beat is the first beat of each bar. If the strong beat comes every 3 beats, then the piece of music you're listening to has three beats in a bar.

The **Time Signature** Shows **How Many** Beats are in a Bar

1) There's always a time signature at the beginning of a piece of music.

2) It goes to the right of the clef and the key signature.

3) It's written using two numbers.

TOP NUMBER
goes between the middle line and the top line

BOTTOM NUMBER
goes between the middle line and the bottom line

The top number tells you how many beats there are in each bar, e.g. a '2' means two beats in a bar, a '3' means three beats in a bar and so on.

The bottom number tells you how long each beat is (see page 16 for the names of the different notes).

If you see a big 'C' in place of the time signature, it stands for 'common time', which means it's in $\frac{4}{4}$. If it's ₵, then it's 'cut common time' — $\frac{2}{2}$.

A 2 at the bottom means each beat is 1 minim long.

$2 = \textngroup$

A 4 at the bottom means each beat is 1 crotchet long.

$4 = \textngroup$

An 8 at the bottom means each beat is 1 quaver long.

$8 = \textngroup$

A 16 at the bottom means each beat is 1 semiquaver long.

$16 = \textngroup$

If the **Beat Changes**, the **Time Signature Changes**

1) The time signature usually stays the same all the way through a piece of music. If it does, it's written just once, at the beginning.

2) Sometimes the beat changes during a piece. If it does, the new time signature's written in the bar where it changes.

3) Not all pieces start on the first beat of the bar — some start on an unaccented beat called an anacrusis (or upbeat).

You can practise listening for the beat any time...

Every time you listen to music, practise listening for the beat and work out the time signature.

Counting the Beat

Counting the beat's fairly easy, but it's a crucial skill. It can help you work out how to <u>play</u> a new piece and how to <u>write a tune down</u> when you've only heard it on a CD or in your head.

In **Simple Time** You Count **All the Beats**

1) <u>Simple</u> time signatures have <u>2</u>, <u>3</u> or <u>4</u> as their <u>top</u> number.

2) In simple time, if you're counting to the music, you count <u>every beat</u>. For $\frac{4}{4}$ you'd count, "<u>One, two, three, four</u>." For $\frac{3}{2}$, you'd count, "<u>One, two, three</u>."

3) If you want to count out the rhythm of <u>smaller notes</u> as well as the beats, try using "<u>and</u>", "<u>eye</u>" and "<u>a</u>" — it seems to make the rhythm come out just right.

> Count "<u>One and two and</u>" for quavers, and "<u>One eye and a</u>" for semiquavers.
>
> $\frac{2}{4}$
>
> 1   2   1 and 2 and   1 eye and a   2 eye and a

4) Any shorter notes are usually a <u>half</u>, a <u>quarter</u>, an <u>eighth</u> or a <u>sixteenth</u> of the main beat.

In **Compound Time** Only Count the **Big Beats**

1) Compound time signatures have <u>6</u>, <u>9</u> or <u>12</u> as their <u>top</u> number — you can always divide the top number by <u>three</u>.

2) If the music is fairly fast, it's too <u>awkward</u> to count to nine or twelve for every bar. You end up with so many little beats that the rhythm sounds <u>mushy</u>.

3) To make the rhythm <u>clear</u>, you can just count the <u>main beats</u>:

4) If you were counting out the main beats in $\frac{6}{8}$, you'd count "One, two".

$\frac{9}{8}$ would go "One, two, three".

5) To count the <u>in-between notes</u>, use "<u>&</u>" and "<u>a</u>".

6) Shorter notes are made by dividing by three — so they're <u>thirds</u>, <u>sixths</u>, <u>twelfths</u>, etc. of the main beat.

7) Music in compound time <u>sounds different</u> from music in simple time because the beat is divided into threes — <u>practise</u> spotting the difference.

$\frac{6}{8}$ 1   2

$\frac{9}{8}$ 1   2   3   1 & a   2 & a   3 & a

The **Patterns** the Beats Make are Called the **Metre**

Depending on the time signature, the beats make different <u>patterns</u>.
The pattern is known as the <u>metre</u>. Metre can be:

Regular	Irregular	Free
The strong beats make the <u>same pattern</u> all the way through. <u>two</u> beats per bar = <u>duple</u> metre <u>three</u> beats per bar = <u>triple</u> metre <u>four</u> beats per bar = <u>quadruple</u> metre	There could be <u>five</u> beats in a bar grouped in twos and threes, or <u>seven</u> beats in a bar grouped in threes and twos or fours.	Music with <u>no particular metre</u>. This one's fairly unusual.

You can describe a time signature based on its beat and metre — e.g. a piece in $\frac{4}{4}$ is in simple quadruple time, and a piece in $\frac{6}{8}$ is in compound duple time.

One and a, two and a, three and a, four and a...

Counting the beat's not really that hard. The tricky bit on this page is the stuff about <u>metre</u>. You could get asked about the metre of a piece in your listening exam, so learn <u>all three sorts</u>.

Rhythms and Metres

When <u>different rhythms</u> are played at the <u>same time</u>, some of them <u>fit together</u> well, but some of them <u>don't</u>. Rhythms that <u>don't fit</u> can create interesting and crazy <u>effects</u>.

Hemiola Gives the Impression of a Different Metre

1) <u>Hemiola</u> is a <u>rhythmic device</u> used to create <u>contrast</u> within a piece. Music <u>written</u> in <u>duple</u> metre (see p.13) is temporarily <u>accented</u> to make it <u>feel</u> like it's in <u>triple</u> metre, or <u>vice versa</u>.

2) In $\frac{6}{8}$ time there are <u>two beats</u> in a bar, each the length of a dotted crotchet. <u>Hemiola</u> is created by playing a bar of <u>three crotchets</u>, giving the impression of $\frac{3}{4}$ time instead.

3) In $\frac{3}{4}$ time, <u>hemiola</u> is created by <u>accenting every other beat</u> for <u>two bars</u>. This gives the impression of <u>three bars</u> of $\frac{2}{4}$ time, rather than two bars of $\frac{3}{4}$.

Different Rhythms Can be Played at the Same Time

1) When two or more <u>contrasting rhythms</u> are played at the <u>same time</u>, the music is <u>polyrhythmic</u>. A polyrhythm made up of just <u>two</u> different rhythms is known as a <u>bi-rhythm</u>. Lots of <u>African</u> music is polyrhythmic — see p.133.

2) <u>Polyrhythms</u> can be created by a number of performers playing <u>different instruments</u>. A drummer can also create polyrhythms by playing a <u>different rhythm</u> with <u>each hand</u>.

- The rhythms will often have <u>accents</u> in different places. <u>Hemiola</u> might be used in one or more parts, giving the impression of instruments playing in <u>different time signatures</u> (this is known as <u>vertical hemiola</u>).

- Another polyrhythmic device is to use <u>triplets</u> against <u>standard notes</u>, e.g. triplet quavers played at the same time as two normal quavers.

- <u>Cross-rhythm</u> occurs when the <u>accents</u> are '<u>out of sync</u>' over a <u>number of bars</u>. This can be used to create <u>tension</u> in the music.

Drum Fills are Little Drum Solos

1) <u>Drum fills</u> are fairly <u>short</u> — they often only last for a <u>few beats</u>.
2) Fills are normally used to <u>build</u> the music up, or to <u>change</u> between <u>sections</u>.
3) They give the drummer a (very short) chance to <u>show off</u>.
4) Most <u>rock</u>, <u>pop</u> and <u>jazz</u> pieces will have drum fills in them.

Rhythms make me very cross...

Listen to 'Skyfall' by Adele and see if you can pick out the drum fills.

Warm-up and Exam Questions

Now have a crack at some questions to see how much you've learnt so far.

Warm-up Questions

1) Draw the symbols for a treble clef, bass clef, vocal tenor clef and C alto clef.

2) Explain what a sharp sign, a flat sign and a natural sign do.

3) Draw a time signature describing three minim beats per bar.

4) How many beats are there per bar if the time signature is $\frac{9}{8}$?

5) What's the difference between simple and compound time?

6) Name the three main types of metre.

Exam Question

This is the type of question you could get in your listening test. You'll need a track from the CD for this question. Use it to test your understanding of the last few pages and as practice for the real thing.

Play the following excerpt **four** times. Leave a short pause between each playing of the excerpt.

 Track 1

It's a good idea to read the whole question through before you listen to the track.

a) Fill in the **8 missing notes** from the vocal part, using the rhythm supplied.

Listen carefully for the direction of the notes — this really isn't as difficult as it seems at first.

[8 marks]

b) Draw a circle around the key signature.

[1 mark]

c) Fill in the time signature.

[1 mark]

d) Here is another part of the same excerpt.

Label the following features:

- the note A♯
- two notes a tone apart
- two notes a semitone apart

[3 marks]

Notes and Rests

Let's face it, you'd be a bit lost reading music if you didn't know what all those funny little dots and squiggles meant. Make sure you know all this stuff <u>better than the alphabet</u>.

The **Symbols** Tell You **How Long** Notes and Rests Are

1) <u>Notes</u> tell you how many beats to hold a <u>sound</u> for.
2) <u>Rests</u> tell you how many beats to hold a <u>silence</u> for.
3) Notes and rests have <u>names</u>, depending on how long they are. Two beats is a <u>minim</u> note or rest. A half-beat is a <u>quaver</u> note or rest.

The length of a note or rest is also called its duration.

Learn this table now — you need to know exactly how to <u>write</u> these out, and how to <u>play</u> them.

NAME OF NOTE	NUMBER OF CROTCHET BEATS	NOTE SYMBOL	REST SYMBOL
semibreve	4	𝅝	▬
minim	2	𝅗𝅥	▬
crotchet	1	𝅘𝅥	𝄽
quaver	½	𝅘𝅥𝅮 or 𝅘𝅥𝅮𝅘𝅥𝅮 if there are 2 or more	𝄾
semiquaver	¼	𝅘𝅥𝅯 or 𝅘𝅥𝅯𝅘𝅥𝅯 if there are 2 or more	𝄿

The **Position** of the Note Tells You the **Pitch**

<u>Just in case</u> you don't know, this is where the notes go in the <u>bass</u> and <u>treble</u> clefs:

In the <u>bottom</u> half of the stave, the tails on the notes go <u>upwards</u>.

There is some overlap — e.g. these are the same note written in different clefs.

In the <u>top</u> half of the stave, the tails on the notes go <u>downwards</u>.

The tail of the note on the <u>middle line</u> can go <u>up</u> or <u>down</u>.

These lines are called <u>ledger lines</u>. You use them to work out how <u>high</u> or <u>low</u> notes <u>above</u> and <u>below</u> the stave are.

'Leger lines' is an alternative spelling for 'ledger lines'.

There's no excuse for not knowing this stuff...

Those of you who were playing the church organ before you could crawl might be feeling a bit like you know this stuff already and you don't need to be told. It's still worth <u>checking over</u> though, I reckon.

Dots, Ties and Triplets

You can only get so far with the note lengths from <u>page 16</u>. If you use <u>dot</u>, <u>tie</u> and <u>triplet</u> symbols you can create more complicated, interesting and sophisticated rhythms.

A **Dot** After a Note or Rest Makes It **Longer**

1) A dot just <u>to the right</u> of a note or rest makes it <u>half as long again</u>.

$$\text{♩} = \mathbf{\frac{1}{beat}} \xrightarrow[1 + ½ = 1½]{1 ÷ 2 = ½} \text{♩.} = \mathbf{\frac{1½}{beats}} \qquad \text{♩} = \mathbf{\frac{2}{beats}} \xrightarrow[2 + 1 = 3]{2 ÷ 2 = 1} \text{♩.} = \mathbf{\frac{3}{beats}}$$

2) A <u>second</u> dot adds on another <u>quarter</u> of the original note length.

♩.. = **1¾ beats**   ♩.. = **3½ beats**

Count these really carefully when you're playing — don't just "add a bit on".

3) In <u>dotted quaver rhythms</u>, you have a <u>dotted quaver</u> (worth ½ + ¼ = ¾ of a beat) followed by a <u>semiquaver</u> (worth ¼ of a beat). Dotted quaver rhythms are common in <u>marches</u>. They're usually written like this:

¾ beat   ¼ beat

4) In a <u>Scotch snap</u>, the rhythm is the <u>other way round</u> — the <u>semiquaver</u> is on the <u>beat</u> (and <u>accented</u>), followed by the <u>dotted quaver</u>, like this:
Scotch snaps are used in <u>Scottish music</u> (e.g. <u>dances</u>) — hence the name.

A **Tie Joins Two Notes** Together

1) A tie is a <u>curved line</u> joining two notes of the <u>same pitch</u> together.

2) It turns them into <u>one note</u>.

3) Ties are often used to make a long note that goes over the <u>end of a bar</u>.

...sounds the same as...

...sounds the same as...

Ties are not the same as slurs. See page 19.

A **Triplet** is **Three Notes** Played in the Time of **Two**

1) A triplet is <u>three</u> notes, all the <u>same length</u>, squeezed into the time of <u>two</u>.

2) Triplets are marked with a '<u>3</u>' above or below the <u>middle</u> of the three notes. Sometimes there's a <u>square</u> bracket or a <u>curved</u> line as well as the three.

3) The notes don't all have to be <u>played</u> — part of a triplet can be <u>rests</u>.

Stick with it, even the tricky bits...

Triplets look so straightforward on the page, but they can be tricky to get just right. The only way to make sure you're playing them properly is to practise with a metronome. Have a go right now.

Tempo and Mood

Composers don't just tell you the notes — they tell you <u>how fast</u> to play them, and what the <u>atmosphere</u> of the piece should be too. You need to understand all the different <u>terms</u> they use.

The **Tempo** is the **Speed** of the Music

Tempo is Italian for "<u>time</u>". In a lot of music the instructions for how fast to play are written in Italian too. Here are the words you're <u>most</u> likely to come across:

Italian word	What it means	Beats per minute
largo	broad and slow	40-60
larghetto	still broad, not so slow	60-66
adagio	bit faster than largo	66-76
andante	walking pace	76-108
moderato	moderate speed	108-120
allegro	quick and lively	120-168
vivace	very lively — quicker than allegro	168-180
presto	really fast	180-200

<u>60</u> beats a minute means each crotchet lasts <u>one</u> second. <u>120</u> beats a minute means each crotchet lasts <u>half</u> a second. And so on...

This is where you put the <u>tempo</u> and <u>beats per minute</u> on the stave. ♩ = 112 means there are 112 crotchet beats per minute. This is called a <u>metronome marking</u>.

Moderato (♩ = 112)

These words tell you how to <u>vary</u> the speed. The <u>words</u> go <u>underneath</u> the stave. The <u>pause</u> symbol goes <u>above</u>.

Italian word	Abbreviation	What it means
accelerando	accel.	speeding up
rallentando	rall.	slowing down
ritenuto	rit.	holding back the pace
allargando	allarg.	slowing down, getting a bit broader
rubato	rub.	can be flexible with pace of music
⌢		pause — longer than a whole beat
a tempo		back to the original pace

Rubato means '<u>robbed time</u>' — you can <u>slow</u> some bits down and <u>speed</u> others up.

To give the <u>impression</u> that the tempo has changed (without actually changing it), composers can use <u>augmentation</u> or <u>diminution</u>. Augmentation is where note lengths are <u>increased</u> in a melody (e.g. by <u>doubling</u> the length of every note — so a <u>crotchet</u> becomes a <u>minim</u>). This has the effect of making the music sound <u>slower</u>. Diminution is the <u>opposite</u> — note lengths are <u>shortened</u>, so the music sounds <u>faster</u>.

Mood is the **Overall** Feel of a Piece

The <u>mood</u> of a piece is usually described in Italian too.

Sometimes parts are marked <u>obbligato</u>, which means they are <u>really important</u> and can't be missed out (obbligato means '<u>obligatory</u>').

Italian word	What it means
agitato	agitated
alla marcia	in a march style
amoroso	loving
calmato	calm
dolce	sweetly
energico	energetic

Italian word	What it means
giocoso	playful, humorous
grandioso	grandly
pesante	heavy
risoluto	strong, confident, bold
sospirando	sighing
trionfale	triumphant

To describe the <u>overall mood</u> put the word at the beginning of the piece.

Andante Grandioso (♩=100)

To describe a <u>change of mood</u> write the word under the stave.

Yes, you do have to learn it all — even the Italian bits...

When you're learning this page, start with words that sound a bit like English — they're easy.

Dynamics and Articulation

More ways for composers to tell players <u>exactly</u> how they want their music to sound...

Dynamic Markings Tell You How Loud or Quietly to Play

Music that was all played at the <u>same volume</u> would be pretty dull.
To get a <u>variety</u> of different volumes you can use these symbols:

Symbol	Stands for	What it means
pp	pianissimo	very quiet
p	piano	quiet
mp	mezzopiano	fairly quiet
mf	mezzoforte	fairly loud
f	forte	loud
ff	fortissimo	very loud
◁	crescendo	getting louder
▷	diminuendo	getting quieter

You might also see dynamics combined together in other ways.
E.g. ***fp*** means you play a sudden loud bit followed by a sudden quiet bit.

For more extreme dynamics, composers might use ***ppp*** or ***fff*** (or even ***pppp*** or ***ffff***).

The markings go <u>underneath</u> the stave.

Crescendos and diminuendos are sometimes called <u>hairpins</u> when they're written like this.

Articulation Tells You How Much to Separate the Notes

In theory all the notes of a bar should add up to one <u>continuous</u> sound — but actually there are <u>tiny gaps</u> between them. If you <u>exaggerate</u> the gaps you get a <u>staccato</u> effect. If you smooth the gaps out, the notes sound <u>slurred</u>.

STACCATO All the dotted notes are played slightly short.

SLUR All the notes below or above the slur are played smoothly, with no breaks between.

<u>Tenuto</u> marks (<u>lines</u> above or below a note) tell you that a note should be held for its <u>full length</u>, or even played slightly <u>longer</u>.

If the articulation goes <u>all the way through</u> a piece, there's an overall instruction at the <u>beginning</u>.

If this piece was marked <u>legato</u> you would have to play smoothly all the way through.

Staccato

Nothing to do with articulated lorries then...

Don't just learn the symbols, learn what they're <u>called</u> too — it'll sound far more impressive if you write about the "dynamics" and "articulation" in your listening exam rather than "loudness and quietness".

More Instructions

Once a composer has told you how <u>fast</u> and how <u>loud</u> to play and how to <u>articulate</u> it, they sometimes put in <u>extra instructions</u>. Things like <u>accents</u>, <u>sforzandos</u> and <u>bends</u> make the music more <u>interesting</u>.

An **Accent Emphasises** a Note

1) An <u>accent</u> is a type of articulation that tells you to <u>emphasise</u> (or <u>stress</u>) a note.

2) On a <u>wind</u> instrument, this is often done by <u>tonguing</u> a note <u>harder</u> than normal.

3) Accents are usually written like this **>** or like this **Λ**.

4) If a whole <u>section</u> should be accented, it can be marked '*marcato*' (which means 'marked').

5) A <u>sforzando</u> is a <u>strongly accented</u> note. It's shown by writing ***sfz*** or ***sf*** underneath the note.

6) A sforzando is often a <u>sudden</u> accent — e.g. a <u>very loud</u> note in a <u>quiet section</u> of a piece. This makes the music more <u>dramatic</u>.

A **Glissando** is a **Slide** Between Notes

1) A <u>glissando</u> is a <u>slide</u> from one note to another. Usually you're <u>told</u> which notes to <u>start</u> and <u>finish</u> on.

2) A glissando can be played <u>effectively</u> on a <u>violin</u> (or other <u>string</u> instrument), <u>piano</u>, <u>harp</u>, <u>xylophone</u> (or similar instrument), <u>timpani</u> and <u>trombone</u>. Other instruments can play them too, but they often <u>won't</u> sound as <u>good</u>.

3) On some instruments (e.g. piano, harp and xylophone), <u>every note</u> is played in the glissando. Think about it — if you were to play a glissando on a xylophone, you'd run your beater over every note, so they'd all be played.

4) On other instruments, like the trombone and strings, the notes you hear <u>aren't fixed notes</u> — the glissando covers all the <u>tiny differences</u> in pitch between the two notes. For example, you <u>can't</u> pick out <u>individual notes</u> in a glissando on the trombone.

5) A glissando can be shown by writing *gliss.* underneath the stave, or by putting a <u>line</u> between <u>two notes</u>.

> A portamento is similar to a glissando — it's more common in singing and on string instruments.

Notes can be **Bent**

1) A <u>bend</u> (or <u>bent note</u>) changes the <u>pitch</u> of the note slightly — it sounds a bit like a <u>wobble</u>.

2) They're often played by starting just <u>above</u> or <u>below</u> the note then <u>bending</u> to it.

3) Bends are often used in <u>jazz music</u>.

4) Bent notes can be played on <u>most</u> instruments — including <u>guitars</u>, <u>trumpets</u>, <u>trombones</u> and <u>harmonicas</u>. <u>Singers</u> can bend notes too.

COMPOSING TIP

Roundabouts, swings, climbing frames, glissandi...

All the things on this page are little <u>extras</u> composers can add to their music to make it more <u>interesting</u> — you could try adding some to your compositions too. I do love a good sforzando.

Warm-up and Exam Questions

Get your brain going with these warm-up questions before tackling the exam question below.

Warm-up Questions

1) Draw a 4-beat note, and write down its full name.

2) Draw a 4-beat rest.

3) Name the following notes and give the time value of each of them.

4) Explain the difference between a tie and a slur.

5) Look at the tempo words below. Write them out in order, fastest first.

Andante   **Largo**   **Presto**   **Moderato**   **Allegro**

Exam Question

Here's another exam-style question for you to try.

Play the following excerpt **three** times. Leave a short pause between each playing of the excerpt.

Track 2

a)   Listen to the rhythm of the opening melody.
Tick one feature that matches what you hear.

Staccato notes ☐

Triplets ☐

Dotted notes ☐

[1 mark]

Turn over

Exam Question

b) Which word best describes the tempo of this piece of music? Underline your answer.

largo   **adagio**   **andante**   **allegro**

[1 mark]

c) Which word describes the dynamic at the opening? Underline your answer.

pianissimo   **piano**   **forte**   **fortissimo**

[1 mark]

d) Which of the following describes the mood of this excerpt? Tick the box.

agitato   ☐

dolce   ☐

energico   ☐

pesante   ☐

[1 mark]

Revision Summary for Section Two

You'll find a page of questions like this at the end of every section. They're <u>not</u> here just to fill up space — they're here to <u>help you</u> test yourself. The basic idea is, if you can answer all the Revision Summary questions without looking back through the section, you can be pretty sure you've understood and remembered all the important stuff. Look back through the section the first and second time you try the questions (if you must), but by the third time you do the questions, you should be aiming to have all the answers <u>off by heart</u>.

1) Does a clef tell you:
   a) how wide the stave is, b) what instrument it's for, or c) how high or low the notes on it are?
2) Draw a stave with a treble clef at the beginning.
3) Draw a stave with a bass clef at the beginning.
4) Which voices read music from the treble clef?
5) Name two instruments that read music from the bass clef.
6) What's the difference between the symbol for a treble clef and the symbol for the vocal tenor clef?
7) Where does middle C go on a vocal tenor clef?
8) Draw staves showing the C clef in both positions and write the correct name by each one.
9) Draw a sharp sign, a flat sign and a natural sign.
10) What does a sharp do to a note?
11) What does a flat do to a note?
12) Draw each of these signs and explain what you do if you see them by a note:
   a) a double sharp   b) a double flat
13) Draw a treble clef stave and add a key signature with one sharp.
14) What do you call a sharp, flat or natural sign when it's in the music but not in the key signature?
15) One beat in the bar usually feels stronger than the others. Which one?
16) What do you call the two numbers at the start of a piece of music?
17) What does the top number tell you about the beats?
18) What does the bottom number tell you about the beats?
19) When a time signature changes in a piece of music, where's the new one written?
20) What's the difference between simple and compound time?
21) What's the difference between regular and irregular metre?
22) What is meant by a cross-rhythm?
23) Draw the symbol for each of the following notes and write down how many crotchet beats it lasts:
   a) semibreve   b) semiquaver   c) crotchet   d) quaver   e) minim
24) What does a dot immediately after a note or rest do?
25) What's the time value of:
   a) a dotted crotchet   b) a dotted minim   c) a dotted semibreve   d) a double dotted minim?
26) What does a 'tie' do?
27) How much time, in crotchet beats, does a crotchet triplet take up?
28) Where do you put the tempo marking on a stave?
29) Which is slower, *allegro* or *moderato*?
30) Where would you write the word *agitato* on the stave?
31) How does a composer show on the written music that the notes should be played smoothly?
32) How are accents usually indicated in a piece of music?
33) What's a glissando?

Major Scales

There are two main types of scales — <u>major</u> and <u>minor</u>. Once you've got the hang of how scales are put together, you should find keys and chords start to make a lot more sense.

Ordinary Scales have **Eight Notes**

The gap between the bottom and top notes of a scale is called an <u>octave</u>. See p.28.

1) An ordinary major (or minor) scale has <u>8 notes</u>, starting and ending on notes of the <u>same name</u>, e.g. C major goes C, D, E, F, G, A, B, C.

2) Each of the eight notes has a <u>name</u>.

1st note	2nd note	3rd note	4th note	5th note	6th note	7th note	8th note
tonic	supertonic	mediant	subdominant	dominant	submediant	leading note	tonic
I	II	III	IV	V	VI	VII	VIII

3) You can just use the <u>numbers</u> or the <u>Roman numerals</u> to name the notes too.

Major Scales Sound **Bright** and **Cheery**

Whatever note they start on, all major scales sound <u>similar</u>, because they all follow the same <u>pattern</u>. This pattern is a set order of <u>tone</u> and <u>semitone</u> gaps between the notes:

I tone II tone III semitone IV tone V tone VI tone VII semitone VIII

This is how <u>C major</u> goes on a keyboard.

Major scales <u>can start on</u> <u>any note</u>, including the black notes, e.g. C♯ major.

All Major Scales Except C have **One or More Black Notes**

<u>C major</u> is the <u>only</u> major scale with <u>no black notes</u>.

<u>All the others</u> need <u>at least one black note</u> to stick to the 'tone-semitone' pattern.

1) <u>G major scale</u> — you have to change <u>F to F♯</u> to make the notes fit the major scale pattern.

2) <u>F major scale</u> — you have to change <u>B to B♭</u> to make the pattern right.

The **Set of Notes** in a **Scale** is Called a **Key**

The key signature goes between the clef and the time signature.

1) The <u>key</u> tells you what <u>sharps and flats</u> there are (if any).

2) Most music sticks to one key. To show what key it's in, all the <u>sharp</u> or <u>flat</u> signs from the scale are written on the beginning of every stave of the piece. This is called the <u>key signature</u>.

3) A key signature can have <u>sharps or flats</u> but <u>NEVER</u> both.

4) If a piece <u>changes</u> key, it's called a <u>modulation</u> — see p.44.

G major's got <u>one</u> <u>sharp</u> note — F♯. You put a <u>sharp</u> symbol on the <u>F line</u>.

Scales — dull but important...

Try playing some major scales starting on <u>different notes</u>. Even if you don't "<u>know</u>" them, you should be able to <u>work out</u> what the notes are, using the <u>tone-semitone</u> pattern and the <u>sound</u>. Give it a go.

Minor Scales

Minor scales have fixed patterns too. There are <u>three</u> different kinds you need to know.

Minor Scales All Sound a Bit Mournful

Minor scales sound <u>completely different</u> from major scales, because they've got a different tone-semitone pattern. There are <u>three</u> types of minor scale, and all of them sound a bit <u>mournful</u>.

1) The Natural Minor has the Same Notes as the Relative Major

These are easy. Start from the <u>sixth</u> note of any major scale. Carry on up to the same note an octave higher. You're playing a <u>natural minor scale</u>.

The sixth note of <u>C major</u> is <u>A</u>. If you play from <u>A to A</u> using the notes of C major, you're playing <u>A natural minor</u> (usually just called '<u>A minor</u>').

Pairs of keys like <u>A minor and C major</u> are called "<u>relative</u>" keys.
A minor is the <u>relative minor</u> of C major.
C major is the <u>relative major</u> of A minor.

All the notes in a natural minor are <u>exactly the same</u> as the ones in the <u>relative major</u>. The <u>key signature's</u> exactly the same too.

2) The Harmonic Minor has One Accidental

1) The <u>harmonic minor</u> has the same notes as the relative major, except for the <u>seventh note</u>.

2) The <u>seventh</u> note is always raised by <u>one semitone</u>.

3) You use the harmonic minor when you're writing <u>harmonies</u>. That <u>sharpened seventh note</u> makes the harmonies work much better than they would with notes from a natural minor. It's probably because it feels like it wants to move up to the <u>tonic</u>.

3) The Melodic Minor has Two Accidentals

1) The <u>melodic minor</u> is just like a natural minor, using the notes from the relative major scale, <u>except for notes 6 and 7</u>.

2) On the way <u>up</u>, notes <u>6</u> and <u>7</u> are each <u>raised</u> by <u>one semitone</u>.

3) On the way <u>down</u>, the melodic minor goes just like the natural minor.

4) The melodic minor is used for writing <u>melodies</u>. The accidental on note 6 makes tunes sound <u>smoother</u> by avoiding the big jump between notes 6 and 7 in the harmonic minor.

And not forgetting the Morris Minor...

All these scales have a <u>minor third</u> between the first and third notes in the scale — that's why they sound melancholy. You need to learn <u>all three</u> — names, notes and what they're used for.

The Circle of Fifths

The circle of fifths looks complicated but it's very <u>useful</u> once you understand how it works — it tells you <u>all the keys</u>, all the <u>relative keys</u> and their <u>key signatures</u>.

The **Circle of Fifths** Shows **All the Keys**

1) Altogether there are <u>12 major keys</u>. They're all shown on the <u>circle of fifths</u>.

2) Don't expect to fully get it if this is the first time you've seen it. Just <u>have a look</u>, then read on.

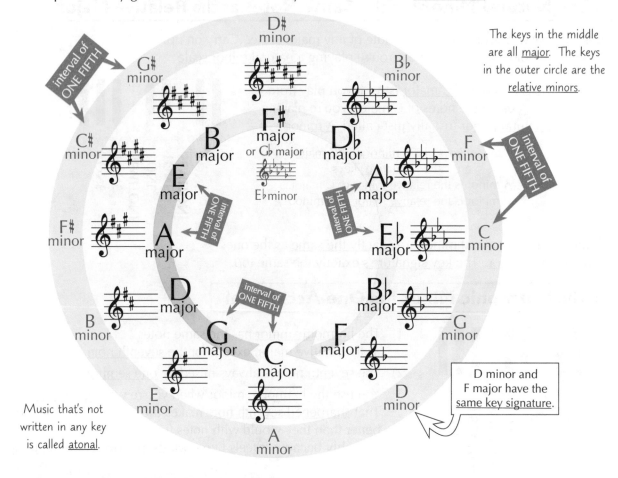

The keys in the middle are all <u>major</u>. The keys in the outer circle are the <u>relative minors</u>.

D minor and F major have the <u>same key signature</u>.

Music that's not written in any key is called <u>atonal</u>.

Each Key **Links** to the Next One

1) The circle <u>starts</u> with <u>C major</u> at the bottom. The next key round is <u>G</u>. G's the <u>fifth note</u> of C major.

2) The fifth note of G major is D, the <u>next</u> key on the circle. This pattern repeats <u>all the way round</u>. That's why the chart's called the circle of fifths.

3) As you go round the circle the number of <u>sharps</u> in the <u>key signature</u> goes up <u>one</u> for each key.

4) When you get to <u>F♯ major</u> at the top there are <u>six sharps</u>. From here, you start writing the key signature in <u>flats</u> — you don't need as many so it's clearer to read.

5) The number of <u>flats</u> keeps going <u>down</u> until you get back to C major, with no sharps and no flats.

The <u>relative minors</u> in the outer circle work just the same way as the major keys — the <u>fifth note</u> of <u>A minor</u> is <u>E</u> and the next minor key's <u>E minor</u>... and so on. Don't forget you can always work out the relative minor by counting up or down to the <u>sixth note</u> of a major scale, (see p.25) or the relative major by counting up to the <u>third note</u> of the minor scale.

Don't worry if it's making your head spin...

You need to be familiar with key signatures with <u>up to four sharps</u> or <u>four flats</u> (both <u>major</u> and <u>minor</u>). Don't worry too much about the others (but there's no harm in learning them too).

Modes and Other Types of Scale

Most music uses notes from a <u>major</u> or a <u>minor scale</u> — and they're the <u>most important</u> ones to learn, but there are a few <u>more unusual scales</u> and <u>modes</u> that you need to know about too.

Modes Follow **Different Patterns** of **Tones** and **Semitones**

Just like scales, you can start a <u>mode</u> on any note.

1) The most common mode is the one you get by playing a <u>major scale</u> (e.g. C major — just play the white notes on a keyboard from C to C). The pattern is <u>tone-tone-semitone-tone-tone-tone-semitone</u>.

2) Another mode can be formed by playing the notes of the same major scale, starting from the <u>second note</u>, e.g. D to D:

3) Starting on E gives you another mode...

This one is used a lot in flamenco music.

4) ...<u>and so on</u>. Each forms its own semitone / tone pattern and they all have different names. You don't need to know them all though — it's more important that you <u>know what they sound like</u>. (E.g. playing the white notes starting from G forms a mode that sounds quite bluesy.)

5) For some examples of pieces written in modes, have a listen to the folk song <u>Scarborough Fair</u>, the theme tune to <u>The Simpsons</u> and REM's <u>Losing My Religion</u>.

Pentatonic Scales are Used a Lot in **Folk** and **Rock Music**

Pentatonic scales use <u>five</u> notes. They're really easy to compose with, because there are <u>no semitone steps</u> — <u>most combinations</u> of notes sound fine. There are <u>two types</u> of pentatonic scale.

1) The <u>major pentatonic</u> uses notes 1, 2, 3, 5 and 6 of a <u>major</u> scale.

2) The <u>minor pentatonic</u> uses notes 1, 3, 4, 5 and 7 of the <u>natural minor</u> scale.

Whole Tone and **Chromatic Scales** Sound **Spooky**

Whole tone scales

Whole tone scales are pretty simple to remember — <u>every step is a tone</u>. From bottom to top there are only <u>six notes</u> in a whole tone scale.

Major and minor scales are known as <u>diatonic scales</u>.

Chromatic scales

Chromatic scales are fairly easy too. On a keyboard you play <u>every white and black note</u> until you get up to an octave above the note you started with. From bottom to top there are <u>12 notes</u>. Basically, <u>every step</u> of a chromatic scale is <u>a semitone</u>.

You know the score...

You <u>could</u> get a piece of music in your <u>listening</u> that's written in a <u>mode</u> or one of the other <u>scales</u>. And you could get <u>asked</u> what kind of scale it's written with. So you'd better learn this page.

Intervals

Not the break halfway through a concert, but the <u>distance</u> between two notes.

An **Interval** is the **Gap** Between **Two Notes**

An interval is the <u>musical word</u> for the <u>gap</u> or <u>distance</u> between <u>two notes</u>.

Notes <u>close together</u> make <u>small</u> intervals. Notes <u>further apart</u> make <u>larger</u> intervals.

There are <u>two ways</u> of playing an interval.

Melodic interval
When one note <u>jumps</u> up or down to another note, you get a <u>melodic interval</u>.

ASCENDING interval   DESCENDING interval

Harmonic interval
When <u>two notes</u> are played at the <u>same time</u>, they make a <u>harmonic interval</u>.

1) You can use the <u>melodic intervals</u> to describe the <u>pattern</u> of a <u>melody</u>.

2) In some melodies, there are only <u>small</u> intervals between the notes — no bigger than a <u>tone</u>.

3) When the notes are <u>close together</u> like this, the melody can be called <u>stepwise</u>, <u>conjunct</u> or <u>scalic</u> (because it moves up and down the notes of a <u>scale</u>).

4) Tunes with <u>big</u> melodic intervals (larger than a tone) are called <u>disjunct</u>.

An Interval has **Two Parts** to its Name...

1) A <u>number</u>

an augmented fifth

2) A <u>description</u>

The **Number** Tells You **How Many Notes** the Interval Covers

1) You get the number by counting up the stave from the bottom note to the top note. You <u>include</u> the bottom and top notes in your counting.

2) C to E is a <u>third</u> because it covers <u>three letter names</u> — C, D and E.

3) C to F is a <u>fourth</u> because it covers <u>four letter names</u> — C, D, E and F.

4) The number of an interval is sometimes called the <u>interval quantity</u>.

The "description" bit is covered at the top of the next page...

The interval between G and D is a <u>fifth</u>.

G	A	B	C	D
1	2	3	4	5

An interval covering <u>eight letters</u> (e.g. A to A) is called an <u>octave</u>.

The interval between D and F sharp is a <u>third</u> (you can just <u>ignore</u> the accidentals when counting).

D	E	F#
1	2	3

Intervals

The **Description** Tells You How the Interval **Sounds**

There are <u>five names</u> for the five main sounds:

| perfect | major | minor | diminished | augmented |

1) To work out the <u>description part</u> of an interval's name, think of the <u>lower note</u> of the interval as the <u>first</u> note of a <u>major scale</u>.

2) If the top note of the interval is part of that major scale it's either <u>perfect</u> or <u>major</u>:

The perfect intervals are the ones that sound 'best' — the notes go together very cleanly.

3) If the top note <u>doesn't</u> belong to the major scale, then it's <u>minor, diminished</u> or <u>augmented</u>.
   If the interval is <u>one semitone LESS</u> than a <u>major interval</u>, then it's <u>minor</u>.
   If the interval is <u>one semitone LESS</u> than a <u>minor</u> or a <u>perfect interval</u>, then it's <u>diminished</u>.
   If the interval is <u>one semitone MORE</u> than a <u>major</u> or a <u>perfect interval</u>, then it's <u>augmented</u>.

Work Out the **Full Name** of an Interval **Step by Step**

1) **HOW MANY LETTER NAMES DOES IT COVER?**
   <u>Six</u> — G, A, B, C, D and E. So the <u>quantity</u> is a <u>sixth</u>.
2) **ARE THE NOTES FROM THE SAME MAJOR SCALE?**
   The bottom note's G. E <u>is</u> in G major — it's the <u>sixth</u> note.
3) **WHAT TYPE OF INTERVAL IS IT?**
   It's the <u>sixth note</u> of G major, and the sixth note always gives a major interval — so it's a <u>major sixth</u>.

1) **HOW MANY LETTER NAMES DOES IT COVER?**
   <u>Three</u> — C, D and E flat. So the <u>quantity</u> is a <u>third</u>.
2) **ARE THE NOTES FROM THE SAME MAJOR SCALE?**
   No.
3) **WHAT TYPE OF INTERVAL IS IT?**
   A third in the major scale is a <u>major</u> interval.
   This interval's one semitone smaller, so it's a <u>minor third</u>.

The **Tritone** Interval **Sounds Odd**

1) The tritone is an interval of <u>three tones</u>. It's <u>dissonant</u> — i.e. it sounds awkward, some would say terrible. It's used in some twentieth century Western art music.

2) <u>Diminished fifths</u> (e.g. G to D flat) and <u>augmented fourths</u> (e.g. G to C♯) are both <u>tritones</u>.

3) Try playing some, so you know what they <u>sound</u> like.

Take it one step at a time and you'll get there in the end...

The tritone interval used to be called '<u>the Devil's interval</u>' — because it has such an awkward, clashing sound. It's supposed to be unlucky, so use it in your composition at your own risk...

Examples

You need to <u>hear</u> the difference between different types of scales and chords. Tracks 3-9 are practical examples of the theory on pages 24-29. Listen to the tracks as you read the info below.

Examples

Track 3   A <u>major scale</u>, with <u>F♯</u> as the tonic, played over two octaves. *(see p.24)*
Try writing out the notes of the scale on a stave. Remember — TTSTTTS.

Track 4   The <u>three</u> different types of <u>minor scale</u> with <u>D</u> as the tonic. *(see p.25)*
    a) The <u>natural minor</u> scale
    b) The <u>harmonic minor</u>
    c) The <u>melodic minor</u>

Track 5   The two different types of pentatonic scale. *(see p.27)*
    a) <u>Major pentatonic</u> scale starting on <u>C</u>
    b) <u>Minor pentatonic</u> scale starting on <u>A</u>
These are relative scales, and because they're pentatonic all the notes are the same.

Track 6   A <u>whole tone</u> scale. *(see p.27)*
It starts off like the major scale, but the 4th and 5th notes are further apart (<u>harmonically distant</u>) than in a major scale, so it sounds odd.

Track 7   A <u>chromatic</u> scale. *(see p.27)*
This one starts on <u>G</u>, but all <u>chromatic</u> scales use all the notes, so they sound nearly the same.

Track 8   The <u>major</u> and <u>perfect</u> intervals. *(see p.29)*
They're played at the same time so they're <u>harmonic</u>.

Track 9   The <u>minor</u> and <u>diminished intervals</u>. *(see p.29)*
    a) Minor 2nd
    b) Augmented 2nd / minor 3rd
    c) Augmented 4th / diminished 5th
    d) Augmented 5th / minor 6th
    e) Augmented 6th / minor 7th

Practice Questions

Now check you've got the hang of it all with these practice questions.

Practice Questions

Track 10 Listen to the four different types of scale. What are they?

a) ....

b) ....

c) ....

d) ....

You can play these tracks more than once — some of them are quite tricky.

Track 11 What type of scale does this tune use?

....

Track 12 Listen to these harmonic intervals. Write down what each of them is called.

a) ....   b) ....

c) ....   d) ....

e) ....   f) ....

g) ....   h) ....

Track 13 Now name these melodic intervals.

a) ....   b) ....

c) ....   d) ....

e) ....   f) ....

g) ....   h) ....

Warm-up and Exam Questions

Time for another round of questions...

Warm-up Questions

1) How many notes would you find in a normal scale?

2) What does a key or key signature tell you about the music?

3) What do the scales of C major and A minor have in common?

4) Name the **three** types of minor scales.

5) Which scale uses only notes 1, 2, 3, 5 and 6 from the major scale?

6) Why is a chromatic scale unusual?

7) What type of interval is formed when two notes are played together at the same time?

8) Which is smaller, a minor 7th or a diminished 7th?

Exam Question

This exam-style question includes a couple of questions on intervals to test your knowledge.

Play the excerpt **three** times. Leave a short pause between each playing.

 Track 14

a) Here are the first three bars.

Exam Question

    i)   How many beats are there in a bar?

....

[1 mark]

    ii)   What is the interval between the notes highlighted in red at letter **a**?

....

[1 mark]

    iii)   What is the interval between the two lower notes in the
left-hand chord indicated at letter **b**?

....

[1 mark]

b)   What key is this excerpt in?

....

[1 mark]

c)   What does the mark ⁻ above a note tell the performer to do?

....

[1 mark]

Chords — The Basics

A <u>chord</u> is two or more notes played together. Chords are great for writing <u>accompaniments</u>.

Only **Some** Instruments **Play Chords**

1) A lot of instruments only play <u>one note at a time</u> — flutes, recorders, trumpets, clarinets, trombones... You can't play a chord with one note, so these instruments <u>don't</u> play chords.

2) You can <u>only</u> play chords on <u>instruments</u> that play <u>more than one</u> note at a time. <u>Keyboards</u> and guitars are both great for playing chords — you can easily play several notes together.

3) Other <u>stringed instruments</u> like violins and cellos can play chords, but not very easily, so chords are only played from time to time.

Don't play chords.

Do play chords.

Some Chords Sound **Great**, Others Sound **Awful**

1) The notes of some chords <u>go together</u> really well — like apple pie and ice-cream.

When you have nice-sounding chords it's called <u>CONCORDANCE</u> or <u>CONSONANCE</u>.

2) Other chords have <u>clashing notes which disagree</u> — more like apple pie and pickled eggs.

When you have horrible-sounding chords it's called <u>DISCORDANCE</u> or <u>DISSONANCE</u>.

The **Best-Sounding** Chords are Called **Triads**

1) You can play <u>any</u> set of notes and make a chord — but most of them sound <u>harsh</u>.

2) An <u>easy, reliable</u> way of getting nice-sounding chords is to play <u>triads</u>.

3) Triads are chords made up of three notes, with <u>set intervals</u> between them.

4) Once you know the intervals, you can easily play <u>dozens</u> of decent chords.

How to make a triad...

1) On a piano, start with any white note — this is called the <u>root note</u>. You <u>build</u> the triad <u>from the root</u>.

2) Count the root as 'first' and the next white note to the <u>right</u>, as 'second'. The <u>third</u> note you reach is the <u>third</u> — the middle note of the triad.

3) Keep counting up and you get to the <u>fifth</u> — the final note of the triad.

4) The intervals between the notes are <u>thirds</u>.

5) If the root note's a <u>B</u>, then you end up with a <u>B triad</u>. If the root note's a <u>C</u>, you end up with a <u>C triad</u>.

6) You can build triads on black notes too, so long as the intervals between notes are <u>thirds</u>.

FIFTH
THIRD
ROOT

C E G

COMPOSING TIP

Good things come in threes...

The next six pages will be useful when it comes to writing your compositions. You'll need to think about which instruments can play chords, and which notes sound nice together.

Triads

There's more than one type of triad...

Triads Use Major and Minor Thirds

1) All triads have an interval of a third between each pair of notes.

2) The intervals can be major or minor thirds.

A major third is four semitones.

A minor third is three semitones.

3) Different combinations of major and minor thirds give different types of triad:

Major triads

- Major triads have a major third followed by a minor third.
- The major third goes between the root and the third.
- The minor third goes between the third and the fifth.

Minor triads

- Minor triads use a major and a minor third too, but in the opposite order.
- The minor third goes between the root and the third.
- The major third goes between the third and the fifth.

DIMINISHED TRIADS use two minor thirds.
AUGMENTED TRIADS use two major thirds.

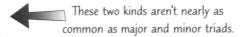

These two kinds aren't nearly as common as major and minor triads.

You Can Add a Note to a Triad to Get a 7th Chord

1) 7th chords are triads with a fourth note added — the seventh note above the root.

2) The interval between the root and the 7th can be a major seventh or a minor seventh — see p.29.

These Symbols Stand for Chords

A special notation is used to represent the various chords. For a triad starting on a C:

C = C major

Caug or **C+** = augmented C chord

C7 = C major with added minor 7th

Cmaj7 = C major with added major 7th

Cm = C minor

Cdim or **C-** or **Co** = diminished C chord

Cm7 = C minor with added minor 7th

Cm maj7 = C minor with added major 7th

For chords other than C, just change the first letter to show the root note.

It's not as hard as it looks and it's VERY useful...

If you play the guitar or play in a band you need to learn these symbols right now. Even if you only ever play classical music they're still worth learning — they're really useful as shorthand.

Fitting Chords to a Melody

There are some basic rules about fitting chords to a melody:

No.1: All the notes in the chords have got to be in the <u>same key</u> as the notes in the melody.

The **Melody** and **Chords** Must be in the **Same Key**

1) A melody that's composed in a certain key <u>sticks</u> to that key.

2) The chords used to <u>harmonise with</u> the melody have got to be in the <u>same key</u> or it'll <u>clash</u>.

3) As a <u>general rule</u> each chord in a harmony should <u>include</u> the note it's accompanying, e.g. a <u>C</u> could be accompanied by a <u>C chord</u> (C, E, G), an <u>F chord</u> (F, A, C) or an <u>A minor chord</u> (A, C, E).

There's a Chord for **Every Note** in the **Scale**

You can make dozens of triads using the notes of <u>major</u> and <u>minor</u> scales as the <u>roots</u>. <u>Every note</u> of <u>every chord</u>, not just the root, has to belong to the scale. This is how <u>C major</u> looks if you turn it into chords:

The odd accidental or ornament in a different key is OK — see p.41.

Chord I	Chord II	Chord III	Chord IV	Chord V	Chord VI	Chord VII	Chord I
Tonic	*Supertonic*	*Mediant*	*Subdominant*	*Dominant*	*Submediant*	*Leading Note*	*Tonic*

1) Chords I, IV and V are <u>major triads</u>. They sound <u>bright and cheery</u>.
   A <u>7th</u> can be added to <u>chord V</u> to give a <u>dominant 7th</u> chord (written V^7).

2) Chords II, III and VI are <u>minor triads</u>. They sound more <u>gloomy</u>.

3) Chord VII is a <u>diminished triad</u>. It sounds <u>different</u> from the major and minor chords. Another name for Chord VII is the <u>leading note chord</u> — it sounds like it should lead on to another chord.

4) Chords built on <u>any</u> major scale, not just C major, follow the <u>same pattern</u>.

5) A <u>series</u> of chords is known as a <u>harmonic progression</u> (also called a <u>chord progression</u> or <u>chord sequence</u>).

6) The <u>speed</u> at which the chords <u>change</u> is called the <u>harmonic rhythm</u>.

The **Primary Chords** are Most **Useful**

1) The three major chords, <u>I</u>, <u>IV</u> and <u>V</u>, are the <u>most important</u> in <u>any</u> key. They're called <u>primary chords</u>. Between them, the primary chords can harmonise with <u>any note</u> in the scale.

2) This is how it works in <u>C major</u>:

note...	C		D	E	F		G		A	B
goes with...	Chord I	Chord IV	Chord V	Chord I	Chord IV	Chord I	Chord V	Chord IV	Chord V
	G	C	D	G	C	G	D	C	D
	E	A	B	E	A	E	B	A	B
	C	F	G	C	F	C	G	F	G

Minor Chords Make Harmony **More Interesting**

1) Primary chords can get a bit <u>boring</u> to listen to after a while — the harmonies are fairly <u>simple</u>.

2) Composers often mix in a few of the other chords — <u>II</u>, <u>III</u>, <u>VI</u> or <u>VII</u> — for a <u>change</u>.

3) Instead of just having endless major chords, you get a mixture of minor and diminished chords too.

Inversions

Inverting triads means changing the order of the notes. It make accompaniments more varied.

Triads with the **Root at the Bottom** are in **Root Position**

These triads are all in root position — the root note is at the bottom.

● = fifth
● = third
● = root

C chord in root position   F chord in root position   G chord in root position

First Inversion Triads have the **Third** at the **Bottom**

These chords are all in first inversion. The root note's moved up an octave, leaving the third at the bottom.

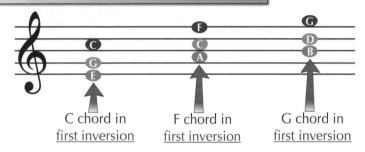

C chord in first inversion   F chord in first inversion   G chord in first inversion

Second Inversion Triads have the **Fifth** at the **Bottom**

Chords can be played in second inversion too.

From the first inversion, the third is raised an octave, leaving the fifth at the bottom.

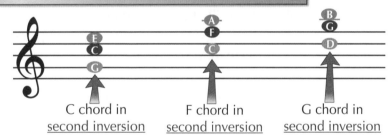

C chord in second inversion   F chord in second inversion   G chord in second inversion

7th Chords Can Go into a **Third Inversion**

1) 7th chords can be played in root position, first inversion or second inversion — just like triads.

2) But there's also a third inversion — where the 7th goes below the standard triad. They have a third inversion because they're four-note chords.

There's a **Symbol** for Each **Inversion**

This means a C chord with E at the bottom.

ROOT POSITION		5/3 chords	because there's a fifth and a third between the notes		Ia	C
FIRST INVERSION	...also known as...	6/3 chords	because there's a sixth and a third between the notes	...and in Roman numerals...	Ib	C/E
SECOND INVERSION		6/4 chords	because there's a sixth and a fourth between the notes		Ic	C/G
THIRD INVERSION		6/4/2 chords	because there's a sixth, a fourth and a second between the notes		Id	Cmaj7/B

...and in good old chord symbols...

These numbers are used in figured bass — see page 57.

Inversions

So now you know what inversions <u>are</u>. Now get to grips with what to <u>do</u> with them too...

Inversions are Handy for **Moving Between Chords**

When you play chords one after another, it sounds <u>nicer</u> if the notes move <u>smoothly</u> from one chord to the next. Inversions help to smooth out any rough patches...

1) Moving from a <u>C chord in root position</u> to a <u>G chord in root position</u> means <u>all</u> the notes have to jump a <u>long way</u>. It sounds <u>clumsy</u> and not all that nice.

Try playing both sets of chords a few times, until you can hear the difference.

2) If you move from a C chord in root position to a <u>G chord</u> in <u>first inversion</u> instead, the transition is much, much smoother.

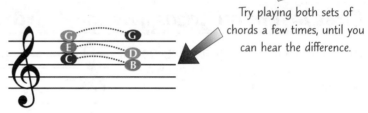

3) You can use <u>second</u> and <u>third inversions</u> too — whatever sounds best.

Unscramble the **Inversion** to Work Out the **Root Note**

This isn't exactly a life-saving skill. But it's <u>dead useful</u>...

If you come across an inverted chord you can <u>work out</u> which is the <u>root note</u>. Once you know that, and you know what <u>key</u> you're in, you can tell whether it's chord IV, VII, II or whatever.

1) Basically you have to turn the chord back into a <u>root position triad</u>.
2) Shuffle the order of the notes around until there's a <u>third interval</u> between each one.
3) When the notes are arranged in <u>thirds</u>, the root will <u>always</u> be at the <u>bottom</u>.

B to D is a THIRD, but D to G is a FOURTH.
You need to <u>move the G</u> to find the root chord.

G to B is a THIRD so the G goes here — <u>G</u>'s the <u>root note</u>.

4) There are no sharps or flats in the key signature, so the piece is in C major. G's the fifth note of C major, so this is <u>chord V</u>.

Unscramble inversions — go back to your roots...

There's a lot to take in when it comes to inversions. Don't go racing through this page — go over it one bit at a time, letting all the facts sink in. Playing the chords for yourself will help.

Different Ways of Playing Chords

So far, the chords in this section have all been written as three notes. It sounds dull if you do it all the time. To liven things up there are chord figurations — different ways of playing the chords.

Block Chords are the Most Basic

This is probably the easiest way to play chords. The notes of each chord are played all together and then held until the next chord.

Rhythmic Chords Give You Harmony and Rhythm

1) Rhythmic chords are chords played to a funky rhythm.

2) You play all the notes of each chord at the same time, like you do for block chords.

3) You don't hold the notes though — you play them to a rhythm that repeats in each bar.

4) Rhythm guitar and keyboards often play rhythmic chords.

In Broken and Arpeggiated Chords the Notes are Separate

Accompanying chords don't have to have to be played at all once. You can play the notes separately.

1) Here's one way of doing it — it goes root, fifth, third, root.

2) This pattern was really popular around the time Mozart was alive (last half of the 1700s). It's called Alberti bass after the composer Domenico Alberti — it usually goes root, fifth, third, fifth.

3) The notes of a chord are sometimes played in order (e.g. root, third, fifth, root) going up or coming down. This is called an arpeggio (are-pedge-ee-o).

4) In an arpeggiated chord, you play the notes one at a time, but in quick succession (imagine strumming a harp). On a piano, you hold down each key as you build up the chord. They're usually written with a wiggly line, like this:

5) A walking bass usually moves in crotchets, often either in steps (see p.28) or arpeggios.

6) A drone is a long, held-on note, usually in the bass, that adds harmonic interest.

7) Pedal notes are a bit different — they're repeated notes, again usually in the bass part. However, the harmony on top of a pedal note changes (whereas a drone sets up the harmony for the whole piece).

Think about using an Alberti bass in your composition...

When you get chord symbols over the music you can play the chords any way you like. Try all these ways of playing chords and think about using them in your compositions.

Examples and Practice

Read on for some more examples of the different kinds of chords.

Examples

Track 15 These are some of the most <u>common</u> chords — learn to recognise them.

a) <u>major</u> triad   b) <u>minor</u> triad

c) <u>diminished</u> triad   d) <u>augmented</u> triad

e) <u>major</u> triad with a <u>major</u> 7th   f) <u>major</u> triad with a <u>minor</u> 7th

g) <u>minor</u> triad with a <u>major</u> 7th   h) <u>minor</u> triad with a <u>minor</u> 7th

Track 16 A <u>sequence</u> of chords, showing different <u>inversions</u>:

What <u>inversion</u> a chord is
depends on which note is on
the <u>bottom</u> — it doesn't matter
how the other notes of the triad
are arranged on top.

*In these first <u>three</u> chords, chords
in the <u>first inversion</u> lead nicely on
to <u>root chords</u> a <u>perfect 4th</u> up. The
<u>semitone</u> steps in the bass make these
progressions sound smooth and logical.*

*At the <u>end</u> of the sequence, listen out
for the <u>third from last</u> note (<u>second
inversion</u> of <u>chord I</u>), which leads into
the <u>cadence</u> that ends the phrase
(see p.42-43 for more on cadences).*

How well do you know your chords... Find out by answering these practice questions.

Practice Questions

Track 17 Describe each of the eight chords on the track, using one of the following words:

major	minor	diminished	augmented

You can play these tracks
more than once.

a) ....   b) ....   c) ....

d) ....   e) ....   f) ....

g) ....   h) ....

Track 18 For each of the following you'll hear a root note, and then an inversion.
Which inversions are they?

a) ....   b) ....   c) ....

d) ....   e) ....   f) ....

g) ....   h) ....

Use Decorations to Vary the Harmony

If you want to <u>liven things up</u> in a harmony you can add a sprinkle of <u>melodic decoration</u>.

Melodic Decoration **Adds Notes** to the Tune

1) <u>Decorative notes</u> are <u>short notes</u> that move between notes or create <u>fleeting clashes</u> (<u>dissonance</u>) with the accompanying chord. They make things sound <u>less bland</u>.

2) Decoration that belongs to the key of the melody (e.g. B in C major) is called <u>diatonic</u>.

3) Decoration that <u>doesn't</u> belong to the key (e.g. F♯ in C major) is called <u>chromatic</u>.

4) There are <u>four</u> main ways of adding melodic decoration.

1) **Auxiliary** Notes are **Higher** or **Lower** than the Notes **Either Side**

1) An auxiliary note is either a <u>semitone</u> or <u>tone</u> <u>above</u> or <u>below</u> the notes either side.

2) The two notes before and after the auxiliary are always the <u>same pitch</u>, and always belong to the accompanying chord.

2) **Passing** Notes **Link** the Notes **Before** and **After**

1) A passing note <u>links</u> the notes before and after. They either belong to the same chord or link one chord with another.

2) They're usually put on <u>weak beats</u>. When they <u>are</u> on the strong beat they're called 'accented passing notes'.

3) **Appoggiaturas Clash** with the Chord

1) An appoggiatura <u>clashes</u> with the accompanying chord. It's written as a <u>little note</u> tied to the note of the chord, and takes <u>half the value</u> of the note it's tied to.

2) The note <u>before</u> it is usually quite a <u>leap</u> away (jumps between notes of more than a <u>2nd</u> are called <u>leaps</u>).

3) The note after the appoggiatura is always <u>just above</u> or <u>below</u>. It's called the <u>resolution</u>. The <u>resolution</u> has to be from the <u>accompanying chord</u>.

4) Appoggiaturas usually fall on a <u>strong beat</u>, so the resolution note falls on a <u>weaker beat</u>.

4) **Suspensions Clash** then Go Back to **Harmonising**

A suspension is a series of three notes called the <u>preparation</u>, <u>suspension</u> and <u>resolution</u>.

1) The <u>preparation</u> note belongs to the accompanying chord. It's usually on a weak beat.

2) The <u>suspension</u> is the <u>same pitch</u> as the preparation note. It's played at the same time as a <u>chord change</u>. It <u>doesn't go</u> with the new chord, so you get <u>dissonance</u>.

3) The <u>resolution</u> note moves up or down (usually down) from the suspension to a note in the accompanying chord. This <u>resolves</u> the dissonance — everything sounds lovely again.

Phrases and Cadences

Notes in a melody fall into 'phrases' just like the words in a story are made up of <u>sentences</u>.
A <u>cadence</u> is the movement from the second-to-last to the last chord of a <u>phrase</u> — it <u>finishes it off</u>.

A **Phrase** is Like a Musical **'Sentence'**

There should be clear <u>phrases</u> in any melody. A tune <u>without</u> phrases would
sound odd — just like a story with no sentences wouldn't make much sense.

1) Phrases are usually <u>two</u> or <u>four</u> bars long.

2) Phrases are sometimes marked with a <u>curved line</u> called a <u>phrase mark</u>, that goes <u>above</u> the stave. Not all music has phrase marks but the phrases are <u>always</u> there. Don't confuse phrase marks and slurs. A phrase mark <u>doesn't</u> change how you play the notes.

Cadences Emphasise the **End of a Phrase**

1) A <u>cadence</u> is the <u>shift</u> between the <u>second-to-last chord</u> and the <u>last chord</u> in a phrase.

2) The <u>effect</u> you get from shifting between the two chords works like a <u>comma</u> or a <u>full stop</u>. It <u>underlines</u> the end of the phrase and <u>gets you ready</u> for the next one.

There are **Four Main Types** of Cadence

These pairs of chords are <u>only</u> cadences when they come at the end of a phrase.
Anywhere else in a phrase, they're <u>just chords</u>.

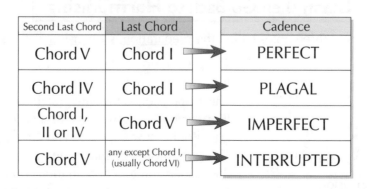

Second Last Chord	Last Chord	Cadence
Chord V	Chord I	PERFECT
Chord IV	Chord I	PLAGAL
Chord I, II or IV	Chord V	IMPERFECT
Chord V	any except Chord I, (usually Chord VI)	INTERRUPTED

More on these on the next page...

Cadences

Learning the <u>names</u> of the different cadences is no use unless you also learn what they're <u>for</u>.

Perfect and Plagal Cadences Work Like Full Stops

1) A <u>perfect cadence</u> makes a piece of music feel <u>finished or complete</u>.

2) It goes from <u>Chord V</u> to <u>Chord I</u> — in C major that's a <u>G chord</u> to a <u>C chord</u>.

3) This is how a perfect cadence goes at the <u>end</u> of 'Twinkle, Twinkle, Little Star':

How I won-der what you are

F chord IV   C chord I   G chord V   C chord I

Here's the <u>perfect cadence</u>.

4) A <u>plagal cadence</u> sounds really different from a perfect cadence but it has a <u>similar effect</u> — it makes a piece of music sound finished.

5) A plagal cadence in C major is an <u>F chord</u> (IV) to a <u>C chord</u> (I). Play it and see what it sounds like. The plagal cadence gets used at the <u>end</u> of lots of <u>hymns</u> — it's sometimes called the '<u>Amen</u>' cadence.

Imperfect and Interrupted Cadences are Like Commas

<u>Imperfect</u> and <u>interrupted</u> cadences are used to end <u>phrases</u> but <u>not</u> at the end of a piece. They work like <u>commas</u> — they feel like a <u>resting point</u> but not an ending.

An <u>imperfect cadence</u> most commonly goes from chord <u>I</u>, <u>II</u> or <u>IV</u> to <u>V</u>. Here's one going from <u>chord I</u> to <u>chord V</u> at the end of the <u>third line</u> of 'Twinkle, Twinkle':

Up a- bove the world so high

C chord I   F chord IV   C chord I   G chord V

Here's the <u>imperfect cadence</u>.

In an <u>interrupted cadence</u> chord V can go to any chord except I, but it usually goes to chord VI. You expect it to go to chord I — so it sounds "interrupted". In C major an interrupted cadence may go from a <u>G chord</u> (V) to an <u>Am chord</u> (VI).

Some Minor pieces Finish with a Tierce de Picardie

1) If a piece of music is in a <u>minor key</u>, you'd expect it to <u>finish</u> with a <u>minor chord</u>.

2) However, some composers (especially <u>Baroque</u> composers) finish a <u>minor piece</u> with a <u>major chord</u>, by using a <u>major third</u> in the last chord. This is known as a <u>Tierce de Picardie</u> (or <u>Picardy third</u>).

This excerpt is from <u>Scarlatti's Piano Sonata in G Minor</u> (<u>Cat's Fugue</u>). Even though the piece is in <u>G minor</u>, it finishes with a <u>G major chord</u>.

REVISION TIP

You need to listen to cadences to understand them...

Cadences probably won't make much sense unless you try playing them. <u>Play</u> the cadences for yourself (or listen to Track 19 — see p.48) until you can <u>hear</u> the differences between them.

Modulation

Most of the notes in a piece of music come from one key — but to vary the melody or harmony you can modulate (change key). It can happen just once, or a few times. It's up to the composer.

The **Starting Key** is Called **'Home'**

1) The key a piece starts out in is called the home key or tonic key.
2) If the music's modulated it goes into a different key.
3) The change of key is usually only temporary. The key goes back to the home key after a while.
4) However much a piece modulates, it usually ends in the home key.

There are **Two** Ways to Modulate

1) Modulation by **Pivot Chord**

1) A pivot chord is a chord that's in the home key and the key the music modulates to.
2) Chord V (G, B, D) in C major is exactly the same as chord I in G major — so it can be used to pivot between C major and G major.
3) Sometimes, the key signature changes to show the new key. More often, accidentals are written in the music where they're needed.

The home key here is C. At the end of the first bar the accompaniment uses the chord G, B, D to pivot into G major:

$\longleftarrow$ C major $\top\!\!\top$ G major $\longrightarrow$

C I   G V/I   D V   G I

Pivot chord

F♯ belongs to G major.

This is called a V/I pivot because it uses V from the home key and I from the key it modulates to.

Related keys...

		Home key		
Relative minor of IV — D minor	IV — F major	I — C major	V — G major	Relative minor of V — E minor
		Relative minor — A minor		

1) It sounds best if you modulate to related keys.
2) The closest keys are (major) keys IV and V and the relative minor.
3) The next closest are the relative minors of keys IV and V.

2) **Abrupt** Modulation

1) In abrupt modulation there's no pivot chord, and no other preparation either. It just happens.
2) Often the modulation is between two keys just one semitone apart, e.g. from C major to C♯ major.
3) Pop songs often modulate up one semitone. It creates a sudden, dramatic effect — it's meant to give the music an excited, uplifting feeling.

You can choose related keys but you can't choose your family...

If you see accidentals it often means the music's modulated, but not always. The accidental could also be there because: 1) the music's written in a minor key — harmonic or melodic (see p.25); or 2) the composer fancied a spot of chromatic decoration (see p.41). That's composers for you...

Texture

Here's one last way composers vary the harmony — by changing the <u>texture</u>. Texture's an odd word to use about music — what it means is how the different parts (e.g. chords and melody) are <u>woven together</u>.

Texture is How the parts Fit Together

1) An important part of music is how the <u>different parts</u> are <u>woven together</u>.
   This is known as <u>texture</u> — it describes how the <u>melody</u> and <u>accompaniment</u> parts <u>fit together</u>.

2) <u>Monophonic</u>, <u>homophonic</u> and <u>polyphonic</u> are all different types of texture.

3) Some textures are made up of the <u>same</u> melodic line that's passed round <u>different parts</u>.
   <u>Imitation</u> and <u>canons</u> are good examples of this.

Monophonic Music is the Simplest

1) In <u>monophonic</u> music there's <u>no harmony</u> — just one line of tune (e.g. a <u>solo</u> with <u>no accompaniment</u>).

2) Parts playing in <u>unison</u> or <u>doubling</u> each other (i.e. the same notes at the same time) are also monophonic.

3) Monophonic music has a <u>thin texture</u>.

Polyphonic Music Weaves Tunes Together

1) <u>Polyphonic</u> music gives quite a complex effect because there's <u>more than one tune</u> being played at once.

2) It's sometimes called <u>contrapuntal</u> music.

3) Parts that move in <u>contrary motion</u> (one goes <u>up</u> and another goes <u>down</u>) are polyphonic.

4) <u>Two-part music</u> (with two separate melodic lines) is also polyphonic.

In Homophonic Music, the Parts Move Together

1) If the lines of music move at more or less the <u>same time</u>, it's <u>homophonic</u> music.

2) A <u>melody with accompaniment</u> (the accompaniment is often <u>chordal</u>) is a good example of homophonic music.

3) <u>Parallel motion</u> (when parts move with the <u>same interval</u> between them, e.g. parallel 5ths) is also homophonic.

In Heterophonic Music the Instruments Share the Tune

In heterophonic music there's <u>one tune</u>. <u>All</u> the instruments play it, but with <u>variations</u>, and often at <u>different times</u>.

<u>Polyphonic</u>, <u>homophonic</u> and <u>heterophonic</u> music all have quite a <u>thick texture</u>.

You might have to write about texture in the exam...

Make sure you know all the proper words to describe texture, and that you can tell the difference between the different types — examiners love asking about it so it'll come in handy...

Texture

When there's <u>one</u> part, the music's <u>pure</u> and <u>simple</u>, but put <u>more parts in</u> and it's much more <u>complex</u>.

Imitation — Repeat a Phrase With **Slight Changes**

1) In <u>imitation</u> a phrase is repeated with <u>slight changes</u> each time.
2) It works particularly well if one instrument or voice imitates <u>another</u> and then <u>overlaps</u>.

Canon — **Same Melody** Different Parts

1) In a <u>canon</u>, each part plays the <u>same melody</u>, but they come in <u>separately</u> and at <u>regular intervals</u>. The parts <u>overlap</u>.
2) A canon is also known as a <u>round</u>. There are some really well-known rounds, e.g. 'London's Burning'.
3) Canons are an example of <u>contrapuntal</u> (or <u>polyphonic</u>) music (see previous page).
4) Composers from the <u>Baroque</u> period (1600-1750) like <u>Bach</u> and <u>Vivaldi</u> used lots of canons.

This excerpt comes from 'Spring' from Vivaldi's Four Seasons. The solo violin and first violin often play in canon.

Another common Baroque texture is the <u>continuo</u> (or <u>basso continuo</u>) — see p.57.

Looping and Layering are Modern Techniques

1) In the <u>1960s</u> and <u>70s</u>, composers like <u>Steve Reich</u> started developing <u>new techniques</u> in their music.
2) They took recordings of sections of <u>music</u>, <u>words</u>, <u>rhythms</u> and <u>other sounds</u> and <u>repeated</u> them over and over again. These are called <u>loops</u>.
3) The loops were often created by <u>cutting</u> pieces of <u>tape</u> and <u>sticking</u> the ends together so they could be played over and over again — this is <u>looping</u>.
4) If there are lots of <u>different loops</u> being played at the <u>same time</u> it's called <u>layering</u>.

A layer of fruit, a layer of sponge, a layer of custard...

There are a few more words on this page that'll be useful if you need to write about musical texture in the listening exam — imitation, canon, looped and layered. Make sure you know what they mean.

Texture

Composers use <u>different textures</u> to <u>vary</u> their music. They can change the <u>number</u> of instruments and whether they play the <u>same notes</u> or in <u>harmony</u>. They can also <u>split</u> tunes between <u>different instruments</u>.

More Than One Part Can Play the Same Melody

1) If there's just <u>one part</u> playing with <u>no accompaniment</u>, there's just a <u>single melody line</u>.

2) If there's <u>more than one</u> instrument playing the <u>same melody</u> at the <u>same pitch</u>, they're playing in <u>unison</u>.

3) If there's <u>more than one</u> instrument playing the <u>same notes</u> but in <u>different ranges</u>, they're playing in <u>octaves</u>.

All of these are examples of <u>monophonic</u> textures.

Some Instruments Play Accompanying Parts

1) The instruments that <u>aren't</u> playing the tune play the <u>accompaniment</u>. Different <u>types</u> of accompaniment give different <u>textures</u>.

2) If the accompaniment is playing <u>chords</u> underneath the melody (or the <u>same rhythm</u> of the melody but <u>different notes</u>), the texture is <u>homophonic</u>. It sounds <u>richer</u> than a single melody line, unison or octaves.

3) If there are <u>two choirs</u> singing at <u>different times</u>, the music is <u>antiphonal</u>. The two choirs will often sing <u>alternate phrases</u> — like <u>question and answer</u> or <u>call and response</u>. A lot of <u>early religious vocal music</u> was antiphonal. You can also get the same effect with two groups of <u>instruments</u>.

Group 1

Group 2

4) If there's <u>more than one</u> part playing <u>different melodies</u> at the <u>same time</u>, the music is <u>contrapuntal</u> (or <u>polyphonic</u>). Contrapuntal parts <u>fit together</u> harmonically.

The examples on this page use the melody from Handel's 'Water Music'.

Would you care to accompany me to the cinema...

There are quite a few tricky <u>textures</u> to learn on this page. Listen to the different types, and try and <u>recognise</u> what they sound like so that you can describe them if they come up in the <u>exam</u>.

Examples

Track 19 should help you get a better idea about cadences, and Track 20 gives you some different examples of modulation. Listen to them lots of times until you can recognise them straight away.

Track 19 You'll hear this bar played **four** times, followed by a different cadence each time.

a) The <u>perfect</u> cadence sounds totally <u>complete</u> — perfect, in fact. You can't imagine it moving on to any other chord.

b) The <u>plagal</u> cadence is sometimes called the "amen cadence" — it sounds <u>peaceful</u> and reassuring.

c) The <u>imperfect</u> cadence is the <u>opposite</u> of the perfect cadence. Instead of bringing things to a close, it seems to open up loads of possibilities.

d) The <u>interrupted</u> cadence starts off like a perfect cadence but ends with a more open, <u>melancholy</u> feel.

Track 20 Listen to these **three** short excerpts. Each one is a different example of a <u>modulation</u> from one key to another. In each excerpt the pattern goes like this:

Note 1 <u>Original</u> key

Note 2 <u>Original</u> key

Note 3 <u>Pivot chord</u> (in the original key and the new key)

Note 4 <u>New</u> key

Practice Questions

Practise your hard-won knowledge of chords, modulation and texture with the questions on this page and the next. Listen to each track a few times to make sure you've heard it properly.

Practice Questions

Track 21 This question is about identifying cadences.
You will hear eight phrases, a)-h), all starting like this:

Write down whether the final cadence is perfect, plagal, imperfect or interrupted.

a) ....

b) ....

c) ....

d) ....

e) ....

f) ....

g) ....

h) ....

Track 22 *For each of the following tracks, fill in the missing notes in the melody, then answer the questions.*

a)

b) The chord in the fourth bar has an A in the bass.
What inversion of chord I is this?

....

c) What type of cadence does the passage end with?

....

Track 23 a)

b) In this passage, the harmony tends to move in time with the melody.
What is the name of this type of musical texture?

....

c) What type of cadence does the passage end with?

....

d) Which note is sustained in the bass in the second-to-last bar?

....

Practice Questions

Practice Questions

Track 24 a)

b) In the first chord in bar 2, the left hand plays the major of chord II. Which note in this chord is not in the scale of the home key?

....

c) What type of cadence does the passage end with?

....

Track 25 a)

b) Circle each auxiliary note in the passage, and say whether each is diatonic or chromatic.

c) Which one of the following best describes the chord in bar 4? Ring your answer.

       1st inversion   **harmonic**   **relative minor**   **suspension**

Track 26 a)

b) What key does this passage start in?

....

c) What key does it finish in?

....

d) The B flat chord at the start of bar 3 comes before the dominant chord of the new key. Give the name of a chord in this position in a modulation.

....

e) Fill in the blanks in the following sentence with the appropriate Roman numerals:

    The B flat chord is chord .... in the home key

    and chord .... in the final key.

Warm-up and Exam Questions

Warm-up Questions

1) Name **two** instruments that are frequently used to play chords.

2) Which **three** chords in a major key produce major triads?

3) If the *root* of a chord is on the top, and the *third* of the chord is on the bottom, which inversion is the chord in?

4) Name **three** different ways of playing chords.

5) What do you call a melodic decoration that belongs to the same key as the main melody?

6) List **three** ways melodies can be decorated to help vary the harmony within a piece of music.

7) At what point in a piece of music would you expect to find an imperfect or interrupted cadence?

8) What's another name for the texture known as polyphonic?

Exam Question

Now practise your exam technique with the question below and over the page.

Track 27

Play the excerpt **four times** then answer the questions on the next page.

Leave a short pause for writing time before each playing.

Here is the complete score for the excerpt:

Exam Question

a) What instrument is playing this piece?

....

[1 mark]

b) How would you describe the way the left hand is playing at **1**?

....

[1 mark]

c) Which of the following best describes the cadence at **2**?
Circle your choice from the options below.

perfect   **plagal**   **imperfect**

[1 mark]

d) Which key is this excerpt in?

....

[1 mark]

e) Look at the key of the piece. How would you explain the sharpened note at **3**?

....

[1 mark]

f) What term is used to describe the dots above the notes at **4**?

....

[1 mark]

g) Which of these options best describes the texture of this music?
Circle your choice.

monophonic   **homophonic**   **heterophonic**

[1 mark]

Revision Summary for Section Three

There's a lot to remember here: four types of triad, four types of triad inversion, cadences, different ways of using decoration with chords, modulation, the something-phonic words... It's too much to tackle all in one go. Test yourself a page at a time and make sure you really know it. You'll know you've done it properly when you can answer all these questions <u>without</u> looking back.

1) How many notes are there in a major scale? How many notes are there in a minor scale?
2) Write out the names of the notes of a scale in words, numbers and Roman numerals.
3) Write down the tone-semitone pattern for a major scale.
4) Which major scale only uses the white notes on the keyboard?
5) What does a key signature tell you?
6) How do you find the 'relative minor' of a major scale?
7) D major has two sharps — F and C. What's the key signature of the relative minor?
8) Write out A minor in each of the three types of minor scale and label the tone and semitone gaps.
9) How many major scales are there altogether?
10) How many minor scales are there altogether?
11) Write down all the major scales in order around the circle of fifths, starting with C major.
12) Write out two common modes.
13) What's a pentatonic scale? What types of music often use pentatonic scales?
14) What are the notes in a G major pentatonic scale?
15) What's a chromatic scale? How many notes are there in a chromatic scale?
16) What's a whole tone scale?
17) What's the difference between a melodic and a harmonic interval?
18) Give the name and number of each of these intervals: a) A to C b) B to F c) C to B d) D to A
19) What's a tritone?
20) What do you call chords with: a) clashing notes b) notes that sound good together?
21) What are the two most common types of triad? Describe how you make each one.
22) What makes a 7th chord different from a triad?
23) Write down the letter symbols for these chords:
    a) G major   b) A minor   c) A minor with a major 7th   d) D diminished triad
24) Draw the scale of G major on a stave, then build a triad on each note. *(Don't forget the F sharps.)*
25) Which three chords of any major or minor scale are known as the 'primary' chords?
26) Write out the notes of the three primary chords in C major, G major and D major.
27) Where do the root, third and fifth go in: a) a first inversion chord b) a second inversion chord?
28) Are these chords in root position, first inversion, second inversion or third inversion?
    a) 6/4   b) C/E   c) IVa   d) 6/4/2
29) Name and describe four different chord figurations.
30) What's the difference between a 'diatonic' decoration and a 'chromatic' decoration?
31) Explain the following terms: a) auxiliary note   b) passing note   c) appoggiatura
32) What is a musical phrase and what job does a cadence do in a phrase?
33) How many chords make up a cadence?
34) Write down the four different types of cadence and which chords you can use to make each one.
35) What do you call it when a piece in a minor key ends on a major chord?
36) What do people mean when they talk about the 'texture' of music?
37) Explain the difference between monophonic music, homophonic music and polyphonic music.

Common Melodic Devices

Melodic devices are methods that composers use to construct melodies.
You need a few good technical words to describe them — like conjunct, disjunct, triadic and scalic.

Melodies can be **Conjunct** or **Disjunct**

1) Conjunct (or stepwise) melodies move mainly by step — notes that are a tone or a semitone apart.

2) The melody doesn't jump around, so it sounds quite smooth.
   This example shows a conjunct melody:

This excerpt's from 'The Silver Swan' by Orlando Gibbons.

3) Disjunct melodies move using a lot of jumps — notes that are more than a major 2nd (a tone) apart.

4) The melody sounds quite spiky as it jumps around a lot.

5) Disjunct melodies are harder to sing or play than conjunct ones.
   This example shows a disjunct melody:

This one's from 'Nessun Dorma' by Puccini.

6) The distance between the lowest and highest notes in any melody is called the range (or compass).

Triadic Melodies Use the Notes of a **Triad**

1) Triads are chords made up of two intervals of a third on top of each other — so triadic melodies usually move between the notes of a triad. (There's more on triads on page 35.)

2) For example, a C major triad is made up of the notes C, E and G. There's a major third between C and E, a minor third between E and G and a perfect fifth between C and G. There's more on intervals on pages 28-29.

3) This example shows a triadic melody:

This excerpt is from the first movement of Haydn's Trumpet Concerto.

Scalic Melodies Use the Notes of a **Scale**

1) A scalic melody moves up and down using the notes of a scale.

2) Scalic melodies are similar to conjunct melodies, but they can only move to the next note in the scale. Conjunct melodies can have a few little jumps in them.

3) Like conjunct melodies, scalic melodies sound quite smooth. Here's an example of a scalic melody (it's also from the first movement of Haydn's Trumpet Concerto):

Some melodies contain all of these melodic devices...

These different types of melody are pretty easy to spot if you have the music in front of you, but it's a bit harder if you're listening to them. Listen out for them in all types of music and practise identifying them.

Common Melodic Devices

Call and response is used a lot in <u>blues</u>, <u>rock</u> and <u>pop</u>, as well as <u>African</u> and <u>Indian</u> music — so it's important that you know what it is. It's used in both <u>instrumental</u> and <u>vocal</u> music.

Call and Response is Like a **Musical Conversation**

1) <u>Call and response</u> is a bit like <u>question and answer</u>. It takes place either between <u>two groups</u> of musicians, or between a <u>leader</u> and the rest of the <u>group</u>.

2) <u>One group</u> (or the <u>leader</u>) plays or sings a <u>short phrase</u>. This is the <u>call</u>. It's then <u>answered</u> by the <u>other group</u>. This is the <u>response</u>.

3) The call <u>ends</u> in a way that makes you feel a response is coming — e.g. it might finish with an <u>imperfect cadence</u> (see page 43).

4) Call and response is very popular in <u>pop</u> and <u>blues</u> music. Often the <u>lead singer</u> will sing the call and the <u>backing singers</u> will sing the response.

In a <u>12-bar blues</u> structure (see p.130), the usual pattern of a call and response would be <u>A</u>, <u>A1</u>, <u>B</u>:

<u>A</u> is the <u>call</u> (4 bars)

<u>A1</u> is the <u>call</u> repeated with <u>slight variations</u> (4 bars)

<u>B</u> is the <u>response</u> (4 bars).

To make things more <u>complicated</u>, sections A and B can have a <u>2-bar</u> call and response of their own:

Indian and **African** Music Use **Call and Response**

1) In <u>Indian</u> music, call and response is usually used in <u>instrumental music</u>. One musician will play a <u>phrase</u> and it'll either be <u>repeated</u> or <u>improvised</u> upon by another musician.

2) <u>African</u> music uses call and response in <u>religious ceremonies</u> and <u>community events</u>. The <u>leader</u> will <u>sing</u> first and the <u>congregation</u> will <u>respond</u>.

3) Call and response is also used in <u>African drumming music</u> (see p.133). The <u>master drummer</u> plays a <u>call</u> and the rest of the drummers play an <u>answering phrase</u>.

Some Melodies Form an **Arch Shape**

1) If a melody <u>finishes</u> in the <u>same way</u> it <u>started</u>, then the tune has an <u>arch shape</u>.

2) The simplest example of this is <u>ABA</u> — where the first section is the same as the last section of the piece. This is extended in some pieces to <u>ABCBA</u>, or even <u>ABCDCBA</u>.

3) This gives a <u>symmetrical</u> melody because the sections are <u>mirrored</u>. It makes the whole piece feel more <u>balanced</u>.

Call and response is used in a lot of music...

... so make sure you can <u>spot</u> it if it comes up in the exam — remember to listen out for it in both <u>instrumental</u> and <u>vocal</u> music. Keep your ears pricked for <u>arch-shaped melodies</u> too.

Common Forms

Form or structure is the way a piece of music is organised as a whole. Strophic form, through-composed form and da capo arias are all song structures. Cyclic form is found in large works like symphonies.

In **Strophic Form** Each **Verse** has the **Same Tune**

1) In strophic form, the same section of music is repeated over and over again with virtually no changes.

2) Strophic form is used in Classical, folk, blues and pop music.

3) In strophic songs, the music for each verse is the same, but the lyrics change in every verse. Hymns are a good example of this.

4) Strophic form can be thought of like this: A, A1, A2, A3, etc. — the same section is repeated but with a small change (the lyrics).

5) The first part of Led Zeppelin's 'Stairway to Heaven' is in strophic form.

In **Through-Composed Form** Each **Verse** is **Different**

1) Through-composed form is the opposite of strophic form — the music changes in every verse.

2) Every verse of lyrics has different music to accompany it, so there's no repetition.

3) Verses can have different melodies, different chords, or both.

4) This form is popular in opera, as the changing music can be used to tell stories. Verses sung by different characters can be completely different.

'Bohemian Rhapsody' by Queen is a through-composed pop song.

5) A lot of film music is through-composed — the music changes to reflect what's happening on-screen.

Baroque Composers Used **Ternary Form** in **Arias**

1) An aria is a solo in an opera or oratorio (see p.86).

2) Arias from the Baroque period (1600-1750) are often in ternary form (see p.81). Arias like this are called 'da capo arias'. Handel wrote lots of these.

After repeating Section A and Section B you come to the instruction da capo al fine. It means "go back to the beginning and play to where it says fine". The fine is at the end of Section A. That's where the piece finishes.

fine   da capo al fine

‖:SECTION A:‖ ‖:SECTION B:‖

Works in **Cyclic Form** Have a **Common Theme**

1) Pieces in cyclic form have common themes in all the movements. These themes link the movements together.

2) Big works like sonatas, symphonies and concertos are sometimes in cyclic form.

3) The linking themes vary in different ways, e.g. they might be played on different instruments, played faster or slower, or played in a different key in different movements. You'll still be able to recognise them though.

4) An example of a common theme in a piece in cyclic form is the four-note theme of Beethoven's Fifth Symphony. It appears in all the movements of the symphony.

5) Film music often has a theme — a bit of melody that keeps popping up throughout the film. The main theme from 'Star Wars®' by John Williams is really easy to recognise.

Don't mind me — I'm just passing through...

Make sure you're completely sorted with the definitions and proper names of all these forms.
Have a listen to the suggested pieces, and check you can spot the features of the forms they're written in.

Common Forms

Continuo and ground bass are both types of bass part. A cadenza is played by a soloist.

A **Continuo** is a **Bass Part**

1) A continuo (or basso continuo) is a continuous bass part. Most music written in the Baroque period has a continuo that the harmony of the whole piece is based on (see p.80).

2) The continuo can be played by more than one instrument, but at least one of the continuo group must be able to play chords (e.g. a harpsichord, organ, lute, harp, etc.). A cello, double bass or bassoon could also be used. The most common combination was a harpsichord and a cello.

3) Continuo parts were usually written using a type of notation called figured bass. Only the bass notes were written on the stave, but numbers underneath the notes told the performers which chords to play. The continuo players would then improvise using the notes of the chord.

4) If there weren't any numbers written, the chord would be a normal triad (the root, the third and the fifth). A 4 meant play a fourth instead of the third, and a 6 meant play a sixth instead of the fifth. A 7 meant that a 7th should be added to the chord.

5) The improvisation is called a realization — the performer would 'realize' a continuo part.

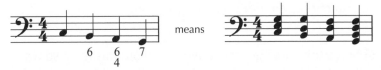

means

Some versions of Handel's Water Music still have the continuo written in figured bass.

Ground Bass Pieces Have **Repetition AND Variety**

1) A ground bass is a repeated bass part that's usually four or eight bars long. It can be played by the left hand on a harpsichord or piano, or by the cello and double bass in a chamber orchestra. A ground bass is a type of ostinato — a short pattern of notes repeated throughout a piece of music.

2) The tune is played over the ground bass part. First you hear the main tune, then a load of variations. The variations are played as one continuous piece — there are no gaps between them.

3) The ground bass part can be varied too. You change the starting note but keep the pattern the same.

First time round, the ground bass tune starts on C.   *Later on you get the same tune starting on G.*

4) The ground bass piece gets more and more complex as it goes on. It can be developed by adding extra, decorative notes to the melody, using more advanced harmonies and adding more instruments to give a richer texture.

A **Cadenza** is Where a **Soloist** can **Show Off**

1) A cadenza is a bit of music that's played by a soloist, usually in the middle of a concerto (see p.91).

2) Almost all concertos have a cadenza — it allows the soloist to show off their technique.

3) Cadenzas started out as improvisations on the main themes of a piece, but now most of them are written out by the composer. However, different musicians will interpret the cadenza in their own way.

Right, that's this page done — better continuo onto the next one...

Listen to a couple of different musicians' performances of Haydn's Trumpet Concerto in E♭ major — the cadenzas will sound different in each one, even though the soloists are playing the same notes.

Popular Song Forms

It's not just <u>Classical</u> music that follows set <u>structures</u> — <u>pop songs</u> do as well.

Pop Songs Usually Have an Intro

Pop tunes almost always start with an <u>intro</u>. It does <u>two jobs</u>:

- It often uses the best bit from the rest of the song to <u>set the mood</u>.
- It grabs people's <u>attention</u> and makes them <u>sit up and listen</u>.

Most Pop Songs Have a Verse-Chorus Structure

<u>After</u> the intro, the structure of most pop songs goes <u>verse-chorus-verse-chorus</u>.

- All the verses usually have the <u>same tune</u>, but the <u>lyrics change</u> for each verse.
- The chorus has a <u>different tune</u> from the verses, usually quite a catchy one. The lyrics and tune of the chorus <u>don't change</u>.
- In a lot of songs the verse and chorus are both <u>8 or 16 bars long</u>.

'What I Go To School For' by Busted has a verse-chorus structure.

The old verse-chorus thing can get repetitive. To avoid this most songs have a <u>middle 8</u>, or <u>bridge</u>, that sounds different. It's an <u>8-bar section</u> in the <u>middle</u> of the song with <u>new chords</u>, <u>new lyrics</u> and a whole <u>new feel</u>.

The song ends with a <u>coda</u> or <u>outro</u> that's <u>different</u> to the verse and the chorus. You can use the coda for a <u>big finish</u> or to <u>fade out gradually</u>.

Pop Songs Can Have Other Structures Too

For example:

CALL AND RESPONSE

This has <u>two bits</u> to it. <u>Part 1</u> is the call — it asks a musical <u>question</u>. <u>Part 2</u>, the response, responds with an <u>answer</u> (p.55).

RIFF

A <u>riff</u> is a <u>short section</u> of music that's <u>repeated</u> over and over again (a bit like an <u>ostinato</u> — see p.83). Riffs can be used to build up a <u>whole song</u>. <u>Each part</u>, e.g. the drums or bass guitar, has its own riff. All the riffs <u>fit together</u> to make one section of the music. They often <u>change</u> for the <u>chorus</u>.

'Flying Without Wings' by Westlife is a pop ballad.

BALLADS

These are songs that tell <u>stories</u>. Each verse usually has the <u>same rhythm</u> and <u>same tune</u>.

32-BAR SONG FORM

This breaks down into <u>four 8-bar sections</u>. Sections 1, 2 and 4 all have the <u>same melody</u>, but may have different lyrics. Section 3 has a <u>contrasting melody</u>, making an AABA structure. The 32 bars may be repeated. The song 'Somewhere Over the Rainbow' from the film 'The Wizard of Oz' has this form.

Verse — chorus — verse — chorus — tea break — chorus...

Songs from <u>musicals</u> follow these structures too. Have a listen to '<u>Any Dream Will Do</u>' from '<u>Joseph and the Amazing Technicolour Dreamcoat</u>', '<u>Bui Doi</u>' from '<u>Miss Saigon</u>' and '<u>Somewhere That's Green</u>' from '<u>Little Shop of Horrors</u>', and look for the structures.

Warm-up and Exam Questions

Warm-up Questions

1) Describe each of the following melody structures:

   Conjunct   **Disjunct**   **Triadic**   **Scalic**

2) What is through-composed form?

3) What is a ground bass, and what instruments often play these parts?

Exam Question

If there are bits you get stuck on in this question, reread the last few pages, then try again.

Play the excerpt **four** times, leaving a short pause between each playing.

 Track 28

a) i) The key signature of the excerpt is shown below.
        What key is the excerpt in?

 ....

[1 mark]

   ii) What is the interval between the notes shown on the right?
       Circle your answer.

   Major third   **Minor third**   **Diminished fourth**

[1 mark]

b) At the very beginning of the excerpt, the singer's lines are answered by
    a group of instruments. What is this back-and-forth movement called?

 ....

[1 mark]

c) Which of these examples is the music that these answering instruments play?
    Tick the box next to your choice.

A:

B:

[1 mark]

Exam Question

Play the excerpt **four** times, leaving a short pause between each playing.

Track 29

a) What musical period was this piece composed in?

....

[1 mark]

b) Name two instruments that play in the excerpt.

....

....

[2 marks]

c) The melody at the start of the excerpt is shown below.

i) Fill in the missing notes in bars 3 and 4.
The rhythm is given above the stave.

[7 marks]

ii) Which word best describes the melodic style in this excerpt?
Circle your choice from the options below.

   Conjunct   **Disjunct**   **Triadic**

[1 mark]

d) What type of bass part is used in this piece?

....

[1 mark]

e) Give one instrument that plays the bass part.

....

[1 mark]

Revision Summary for Section Four

You need to know a lot more about melodies and structures than being able to whistle a few tunes — you'll need to be familiar with all the terms used in this section so you can use them when you need to describe melodies and musical structures in the exam. If you're not sure about any, go back and have another look over the section. And then to really cement this knowledge into your head, go through these questions until you can answer them without looking back.

1) Explain what is meant by each of the following words that are used to describe melodies:
   a) conjunct,
   b) disjunct,
   c) triadic,
   d) scalic.
2) What is call and response?
3) Name two types of music that use call and response.
4) Explain what is meant by an arch-shaped melody.
5) What's the difference between strophic and through-composed form?
6) Give an example of a type of music that's often written in through-composed form, and explain why this form is used.
7) What's a da capo aria?
8) What is cyclic form?
9) What is basso continuo?
10) Explain how figured bass works.
11) Describe the structure of a ground bass piece.
12) What's a cadenza?
13) Why do pop songs have an introduction?
14) Describe verse-chorus structure.
15) What is a bridge?
16) What is a riff?
17) What is the structure of a song in 32-bar form?
18) Name two structures (other than 32-bar form) often used in pop songs.

Brass Instruments

You probably know a lot about <u>your</u> instrument. It's also a good idea to know about the instruments other people play so you can understand what they're up to. <u>Brass</u> first.

Brass Instruments are All Made of Metal

1) Brass instruments include <u>horns</u>, <u>trumpets</u>, <u>cornets</u>, <u>trombones</u> and <u>tubas</u>.

2) They're all basically a length of <u>hollow metal tubing</u> with a <u>mouthpiece</u> (the bit you blow into) at one end and a <u>funnel shape</u> (the <u>bell</u>) at the other.

3) The different <u>shapes</u> and <u>sizes</u> of these parts gives each brass instrument a different tone and character.

4) Brass instruments often play <u>fanfares</u> (short musical <u>flourishes</u>) in orchestral pieces. They're most commonly played on the <u>trumpet</u>, and can be accompanied by <u>percussion</u>. A fanfare might also be played as part of a <u>ceremony</u>.

trumpet

French horn

trombone   tuba

You Get a Noise by 'Buzzing' Your Lips

1) To <u>make a sound</u> on a brass instrument, you have to make the air <u>vibrate</u> down the tube.

2) You do it by '<u>buzzing</u>' your lips into the <u>mouthpiece</u>. You <u>squeeze</u> your lips together, then <u>blow</u> through a tiny gap so you get a <u>buzzing noise</u>.

3) You have to squeeze your lips together <u>tighter</u> to get <u>higher notes</u>.

4) Notes can be <u>slurred</u> (played together <u>smoothly</u>) or <u>tongued</u> (you use your tongue to <u>separate</u> the notes).

Brass Instruments Use Slides and Valves to Change Pitch

1) Squeezing your lips only gets a <u>limited range</u> of notes. To get a decent range, brass instruments use <u>slides</u> (like on a trombone) or <u>valves</u> (like on a trumpet).

2) The <u>slide</u> on a trombone is the <u>U-shaped tube</u> that moves in and out of the main tube. Moving it <u>out</u> makes the tube <u>longer</u> so you get a <u>lower</u> note. Moving it in makes the tube <u>shorter</u> so you get a <u>higher</u> note.

3) <u>Horns</u>, <u>trumpets</u> and <u>cornets</u> use three buttons connected to <u>valves</u>. The valves <u>open</u> and <u>close</u> different sections of the tube to make it <u>longer</u> or <u>shorter</u>. Pressing down the buttons in <u>different combinations</u> gives you all the notes you need.

Brass Players use Mutes to Change the Tone

1) A <u>mute</u> is a kind of <u>bung</u> that's put in the <u>bell</u> of a brass instrument. It's used to make the instrument play more <u>quietly</u> and change the <u>tone</u>. You wouldn't usually use one all the way through a piece — just for a <u>short section</u>.

2) <u>Different shapes</u> and <u>sizes</u> of mute change the tone in different ways, e.g. the <u>wah-wah</u> mute gives the instrument a wah-wah sound.

EXAM TIP

Brass instruments aren't always made of brass...

If you get brass in a listening test and need to say what instrument it is, remember that bigger instruments generally play lower notes and smaller instruments usually play higher notes.

Woodwind Instruments

Some people get woodwind and brass muddled up. If you're one of them, <u>learn the difference</u>.

Woodwind Instruments Used to be Made of Wood

<u>Woodwind</u> instruments got their name because they all use <u>air</u> — wind — to make a sound and once upon a time were all made of <u>wood</u>. Nowadays some are still made of <u>wood</u>. Others are made of <u>plastic</u> or <u>metal</u>. These are the main ones:

Woodwind Instruments Make Sound in Different Ways

To get a <u>sound</u> from a <u>wind</u> instrument, you have to make the <u>air</u> in its tube <u>vibrate</u>. There are <u>three different ways</u> woodwind instruments do this:

1) <u>Edge-tone instruments</u> — <u>flutes</u> and <u>piccolos</u>. Air is blown across an <u>oval-shaped hole</u>. The <u>edge</u> of the hole <u>splits</u> the air. This makes it <u>vibrate</u> down the instrument and make the sound.

2) <u>Single-reed instruments</u> — <u>clarinets</u> and <u>saxophones</u>. Air is blown down a <u>mouthpiece</u> which has a <u>reed</u> (a thin slice of wood/reed/plastic) clamped to it. The reed <u>vibrates</u>, making the air in the instrument <u>vibrate</u>, and creating the sound.

3) <u>Double-reed instruments</u> — <u>oboes</u> and <u>bassoons</u>. The air passes between <u>two reeds</u>, tightly bound together and squeezed between the lips. The reeds <u>vibrate</u> and you get a sound.

Like brass instruments, woodwind instruments can be <u>slurred</u> or <u>tongued</u> as well.

Different Notes are Made by Opening and Closing Holes

1) Wind instruments are covered in <u>keys</u>, <u>springs</u> and <u>levers</u> (or just holes for some instruments). These operate little <u>pads</u> that <u>close</u> and <u>open</u> holes down the instrument.

2) Opening and closing holes effectively makes the instrument longer or shorter. The <u>shorter</u> the tube, the <u>higher</u> the note. The <u>longer</u> the tube, the <u>lower</u> the note.

I can't see the woodwind for the clarinets...

Flutes and saxophones are made of metal but they're still woodwind instruments. If you're still confused, remember that woodwind instruments sound more breathy than brass instruments.

Orchestral Strings

Orchestral strings are the <u>heart</u> of the orchestra — or so string players would have you believe.

The **Double Bass, Cello, Viola**
and **Violin** are Very Alike

violin

viola

cello

double bass

These are all <u>made</u> and played in a <u>similar way</u>. The main differences are the <u>size</u> and <u>pitch</u>.

The <u>bigger</u> the instrument is, the <u>lower</u> the sounds it makes. So the double bass plays the lowest notes and the violin plays the highest.

Stringed Instruments can be **Bowed** or **Plucked**

bow (made of wood and hair). The hair is drawn across the strings.

When the <u>strings vibrate</u>, the air inside the instrument <u>vibrates</u> and amplifies the <u>sound</u>. There are two ways to get the strings vibrating:

1) <u>Bowing</u> — drawing a bow across the string. *Con arco* (or just *arco*) means '<u>with bow</u>'.

2) <u>Plucking</u> the string with the tip of your finger. The posh word for this is *pizzicato*.

The **Strings** are '**Stopped**' to Make **Different Notes**

1) You can get an "<u>open note</u>" just by plucking or bowing one of the four strings.

2) To get all the other notes, you have to change the <u>length</u> of the strings. You do this by <u>pressing down</u> with your finger. It's called <u>stopping</u>.

3) If you stop a string <u>close to the bridge</u>, the string's short and you get a <u>high</u> note.

4) If you stop a string <u>further away</u> from the bridge, the string's longer and you get a <u>lower</u> note.

5) <u>Double-stopping</u> is when <u>two</u> notes are played at the same time. Both strings are <u>pressed</u> (not open).

6) If you just <u>touch</u> a string <u>lightly</u> at certain points (instead of stopping), you can produce a series of <u>higher</u>, <u>fainter-sounding notes</u> called <u>harmonics</u>.

You Can Get **Very Varied** Effects with Stringed Instruments

mute

strings

bridge

1) **Tremolo** The bow's moved <u>back and forth</u> really <u>quickly</u>. This makes the notes sort of trembly. It's a great effect for making music sound <u>spooky</u> and <u>dramatic</u>.

2) **Col legno** The <u>wood</u> of the bow (instead of the hair) is tapped on the strings. This makes an <u>eerie</u>, <u>tapping</u> sound.

3) **Con sordino** A <u>mute</u> is put over the <u>bridge</u> (the piece of wood that supports the strings). It makes the strings sound <u>distant</u> and <u>soft</u>. Mutes are made of <u>wood</u>, <u>rubber</u> or <u>metal</u>.

4) **Vibrato** By <u>wobbling</u> the finger used to stop a string, a player varies the <u>pitch</u> slightly, creating a <u>rich tone</u>. This technique is also used on the <u>guitar</u> (see next page).

The **Harp** is Different...

1) The harp's <u>always plucked</u> — not bowed.

2) Most have <u>47</u> strings. Plucking each string in order on a concert harp is like playing up the <u>white notes</u> on a piano.

3) It has <u>seven pedals</u>. Pressing and releasing these lets you play <u>sharp</u> and <u>flat</u> notes.

4) You can play <u>one</u> note at a time, or play <u>chords</u> by plucking a few strings together.

EXAM TIP

Don't stop now, there are lots more instruments to come...

Make sure you learn the different string effects — you might need to identify them in the exam.

Guitars

Guitars are <u>everywhere</u> so it's best to know a bit about how they work.

An **Acoustic Guitar** has a **Hollow Body**

The <u>acoustic guitar</u> makes a sound the same way as the orchestral strings — by vibrating air in its belly.
Slightly different types are used by pop, folk and classical guitarists, but the <u>basic design</u> is similar.

HOLLOW BODY makes the string vibrations <u>resonate</u>, giving a louder sound.

acoustic guitar

STRINGS tuned to the notes E(low)-A-D-G-B-E(high). Low E is the string nearest your head as you're playing. Played with <u>fingers</u> or a <u>plectrum</u>.

FRETS (the little metal strips on the fingerboard/neck) help the player find the <u>correct finger position</u> for different notes.

There are three different kinds of acoustic guitar:

1) The <u>classical</u> or <u>Spanish</u> guitar has <u>nylon strings</u> (the thickest three are covered in <u>fine wire</u>).
2) The <u>acoustic guitar</u> has <u>steel strings</u> and is used mainly in <u>pop</u> and <u>folk music</u>.
3) The <u>12-stringed guitar</u> is often used in <u>folk music</u>. There are <u>two</u> of each string, giving a '<u>thicker</u>' sound which works well for accompanying <u>singing</u>.

Some guitar music is written in <u>tablature</u> (tab for short) — the numbers tell guitarists which frets to place their fingers at for each string.

```
E ──────────────
B ──────────────
G ──────────────
D ──────0──0────
A ──2───────2───
E ──────────────
```

This means play the 2nd fret on the A string, then the open D string, then both at the same time.

Electric Guitars Use an **Amplifier** and a **Loudspeaker**

electric guitar

1) An <u>electric guitar</u> has <u>six strings</u>, just like an acoustic guitar, and is <u>played</u> in a similar way.
2) The main difference is that an electric guitar has a <u>solid body</u>.
   The sound's made louder <u>electronically</u>, using an <u>amplifier</u> and a <u>loudspeaker</u>.
3) A <u>combo</u> (short for combination) is an <u>amplifier</u> and <u>loudspeaker</u> '<u>all in one</u>'.

The **Bass Guitar** has **Four Strings**

1) The <u>bass guitar</u> works like a guitar except it usually has <u>four strings</u>, not six.
2) They're tuned to the notes <u>E-A-D-G</u> (from lowest note to highest).
3) It's <u>lower pitched</u> than other guitars because it has <u>thicker and longer</u> strings.
4) Most bass guitars have frets, but there are some (imaginatively named <u>fretless basses</u>) that don't.

Like ordinary guitars, you can get electric or acoustic basses.

Guitar Strings are **Picked** or **Strummed**

1) Plucking <u>one string</u> at a time is called <u>picking</u>. <u>Classical</u> and <u>lead guitarists</u> pick the notes of a <u>melody</u>. <u>Bass</u> guitarists almost <u>always</u> pick out the individual notes of a bass line. They <u>hardly ever strum</u>.
2) Playing <u>two or more</u> strings at a time in a sweeping movement is called <u>strumming</u>. It's how <u>chords</u> are usually played. <u>Pop</u> and <u>folk guitarists</u> tend to play <u>accompaniments</u> rather than tunes, so they do more strumming than picking.
3) A <u>plectrum</u> is a small, flat piece of plastic that guitarists can use to pluck or strum with.
4) '<u>Hammer-on</u>' (<u>ho</u>) and '<u>pull-off</u>' (<u>po</u>) are techniques that allow a guitarist to play notes in <u>quick succession</u> — they create a <u>smoother</u>, more <u>legato</u> sound than picking.
5) Another guitar technique is '<u>palm muting</u>' (<u>pm</u>) — <u>dampening</u> the sound with your hand whilst <u>plucking</u> the strings. This can be done on <u>bass guitars</u> too.
6) To produce a <u>different</u> sound on the bass guitar, you can <u>strike</u> the strings with your <u>thumb</u> (instead of <u>plucking</u> with your <u>fingers</u>), which gives a more <u>percussive</u> sound. This is known as <u>slap bass</u>.
7) Guitarists can also press a <u>tube</u> (usually made of <u>metal</u>) called a <u>slide</u> or <u>bottleneck</u> against the strings. The player can move <u>smoothly</u> between <u>notes</u> by <u>sliding</u> this up or down the neck of the guitar.

Keyboard Instruments

The actual <u>keyboard</u> looks much the same on most keyboard instruments, but the wires and mysterious levers <u>inside</u> vary quite a bit. That means the <u>sounds</u> they make vary too.

Harpsichords, Virginals and Clavichords Came First

harpsichord

1) Harpsichords were invented long before pianos. They're still played today but they were <u>most popular</u> in the <u>Baroque</u> and <u>early Classical</u> periods.

2) Harpsichords have quite a <u>tinny</u>, <u>string</u> sound. When you press a key a string inside is <u>plucked</u> by a lever. You can't vary the <u>strength</u> of the pluck, so you <u>can't</u> vary the <u>dynamics</u>.

3) A <u>virginal</u> is a <u>miniature</u> table-top version of a harpsichord. In the <u>sixteenth century</u>, virginals were really popular in England.

4) The <u>clavichord</u> is another early keyboard instrument. Clavichords are small and have a <u>soft</u> sound. The strings are <u>struck</u> with hammers (called "blades"), not plucked, so you can <u>vary</u> the dynamics a <u>little bit</u>.

The Most Popular Keyboard Instrument Now is the Piano

1) The piano was invented around <u>1700</u>. The <u>technology</u> is <u>more sophisticated</u> than it was in earlier keyboard instruments. When a key's pressed, a hammer hits the strings. The <u>harder</u> you hit the key, the <u>harder</u> the hammer hits the strings and the <u>louder</u> the note — there's a big range of <u>dynamics</u>.

2) Pianos have a wide range of <u>notes</u> — up to <u>seven and a half octaves</u>.

3) Pianos have <u>pedals</u> that let you change the sound in different ways.

The <u>soft</u> pedal on the left <u>mutes</u> the strings, making a softer sound.

The <u>sustain</u> pedal on the right <u>lifts</u> all the <u>dampers</u>. This lets the sound <u>ring on</u> until you release the pedal.

For more detail on the piano, have a look at page 100.

<u>Grand pianos</u> have a <u>middle pedal</u> too. This lets the player <u>choose</u> which notes to sustain. Modern pianos might have an extra mute pedal for <u>very quiet</u> practising.

Traditional Organs Use Pumped Air to Make Sound

1) The traditional organ (the <u>massive instrument</u> with hundreds of metal pipes that you see in churches and concert halls) is one of the most <u>complicated</u> instruments ever designed.

2) Sound is made by <u>blowing air</u> through sets of pipes called <u>ranks</u>. The air is pumped in by <u>hand</u>, <u>foot</u> or, on more recent organs, <u>electric pumps</u>.

3) The pipes are controlled by <u>keyboards</u> (called <u>manuals</u>) and lots of <u>pedals</u> which make a keyboard for the player's feet.

4) <u>Pressing</u> a key or pedal lets air pass through one of the pipes and play a note. <u>Longer</u> pipes make <u>lower</u> notes. <u>Shorter</u> pipes make <u>higher</u> notes.

5) Organs can play <u>different types of sound</u> by using differently designed pipes. Buttons called <u>stops</u> are used to select the different pipes. One stop might select pipes that make a <u>trumpet</u> sound, another might select a <u>flute</u> sound...

6) Modern <u>electronic organs</u> don't have pipes. Sound is produced <u>electronically</u> instead. These organs are much <u>smaller</u> and <u>cheaper</u> to build.

You've got to learn it all...

Listen to music played on each of these instruments so that you know how they all sound — harpsichords have a more <u>jangly</u> tone than pianos, and organs are fairly easy to spot as well.

Percussion

A percussion instrument is anything you have to <u>hit</u> or <u>shake</u> to get a sound out of it. There are <u>two types</u>: those that play tunes are called <u>tuned percussion</u>, and the ones you just hit are <u>untuned</u>.

Tuned Percussion Can Play Different Notes

XYLOPHONES have <u>wooden</u> bars. The sound is '<u>woody</u>'.

GLOCKENSPIEL — Looks a bit like a xylophone but the bars are made of <u>metal</u>. Sounds <u>tinkly</u> and <u>bell-like</u>.

CELESTA — a bit like a glockenspiel except that you use a <u>keyboard</u> instead of whacking it with a hammer.

TUBULAR BELLS — Each of the <u>hollow steel tubes</u> plays a different note. Sounds a bit like <u>church bells</u>.

TIMPANI — also called <u>kettledrums</u>. The handles on the side or the foot pedal can be used to tighten or relax the skin, giving <u>different notes</u>.

VIBRAPHONE — This is like a <u>giant glockenspiel</u>. There are long tubes called <u>resonators</u> below the bars to make the notes <u>louder</u> and <u>richer</u>. <u>Electric fans</u> can make the notes <u>pulsate</u>, giving a warm and gentle sound.

There are Hundreds of Untuned Percussion Instruments

<u>Untuned percussion</u> includes any instrument that'll <u>make a noise</u> — but <u>can't</u> play a tune. These are the instruments that are used for <u>pure rhythm</u>. It's pretty much <u>impossible</u> to learn <u>every</u> untuned percussion instrument, but try and remember the names of these.

Percussion instruments make different sounds depending on what you hit them with. e.g. hard wooden drumsticks, mallets, beaters (sticks with hard or soft round heads), brushes...

Remember — xylophones are wooden, glockenspiels are metal...

In a band, the drummer's job is to make a song sound like it's going somewhere and keep everyone in <u>time</u>. In an orchestra, percussion emphasises the <u>rhythm</u> of the piece and also adds <u>special effects</u> — you can imitate thunder with a drum roll on the timpani, or the crashing of waves with clashes of the cymbals.

The Voice

There are special names for male and female <u>voices</u> and <u>groups</u> of voices.

Female Singers are Soprano, Alto or Mezzo-Soprano

1) A singer with a particular type of voice is expected to be able to sing a certain <u>range</u> of notes.

2) The range of notes where a particular singer is most <u>comfortable</u> is called the <u>tessitura</u>. This term can also describe the <u>most commonly used</u> range of notes within a vocal or instrumental part of a piece.

3) A <u>high</u> female voice is called a <u>soprano</u>. The main female parts in operas are sung by sopranos.

4) A <u>lower</u> female voice is called an <u>alto</u> — short for <u>contralto</u>.

5) <u>Mezzo-sopranos</u> sing in the <u>top</u> part of the <u>alto</u> range and the <u>bottom</u> part of the <u>soprano</u> range.

Male Voices are Tenor or Bass

1) <u>Higher</u> male voices are called <u>tenors</u>.

2) <u>Low</u> male voices are called <u>basses</u> (it's pronounced "bases").

3) <u>Baritones</u> sing the <u>top</u> part of the <u>bass</u> range and the <u>bottom</u> part of the <u>tenor</u> range.

4) Men who sing in the <u>female vocal range</u> are called <u>countertenors</u>.

5) Some tenors, baritones and basses can push their voices <u>higher</u> to sing some of the same notes as a <u>soprano</u>. This is called <u>falsetto</u> singing.

Children's Voices are Either Treble or Alto

1) A <u>high child's</u> voice in the <u>same range</u> as a <u>soprano</u> is called a <u>treble</u>.

2) A <u>low child's</u> voice is called an <u>alto</u>. They sing in exactly the <u>same range</u> as an adult alto.

3) <u>Girls'</u> voices <u>don't change much</u> as they get older. <u>Boys'</u> voices <u>drop</u> to a <u>lower range</u> when they hit puberty.

When Several Voices Sing Each Part It's a Choir

1) A <u>choir</u> is a group of singers. Each part is performed by <u>more than one</u> singer.

2) A <u>mixed voice choir</u> has sopranos, altos, tenors and basses (<u>SATB</u> for short).

3) An <u>all-male choir</u> has trebles, altos, tenors and basses — a treble has the same range as a soprano, so it's basically SATB.

4) A <u>male voice choir</u> is slightly different — it tends to have two groups of <u>tenors</u>, as well as <u>baritones</u> and <u>basses</u> (<u>TTBB</u> for short), with no higher parts.

5) An <u>all-female choir</u> has <u>two groups of sopranos</u> and <u>two groups of altos</u> (<u>SSAA</u> for short).

6) When a choir sings <u>without</u> an instrumental <u>accompaniment</u>, this is known as '<u>a cappella</u>'.

7) Music written for a choir is called <u>choral music</u> — see page 85.

These are the names for smaller groups:
2 singers = a **duet**
3 singers = a **trio**
4 singers = a **quartet**
5 singers = a **quintet**
6 singers = a **sextet**

No excuses — get on and learn all the voices...

The different voices don't just sound different in pitch — they've got different characters too, e.g. sopranos usually sound very clear and glassy, and basses sound more rich and booming.

Wind, Brass and Jazz Bands

In your listening exam, you'll get marks for saying what type of <u>group</u> (or <u>ensemble</u>) is playing.
<u>Wind</u>, <u>jazz</u> and <u>brass</u> bands can sound quite <u>similar</u>, so make sure you know the differences.

Wind Bands have Woodwind, Brass and Percussion

1) Wind bands are <u>largish groups</u>, made up of 'wind' instruments —
woodwind and brass — and percussion instruments.

2) There's <u>no string section</u>. If there was it would be an orchestra...

3) <u>Military bands</u> are wind bands. They tend to play <u>marches</u> — pieces with a
<u>regular rhythm</u> (usually $\frac{4}{4}$ or $\frac{2}{4}$ time) that can be marched to.

Brass Bands have Brass and Percussion

1) A brass band is a group of <u>brass</u> and <u>percussion</u> instruments.

2) A typical brass band would have <u>cornets</u>, <u>flugelhorns</u>, <u>tenor</u> and <u>baritone horns</u>,
<u>tenor</u> and <u>bass trombones</u>, <u>euphoniums</u> and <u>tubas</u>.

3) The exact <u>percussion instruments</u> depend on the piece being played.

4) Brass bands have been popular in <u>England</u> for <u>years</u>.

5) <u>Contests</u> are organised through the year to find out which bands are 'best'.
There's a <u>league system</u> similar to football. The divisions are called <u>sections</u>.
There are <u>five sections</u> and bands are <u>promoted</u> and <u>demoted</u> each year
depending on how they do at the <u>regional</u> and <u>national</u> contests.

Jazz Bands are Quite Varied

1) Jazz bands have <u>no fixed set of instruments</u>.

2) Small jazz groups are known as <u>combos</u>. A typical combo
might include a <u>trumpet</u>, <u>trombone</u>, <u>clarinet</u>, <u>saxophone</u>, <u>piano</u>,
<u>banjo</u>, <u>double bass</u> and <u>drum kit</u> — but there's no fixed rule.
Combos play in small venues like <u>clubs</u> and <u>bars</u>.

3) Larger jazz bands are known as <u>big bands</u> or <u>swing bands</u>. Instruments are doubled and tripled
up so you get a <u>much bigger sound</u>. Big bands were really popular in the <u>1930s</u> and <u>1940s</u>.
They played live at <u>dance halls</u>.

4) A large jazz band with a string section is called a <u>jazz orchestra</u>.

Jazz Bands have a Rhythm Section and a Front Line

In a jazz band, players are either in the <u>rhythm section</u> or the <u>front line</u>.

1) The <u>rhythm section</u> is the instruments responsible for <u>keeping the beat</u> and
<u>adding the harmony parts</u>. The rhythm section's usually made up of the
<u>drum kit</u> with a <u>double</u> or <u>electric bass</u>, <u>electric guitar</u> and <u>piano</u>.

2) The instruments that <u>play the melody</u> are the <u>front line</u>. This is usually
<u>clarinets</u>, <u>saxophones</u> and <u>trumpets</u>, but could also be guitar or violin.

Keep at it — there are more groups to come...

You need to know the differences between wind, brass and jazz bands — if you reckon you've got it sorted,
test yourself by covering up the page and writing down the instruments that play in each type of band.

Chamber Music

Chamber music is music composed for <u>small groups</u> and it's pretty formal stuff.

Chamber Music was Originally 'Home Entertainment'

1) '<u>Chamber</u>' is an old word for a room in a posh building like a palace or a mansion.

2) <u>Rich people</u> could afford to <u>pay musicians</u> to come and play in their 'chambers'. Musical families could play the music for themselves. The music written for these private performances is called <u>chamber music</u>.

3) Nowadays, you're more likely to hear chamber music in a <u>concert hall</u> or on a <u>CD</u> than live at someone's house. Let's face it — most people haven't got the cash to hire musicians for the evening, and they can download any music they want to listen to.

Chamber Music is Played by **Small Groups**

1) The rooms where musicians came to play were nice and <u>big</u> — but <u>not enormous</u>. Limited space meant that chamber music was written for a <u>small number</u> of musicians — between <u>two</u> and <u>eight</u>.

2) There's a <u>name</u> for each size of group:

> **Duet** = two players
> **Trio** = three players
> **Quartet** = four players
> **Quintet** = five players
> **Sextet** = six players
> **Septet** = seven players
> **Octet** = eight players

Have a look at the names for singing groups on p.68 — they're much the same.

These instruments make up a 'piano trio' — see below.

3) With so <u>few people</u> in chamber groups, you <u>don't</u> need a conductor. Instead, one of the players <u>leads</u>. The others have to <u>watch</u> and <u>listen</u> carefully, to make sure the <u>timing</u>, <u>dynamics</u> and <u>interpretation</u> are right.

4) Each part in the music is played by <u>just one person</u>.

Some **Chamber Groups** are **Extra-Popular** with Composers

Chamber music is written <u>more often</u> for some instrumental groups than others.
These are some of the most <u>popular</u> types of chamber group:

String trio	— violin, viola, cello
String quartet	— first violin, second violin, viola, cello
Piano trio	— piano, violin, cello (<u>not</u> three pianos)
Clarinet quintet	— clarinet, first violin, second violin, viola, cello (<u>not</u> five clarinets)
Wind quintet	— usually flute, oboe, clarinet, horn and bassoon

Chamber groups are small...

Learn the instruments that play in all the different chamber groups. Keep a special eye out for the piano trio and clarinet quintet — they're not what you'd expect. And finally, don't forget there's no conductor.

The Orchestra

If you go to a classical concert, more often than not there'll be an <u>orchestra</u> up there on stage. Loads and loads of classical music has been written for orchestras.

A **Modern Orchestra** has **Four** Sections

If you go and see a <u>modern symphony orchestra</u>, it'll have <u>four sections</u> of instruments — strings (p.64), woodwind (p.63), brass (p.62) and percussion (p.67). The strings, woodwind, brass and percussion always sit in the <u>same places</u>.

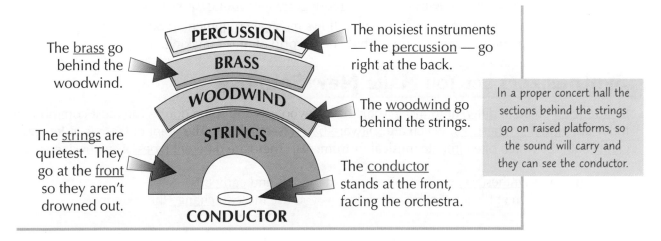

The <u>brass</u> go behind the woodwind.

The noisiest instruments — the <u>percussion</u> — go right at the back.

PERCUSSION
BRASS
WOODWIND
STRINGS

The <u>woodwind</u> go behind the strings.

In a proper concert hall the sections behind the strings go on raised platforms, so the sound will carry and they can see the conductor.

The <u>strings</u> are quietest. They go at the <u>front</u> so they aren't drowned out.

CONDUCTOR

The <u>conductor</u> stands at the front, facing the orchestra.

The **Conductor** has a **Complete Overview**

1) The conductor has a <u>score</u> — a version of the piece with <u>all the parts</u>. The <u>parts</u> are arranged in a <u>standard order</u>, one on top of the other, so that it's easy to see what any part is doing at any time. Woodwind parts are written at the <u>top</u>, followed by brass, percussion, and strings at the <u>bottom</u>.

2) The conductor <u>controls the tempo</u> by beating time with their hands, or a <u>baton</u> — a pointy white stick that's easy to see. There's a different way of beating time for each <u>time signature</u>.

3) The conductor '<u>cues in</u>' musicians — especially helpful for <u>brass</u> and <u>percussion</u>, who sometimes don't play anything for <u>hundreds of bars</u>, then suddenly have to play a <u>really loud, important bit</u>.

4) The conductor <u>interprets</u> the music. A conductor can decide whether to play one bit <u>louder</u> than another, whether to play a section in a <u>moody</u> or a <u>magical</u> way, and whether to make a piece sound very <u>smooth</u> or very <u>edgy</u>. They're a bit like a <u>film director</u> deciding the best way to <u>tell a story</u>.

An **Orchestra** is Any **Large Group with Strings**

<u>Symphony orchestras</u> (above) are the biggest type of orchestra. There are <u>other</u> smaller kinds too:

1) <u>String orchestra</u> — an orchestra with <u>stringed instruments</u> only.

2) <u>Chamber orchestra</u> — a <u>mini-orchestra</u>. It has a small string section, a wind and brass section with <u>one or two</u> of each instrument (but <u>no</u> tubas or trombones) and a small percussion section.

3) <u>Jazz orchestra</u> — a largish jazz group with an added string section.

You have to do what the conductor tells you...

Copy out the diagram of the orchestra, but don't copy the labels. Close the book and see if you can fill in the different instrument sections in the right places. Then learn all about the conductor.

Music Technology

Modern technological and 'virtual' instruments allow a huge variety of sounds to be created.

MIDI lets you Connect Electronic Musical Instruments

1) MIDI was invented in 1983. It stands for Musical Instrument Digital Interface. It's a way of connecting different electronic instruments.

2) MIDI equipment is connected by MIDI cables.

3) MIDI data is digital information (i.e. in zeroes and ones). It's sent down the MIDI cables. MIDI instruments turn MIDI information into sound (or vice versa).

4) One important advantage of MIDI is that it allows musical equipment to be linked with computers, opening up a whole new world of music-making.

Synthesizers Let You Make New Sounds

Synthesizers come in different forms — some have keyboards and some don't. The most common ones today are virtual synthesizers, which are software-based (see below). The point of them is to let you create sounds, which often imitate musical instruments. There are different types of synthesizers:

1) Analogue synthesizers were mainly made in the 70s and early 80s. They've often got lots of knobs and sliders — you use these to change the sound.

2) Digital synthesizers started to be popular in the 80s. Most modern synthesizers are digital, though some of them try to mimic analogue synths. Digital synths usually have fewer knobs and sliders than analogue ones.

3) Software synths started to become popular in the late 90s. Software synths are computer programs (often linked to a sequencer — see below). They often have graphical sliders and knobs that you can move with a mouse. Some of them try to be like analogue and early digital synthesizers. They also try to recreate classic electric instruments like the Hammond organ.

Sequencers Let You Record, Edit and Replay Music

1) Sequencer is the posh word for equipment that can record, edit (mess about with) and replay music stored as MIDI or audio information. A "sequenced composition" is a musical piece produced mainly from synthesized sounds using a sequencer.

2) Modern sequencers are usually computer programs, which often include synthesizers and samplers.

3) Most sequencers can record audio (real sounds) as well as the MIDI stuff, so you can create synthesized music and then record your own voice or instruments along with it. If you're unhappy with part of a recording, it's easy to replace that section with a re-take.

4) Modern sequencers are multi-track recorders. This allows the various lines of music, such as those played by different instruments, to be recorded on separate tracks. The individual tracks can then be edited separately to achieve the perfect balance of sounds.

5) One of the big advantages of a sequencer is that it shows your music as actual notation or as representative boxes — this makes it much easier to change and try out new ideas.

6) Drum machines are special sequencers that play back rhythm patterns using built-in drum sounds.

This can all be a bit confusing...

Some of this stuff is quite technical — but don't panic. You don't need to have an in-depth understanding of how the different types of technology work — as long as you know what they do and what people use them for. You can even have a go at using them in your compositions.

Music Technology

Sampling is a very popular way of putting different sounds into your music.
Samples can be fiddled with and looped to make long repeated sections.

Samplers let you 'Pinch' Other People's Sounds

1) A sampler is a piece of equipment that can record, process (change) and play back bits of sound.

2) These sections of sound are called samples.

3) Samplers are often used to take a bit of a piece of music that's
   already been recorded to use in some new music.

4) You can sample anything from instruments to birdsong — even weird things like a car horn.

5) Today, samplers are most often used to reproduce the sound of real instruments,
   such as strings or piano. Most pop music is sampled.

6) Pop stars often use samples of other people's music in their own music
   — anything from other pop songs to bits from Classical pieces. For example:

   • Madonna used a sample of ABBA's 'Gimme! Gimme! Gimme! (A Man After Midnight)'
     in her 2005 hit 'Hung Up'.
   • Take That used a sample from Verdi's Requiem (see p.103) in 'Never Forget' (1995).
   • Fallout Boy used a sample of 'Tom's Diner' by Suzanne Vega in their song 'Centuries' in 2014.

Samples Can be Added to Other Pieces

1) You don't have to create a piece made up entirely of samples — you can just add one or
   two, or use a whole range to create a collage of sound. The collage can then be put over
   the top of a repeating drum and bass loop.

2) DJs and producers often do this when they make a dance remix of a piece.

   > REMIX is a term used for a different version of a piece of music.
   > They're often used to turn pop or rock tunes into dance music
   > — e.g. by speeding them up and giving them a fast drum beat.

3) Samples can be added to a piece by over-dubbing — adding tracks over the top of other tracks.
   You can record a drum track, then overlay the guitar part, then the vocal part, etc.

DJs Choose, Play and Alter Music

1) DJs (disc jockeys) choose which tracks (lines of music) to play, and change bits of them (e.g. by adding
   samples). They choose compatible tracks — ones that work well together, e.g. tracks in the same key.

2) DJs play music in clubs and on the radio.

3) At a live performance in a club, the DJ sometimes adds extra sounds using samples, keyboards
   or a drum machine to build the piece up. Some DJs also rap over the top of the music.

4) DJs use a mixing desk to combine different tracks and add extra sounds to the music,
   and a set of decks to play their music.

5) The amplification is important — DJs need to make sure the right parts stand out,
   and that all parts can be heard. The amplification can be changed in live performances.

There's even a dance remix of Beethoven's 5th Symphony...

Again, there's lots of technical bits on this page. You might choose to use some samples in your own
compositions, but even if you don't, you need to know how other people (like DJs) might use them.

Timbre

When you're listening to music, you can pick out <u>individual instruments</u> because of their <u>unique sound</u> — e.g. a trumpet sounds nothing like a violin. This is all down to a little thing called <u>timbre</u>.

Every Instrument Has its Own **Timbre**

1) <u>Timbre</u> is the <u>type of sound</u> that different instruments make. It's also known as <u>tone colour</u>.

2) <u>Musical notes</u> (and all sounds) are made by <u>vibrations</u>. Different instruments produce vibrations in <u>different ways</u>. For example, on a <u>string</u> instrument, the <u>bow</u> is drawn across the <u>string</u> to make it vibrate. On a <u>brass</u> instrument the vibrations are produced when the player '<u>buzzes</u>' their lips. The different <u>vibrations</u> make the <u>timbres</u> different.

3) The <u>size</u> and <u>material</u> of the instrument alter the timbre as well — e.g. a <u>cello</u> has a different timbre to a <u>violin</u> because it's <u>bigger</u>, and <u>wooden</u> flutes sound different from <u>metal</u> ones.

4) The same instrument can sound <u>different</u> depending on who's playing it. The <u>tone</u> (or quality) of the sound is affected by an individual's <u>playing style</u> and can be described as <u>rich</u>, <u>full</u>, <u>strong</u>, etc.

5) The overall nature of the sound produced by an instrument is called its <u>sonority</u>. <u>Timbre</u> and <u>tone</u> contribute to this, along with the <u>dynamics</u> and <u>articulation</u> of the music.

Instruments From the **Same Family** Have **Similar Timbres**

Even though each instrument has a <u>unique</u> timbre, it can still sometimes be <u>hard</u> to tell ones from the <u>same family</u> apart. Different families of instruments <u>change</u> the <u>timbre</u> in <u>different ways</u>:

STRING INSTRUMENTS

- String instruments (like the <u>violin</u>, <u>viola</u>, <u>cello</u> and <u>double bass</u>) have a <u>warm</u> sound. Notes are produced by making the <u>strings vibrate</u>, either using a <u>bow</u> or the <u>fingers</u>.
- All string instruments can be played *con arco* (with a bow), *pizzicato* (plucked), *con sordino* (muted) or *sul ponticello* (close to the bridge).
- <u>Double stopping</u> is when <u>two strings</u> are pressed at the <u>same time</u>, so <u>two notes</u> can be played at once.
- <u>Tremolo</u> sounds like <u>trembling</u> — the bow is moved <u>back and forth</u> very quickly.

PIANO

- When you press the <u>keys</u>, a <u>hammer</u> hits the strings inside the piano, making them <u>vibrate</u>.
- The timbre of the piano can be <u>changed</u> by using the <u>soft</u> or <u>sustain pedals</u>.

There's more on families of instruments and types of ensembles on pages 62-71.

WOODWIND INSTRUMENTS

- Wind instruments (e.g. <u>flute</u>, <u>clarinet</u>, <u>oboe</u> and <u>bassoon</u>) have a <u>soft</u>, <u>mellow</u> sound.
- <u>Edge-tone</u> instruments (e.g. flutes) make a <u>softer</u>, <u>breathier</u> sound than <u>reed</u> instruments (e.g. clarinets).
- Clarinets and oboes can <u>alter</u> their timbre by using a technique called '<u>bells up</u>', where the player <u>points</u> the end of the instrument <u>upwards</u>. This produces a <u>harsher</u> sound.

BRASS INSTRUMENTS

- Brass instruments (like the <u>trumpet</u>, <u>French horn</u>, <u>trombone</u> and <u>tuba</u>) have a <u>bright</u>, <u>metallic</u> sound.
- Playing <u>with a mute</u> (*con sordino*) can change the timbre.

PERCUSSION INSTRUMENTS

- Percussion instruments (e.g. <u>drums</u> and <u>xylophones</u>) make a sound when they're <u>struck</u>.
- What you hit them with can <u>change</u> the <u>timbre</u> — e.g. whether you use <u>sticks</u>, <u>brushes</u> or your <u>hands</u>.

SINGERS

- Singers produce notes when their <u>vocal cords</u> vibrate.
- The <u>speed</u> that they vibrate changes the <u>pitch</u> and the <u>timbre</u> — e.g. <u>bass</u> voices sound very <u>different</u> to <u>sopranos</u>.
- Techniques like <u>vibrato</u> (making the note <u>wobble</u>) can give a <u>richer</u> sound.
- <u>Falsetto</u> singing produces a much <u>thinner</u> sound.

I'm picking up good vibrations...

You may be asked to <u>describe</u> the timbre of different instruments that crop up in your exam.

Timbre

Electronic effects can be used to alter the timbre of an instrument or voice.

There are Lots of Different **Electronic Effects**

1) There are loads of different ways to change the sound of an instrument.

2) These effects are often used with electric guitars — they're really popular with rock bands, especially during guitar solos. Guitarists use pedals (e.g. a wah-wah pedal) to alter the tone or pitch.

3) The effects can also be used to change the sound of recorded music during mixing or post-processing.

4) Electronic effects (also called studio effects) include:

- **DISTORTION** distorts the sound.
- **REVERB** adds an echo to the sound.
- **CHORUS** makes it sound as if there's more than one player or singer — copies of the original sound are mixed together, with slight changes in timing and pitch.
- **PHASER** creates a 'whooshing' effect (a bit like the noise an aeroplane flying overhead makes).
- **FLANGER** similar to a phaser, but makes a more intense sound. The effect is created by combining the original sound with a copy, and varying the delay between them. It's used a lot in sci-fi programmes.
- **PITCH SHIFTING** used to bend the natural note or add another harmony.
- **OCTAVE EFFECTS** creates octaves above or below the note being played.

Synthesized Sounds have **Different Timbres** to **Real Sounds**

1) The natural sound of an instrument can be digitally reproduced to create a synthesized sound.

2) Electronic keyboards have different settings, so they can be made to sound like pretty much any instrument, from violins to percussion.

> One big difference between real and synthesized sounds is what happens to the timbre when the volume changes. When a real instrument is played louder, it has a different timbre to when it's played quietly. However, a synthesized sound has the same timbre at any volume — it's just the loudness that changes.

Sampling Uses **Recordings** of **Real Instruments**

1) The most effective way to recreate the sounds of real instruments is to use sampling (see p.73).

2) Sampling is where you record an instrument and use the recording (called a sample) in your music.

3) The samples can be altered to create different effects — there are lots of different computer programs that help you do this.

4) Samples can be looped (played over and over again), and other samples can be added over the top.

5) Most electronic music produced today uses looping, especially drum patterns.

6) It's not just instruments that can be sampled — you can take samples of anything you like, e.g. traffic noises or doorbells.

7) Lots of pop songs use samples — Kanye West sampled Ray Charles' 'I Got A Woman' in his 2005 hit 'Gold Digger'.

I'd like a sample of that cake please...

Have a listen to the 2005 hit 'Gold Digger' by Kanye West — he uses a sample of 'I Got A Woman' by Ray Charles (which was released more than 50 years earlier, in 1954).

Warm-up and Exam Questions

The questions on these pages are great for finding out what you know — don't ignore them.

Warm-up Questions

1) For each of the words below, name an instrument that links with the word:

    slide   **single reed**   **double reed**   **pizzicato**   **wooden bars**

2) Explain each of these words and phrases:

    tremolo   **con sordino**   **tenor**   **falsetto**

3) Name the **three** main types of guitar and briefly describe each of them.

4) In which period was the harpsichord the most popular keyboard instrument?

5) Explain the difference between a military band, a brass band and a jazz band.

6) List all the instruments that play in a piano trio and a clarinet quintet.

7) Define the following terms:

    MIDI   **sampler**   **remix**   **sequencer**

Exam Question

Brush up on your exam technique with this question.

This question is about two excerpts, Track 30 and Track 31.

First play Track 30 **three** times, leaving a short pause for writing time between each playing.

a) Name the solo woodwind instrument that plays at the beginning.

....

[1 mark]

b) What is the other instrument that plays in the excerpt?

....

[1 mark]

Exam Question

c) Tick **one** box to indicate which shape best represents the opening of the melody played by the solo instrument.

Shape A ☐

Shape B ☐

Shape C ☐

[1 mark]

d) Describe the relationship of the two instruments heard here. Refer to the **texture** and any other interesting features.

....

....

[2 marks]

Two marks available means you need to make two points. Don't forget to write about <u>texture</u>.

(Track 31)

Now play Track 31 **three** times, leaving a short pause for writing time between each playing.

e) Name the two solo woodwind instruments which play the melody at the beginning of this excerpt.

....

....

[2 marks]

Make sure you write about the <u>melody</u>, not the accompaniment.

Turn over

Exam Question

f)   Name the family of instruments playing throughout this excerpt.

....

[1 mark]

g)   Ring the word that describes the scale used throughout the excerpt.

major   **minor**   **chromatic**

[1 mark]

h)   Tick one of the following to represent the backing melody played by the two wind instruments.

A   ☐

B   ☐

C   ☐

[1 mark]

i)   Ring **one** feature that you can hear in this excerpt.

accelerando   **crescendo**   **ritardando**

[1 mark]

Revision Summary for Section Five

This section should be easy where it's talking about your own instruments. Don't ignore the other instruments. You'll need to know enough about them to be able to describe them in the listening test. And you might need to write parts for other instruments for your composition — it'll be a big help to know what they can and can't do. Go through the questions and check you can answer them all.

1) Name three brass instruments.
2) How do you vary the pitch on a brass instrument?
3) Are all woodwind instruments made of wood?
4) Name three woodwind instruments.
5) What are the three different mouthpieces used on woodwind instruments called? How do they work?
6) What are all those little keys, springs and levers for on a woodwind instrument?
7) What's the smallest orchestral string instrument?
8) What's the biggest string instrument that you play with a bow?
9) How do you make different notes on a string instrument?
10) What makes a harp different from the other string instruments? Give three differences.
11) Where would you put a mute on a bowed string instrument and what effect would it have?
12) How many strings are there on:
    a) an acoustic guitar   b) an electric guitar   c) a bass guitar?
13) What do you call those metal bits on the fingerboard of a guitar? Do you get them on a bass?
14) What's the proper word for twanging a guitar string with a plectrum?
15) Name three different keyboard instruments.
16) What's the biggest type of keyboard instrument?
17) What's the most popular keyboard instrument?
18) How could you tell you were listening to a church organ and not a harpsichord?
19) Name three tuned percussion instruments and six untuned percussion instruments.
20) What's the highest type of singing voice?
21) What's the lowest type of singing voice?
22) What do you call a boy's voice when it's got the same range as a soprano?
23) How can you tell the difference between a wind band and a brass band?
24) How can you tell the difference between a wind band and a jazz orchestra?
25) What are the two sections of a jazz orchestra called, and what are their jobs?
26) Why's chamber music called chamber music?
27) How many people are there in: a) a trio   b) a sextet   c) a quartet   d) an octet?
28) How many clarinets are there in a clarinet quintet?
29) Sketch a plan of a standard symphony orchestra. Label the different sections and the conductor.
30) What sections are there in a string orchestra, chamber orchestra and jazz orchestra?
31) How is MIDI information stored?
32) What do sequencers do?
33) What are samples? How can they be used in tracks?
34) Explain how the sound is produced on:
    a) a string instrument b) a piano c) a brass instrument?
35) Name four different electronic effects.

The Baroque Style

You need to know all about the <u>features</u> and <u>development</u> of <u>Western classical music</u> between <u>1650</u> and <u>1910</u>. Let's start with the musical style from the start of that period — <u>Baroque music</u>.

Baroque has a Recognisable Sound

The <u>Baroque</u> period was from about <u>1600-1750</u>. Key composers include <u>Bach</u>, <u>Handel</u>, <u>Vivaldi</u> and <u>Purcell</u>. Baroque music's pretty <u>easy to recognise</u>. These are the <u>main things</u> to look out for:

1) The <u>melodies</u> are built up from <u>short musical ideas</u> (called <u>motifs</u>), so you get quite a bit of <u>repetition</u>.

2) The <u>harmonies</u> are simple, with a fairly narrow range of chords — mainly <u>I</u> and <u>V</u>.

3) The melody is packed with <u>ornaments</u>, added in to make it sound more <u>interesting</u> (see p.84).

4) The <u>music</u> often involves <u>counterpoint</u> — where <u>two or more different lines of melody</u> are played at the same time. This <u>texture</u> is described as <u>contrapuntal</u> (or <u>polyphonic</u> — see p.45).

5) The <u>dynamics change suddenly</u>. Each bit is either <u>loud</u> or <u>soft</u> — this is called <u>terraced</u> or <u>stepped</u> dynamics. You <u>won't</u> hear any <u>gradual changes</u> in volume (no <u>crescendos</u> or <u>diminuendos</u>). This is mainly due to the prominence of the <u>harpsichord</u> in Baroque music — harpsichords could <u>either</u> play loud or soft, but couldn't change <u>gradually</u> between the two.

6) Baroque music is <u>tonal</u>:

> • From about 1600, Western composers used <u>major</u> and <u>minor keys</u> to write <u>tonal</u> music — this replaced <u>modal</u> music (see p.27).
>
> • Composers used <u>modulation</u> to switch between keys (see p.44) — this created <u>contrast</u> in their music.
>
> • Compositions were often made up of <u>sections</u> in <u>different keys</u>, with modulation between them. <u>New structures</u> were developed for organising pieces of music with a number of sections, e.g. <u>binary</u> and <u>ternary</u> forms (see next page).

String and Keyboard Instruments Played Key Roles

1) <u>String instruments</u> were dominant in a Baroque orchestra (just like today) — <u>violins</u>, <u>violas</u>, <u>cellos</u> and <u>double basses</u> were all used. (If you see '<u>violone</u>' in the score, it's played by a double bass today.)

2) <u>Keyboard</u> instruments such as the <u>harpsichord</u> and <u>organ</u> were also very important in Baroque music.

3) Woodwind instruments such as the <u>flute</u>, <u>recorder</u>, <u>oboe</u> and <u>bassoon</u> were also used.

4) The instruments available were much more <u>limited</u> than in the later musical periods. There were some early forms of <u>brass</u> instruments, such as <u>trumpets</u> and <u>horns</u>, but they didn't have any <u>valves</u> so could only play a <u>limited range</u> of notes.

5) <u>Orchestras</u> were generally <u>small</u> compared to modern orchestras. The size of an orchestra depended on the <u>resources</u> available, and the performance <u>space</u>. Music was often performed by <u>chamber groups</u> (see p.70) with a small number of musicians, but there were <u>larger orchestras</u> too.

Baroque Music Often Had a Basso Continuo

> 1) A <u>basso continuo</u> is a <u>continuous bass part</u> (see page 57). It's played throughout a piece, and is based on the <u>chords</u> of the piece.
>
> 2) It was often played on an <u>organ</u> or <u>harpsichord</u>, but could also feature additional instruments — e.g. <u>cellos</u>, <u>double basses</u> or <u>bassoons</u>.

'Baroque Around the Clock' was a huge hit...
You have to spot key features of Baroque music in the exam so make sure you learn them.

Baroque Structures

Baroque composers used various standard structures to construct their music.

The **Concerto Grosso** was a **Popular Form** of **Orchestral Music**

1) In a concerto grosso, a small group of soloists (called the concertino) is contrasted with the rest of the orchestra (the ripieno) and the basso continuo. The ripieno is usually a string orchestra. Handel wrote several concerto grossi (plural for grosso) — in his Concerto Grosso No. 5 (Op. 6), the concertino is made up of two violins and a cello, the ripieno is a string orchestra, and the continuo is played on the harpsichord. J.S. Bach's Brandenburg Concertos are concerto grossi.

2) Baroque composers also wrote solo concertos. Here a single solo instrument is 'showcased', allowing its performer to demonstrate the instrument's capabilities, accompanied by an orchestra. Vivaldi's 'Four Seasons' is a solo concerto for the violin. It was this type of concerto that was further developed by composers such as Mozart and Haydn in the Classical period — see p.91.

Binary and **Ternary Forms** are Made Up of **Different Sections**

1) Binary means something like 'in two parts' — binary form has two sections.
2) Binary form is usually used for Baroque dances, e.g. bourrée, minuet, gavotte, sarabande and gigue.
3) Each section is repeated. You play Section A twice, and then Section B twice, so it goes AABB.
4) Section B contrasts with Section A — the two bits should sound different.
5) The contrast is often made by modulating to related keys. Pieces in a minor key usually modulate to the relative major, e.g. A minor to C major. Pieces in a major key usually modulate to the dominant key (V), e.g. C major to G major.

1) Ternary form has three sections. The general structure is ABA, but the sections are often repeated, producing structures such as AABBAA.
2) Section A ends in the home key, normally with a perfect cadence (see pages 42-43). This makes it sound like a complete piece in itself.
3) In Section B the music often modulates to a related key, like the dominant or relative minor, and then goes back to the home key before it ends.
4) The last section can be exactly the same as Section A, or a slightly varied version. If it is varied, you call it A1 instead of A.

In a ritornello, the same musical idea or theme is repeated at various points in the piece. A more formal structure of this type is a rondo, where a main theme (A) is repeated, separated by a number of different sections, creating forms such as ABACA (see p.93).

Some **Works** Have an **Introduction** Called a **Prelude**

1) In the Baroque period, a prelude was a short, relatively simple piece of music. It usually served as an introduction to a longer piece or to a number of pieces of music.
2) The first movement of a suite (a set of dances) is often a prelude.
3) A prelude was often used as an introduction to a more complex piece such as a fugue. Bach wrote a prelude and fugue in each of the 24 keys in 'The Well-Tempered Clavier' — a collection of solo pieces for keyboard instruments.
4) In the Romantic period (see p.99-100), the term came to be used to describe a short, stand-alone piece.

This page is just a prelude to yet more fascinating structures...

You need to be able to spot these various structures, so make sure you learn all their features. If you're struggling to identify the different sections, listen out for a change of key — it'll probably be a new section.

Baroque Structures

Variations are pieces which start with one pattern or tune, and then change it in different ways.
There are two main structures for variations. They're called 'theme and variation' and 'ground bass'.

Theme and Variation Form Varies the Melody

1) In theme and variation form, the theme's usually a memorable melody.

2) The theme is played first. There's a short pause before the first variation is played, then another pause before the next variation. Each variation is a self-contained piece of music. There can be as many or as few variations as the composer wants.

3) Each variation should be a recognisable version of the main theme, but different from all the others.

You can vary a melody in loads of simple ways:

1) Start off with a basic theme...

2) Add notes to make the melody more complex.

3) Remove notes to simplify the melody.

4) Change the metre — e.g. from 2 beats in a bar to 3.

5) Add a countermelody — an extra melody over the top of the theme.

6) You can also change the tempo, change the key (from major to minor or vice versa), change some or all of the chords or add a different type of accompaniment instead of block chords.

A fantasia is a composition with an improvised feel — the composer uses their imagination and skill to compose a piece that doesn't follow a set structure. Fantasias often involve variations on a theme.

Ground Bass Form Varies Ideas Over a Fixed Bass Part

Ground bass is a continuous set of variations — there are no pauses. The main theme (called the ground) is a bass line which repeats throughout the piece — it is also known as basso ostinato. Varying melodies and harmonies which become gradually more complex are played over the ground. There are two types of Baroque dance that are in ground bass form — the chaconne and passacaglia. They're quite slow and stately.

Freshly ground bass — it goes all powdery...

Make sure you've learnt all the ins and outs of these structures. The examples of variations on this page are fairly simple, but they can become quite complex and require a lot of skill and practice to play well.

Baroque Melody Patterns

Composers often create a melody by starting with a <u>key phrase</u>, then <u>adapting</u> it using different <u>techniques</u>.

Melodic Inversion — Turning the Tune **Upside Down**

With <u>melodic inversion</u> you keep the <u>same intervals</u> between the notes, but they go in the <u>opposite</u> <u>direction</u>, i.e. down instead of up, and up instead of down. Basically you turn the tune on its head.

The first melody goes <u>up a major third</u> from C to E, then <u>up a minor third</u> to G.

In the inversion the melody goes <u>down a major third</u> to A♭, then <u>down a minor third</u> from A♭ to F.

Retrograde — Playing the Tune **Backwards**

Playing the notes <u>in reverse order</u> but with the same rhythm is called <u>retrograde</u>. This is the retrograde version of the first melody (above).

If you switch the notes so they're in reverse order <u>and</u> inverted, you get a <u>retrograde inversion</u>. This is the retrograde inversion of the first melody.

Sequencing — Repeat a **Pattern**, Vary the **Pitch**

1) Repeat the <u>pattern</u> of a phrase but start on a <u>different note</u>, higher or lower. This is called a <u>sequence</u>.

2) <u>Ascending</u> sequences go up in pitch.
   <u>Descending</u> sequences go down.

Imitation — Repeat a Phrase With **Slight Changes**

1) In <u>imitation</u>, a phrase is repeated with <u>slight changes</u> each time.

2) It works really well if one instrument or voice imitates <u>another</u> and then <u>overlaps</u>.

original phrase

original phrase, one octave higher

imitation with modulation

overlap starts in relative minor

Ostinato — Keep **One Pattern** the **Same**, Change the Rest

1) An ostinato is a pattern that's played <u>over and over</u> again.

2) The rest of the piece <u>changes around it</u>.

3) An ostinato is usually in the <u>bass</u> line, but it can be in other parts too.

4) <u>Ground bass form</u> (p.82) features ostinato <u>phrases</u> in the bass line — the repeated phrases can be quite <u>long</u>.

Here's the repeating pattern

Ornaments in Baroque Music

Ornaments are short extra notes that liven up the main melody — Baroque composers used them a lot in their music. There are a few different types of ornament...

A Trill is Lots of Tiny Quick Notes

1) In Baroque music, the trill starts one note above the written note then goes quickly back and forth between the written note and the note you started on.

2) Sometimes a trill ends with a turn (see below).

3) If the note above the written note doesn't belong to the key signature, there'll be a sharp, flat or natural sign above the trill symbol.

4) A trill is slightly different in Classical music — it starts on the written note and goes up to the note above.

This is how you play a trill in Baroque music...

OR =

The trill lasts the same length of time as the written note.

An Appoggiatura is an Extra Note in a Chord

1) The appoggiatura starts on a note that clashes with the chord, then moves to a note that belongs in the chord (this is called the resolution).

2) The two notes are usually just one tone or semitone apart.

3) It normally takes half the time value of the note it 'leans' on.

Squeezing in a Tiny Note is Called Acciaccatura

"Acciaccatura" means crushing in. An acciaccatura is a note that's squeezed in before the main note and played as fast as possible.

Mordents and Turns are Set Patterns of Notes

MORDENTS

Mordents start off like trills.

The difference is they end on the written note, which is played a bit longer than the trilled notes. There are loads of different mordents but these two are the most common.

upper mordent

= OR

lower mordent

= OR

TURNS

Start on the note above the written note, then play the written note, followed by the note below the written note. End back on the written note. =

For an inverted turn play the note below the written note, the written note, the note above that and finally the written note. OR OR =

COMPOSING TIP

I've done my bit — now it's your turn...

Take a look at p.41 for more on decoration. You might even want to add some of these ornaments to your compositions to make them more exciting (don't go overboard though).

Choral Music

Choirs have been around for ages. They vary in size from just a few singers to hundreds, and perform anywhere from school halls and churches to concert halls, theatres and cathedrals.

Choral Music has Been Around for Over 600 Years

1) The first choral pieces were sung in churches in the 14th century.
   Before that, monks used to sing plainsong (a unison chant).

2) Most choral music in Renaissance and Baroque times was sacred (church music). Some was sung a cappella (without accompaniment) and some was accompanied by an instrument, such as an organ.

3) Masses were sung in Catholic churches. They were part of the church service.
   A requiem was a mass for the dead. There's more about masses and requiems on p.103.

4) Oratorios are Bible stories set to music (see next page). Masses, requiems and oratorios are all sacred music. They're made up of choir sections and solo sections.

5) Secular (non-religious) choral music is mainly made up of choruses in operas (see next page).
   Operas often tell love stories and are performed on stage. The chorus emphasises important bits.

Choirs Were Originally All Male

There's more on the different types of voice on p.68.

1) Baroque choirs were fairly small — they'd sometimes have just one singer on each part.
   All parts were sung by men (women were banned from singing in church).

2) Most choir music was written for 4 different voices: treble (a boy soprano), countertenor or alto (a high-pitched voice known as falsetto), tenor (a high male voice) and bass (a low male voice).

3) By the Victorian era, choirs were huge — they'd often have over 100 members (it was a popular Victorian hobby). The Huddersfield Choral Society was started in 1836 and still exists today.

4) Some choirs are mixed-sex, with music arranged for SATB voices: soprano (a high female voice), alto (a lower female voice), tenor (a high male voice) and bass (a low male voice).

5) All-female choirs are usually SSAA (2 soprano parts and 2 alto parts) or SSA (2 soprano parts and 1 alto part). Male voice choirs are often TTBB (2 tenor parts, 1 baritone part and 1 bass part).

Choral Singing is Still Popular Today

1) 20th and 21st century choirs are generally smaller than the large Victorian choirs — they'll often have around 80 members though. Some can have as many as 130 members.

2) Lots of 20th century choral works are written for chamber choir and chamber orchestra. These are just small versions of choirs and orchestras (they're called 'chamber' because they used to perform in rooms or chambers, rather than a concert hall). Chamber choirs normally have 20-25 members.

3) Chamber choir pieces may have been a reaction against 19th century composers, who often composed pieces for massive choirs.

Choirs Have Soloists Too

There are sometimes solo sections in choral works — the soloist might be accompanied by the rest of the choir, or just sing on their own, with or without orchestral accompaniment. The main solo voices are:

- Soprano, alto, tenor or bass (as described above).
- Mezzo-sopranos (a female voice that's lower than a soprano but higher than an alto), baritones (a male voice that's lower than a tenor but higher than a bass) or contralto (the lowest female voice that has a similar range to a countertenor).

Requiems, oratorios — there's Masses of stuff on this page...

J.S. Bach and Handel wrote a lot of choral music in the Baroque period — both sacred and secular. There's a whole page on Handel's oratorios and anthems on p.87 (but Bach doesn't get a page — sorry Bach).

Operas and Oratorios

Operas and oratorios are large vocal works, both made up of solo and chorus sections.

Operas are Like **Plays** Set to **Music**

1) An opera is a story set to music with singing and acting. Most operas are divided up into three parts (or 'Acts'). Operas are secular (non-religious).

2) The main characters are played by solo singers and are supported by a chorus and an orchestra.

3) The story is acted out — usually with lavish sets, costumes and special effects.

4) In some operas every single word is sung (this is known as sung-through) — in others there's a bit of talking from time to time.

5) Some operas have really serious, tragic themes. Others are more light-hearted and comic. These are the names for the main types:

6) The words of an opera are called the 'libretto'. This is often written by a 'librettist' working alongside the composer.

Grand opera	serious, set entirely to music (sung-through)
Opera seria	formal, serious opera, often mythological themes
Opera buffa	comic opera with lighter, more everyday themes
Opéra comique	like opera buffa but with some spoken dialogue
Operetta	shorter than a proper opera, lighter themes

In Opera There are **Three Types** of **Song**

ARIA

1) An aria is a solo vocal piece, backed by the orchestra.

2) Arias are used to show the thoughts and emotions of the main characters.

3) The arias have the memorable, exciting tunes. They're challenging for the performers and let them show their vocal tone and agility.

In England and France, arias are sometimes known as 'airs'.

RECITATIVE

1) A recitative is a song for a soloist that tells the story and moves it along. The rhythm of the words tends to imitate the rhythm of normal speech.

2) A recitativo secco is a recitative that's unaccompanied or backed by simple chords.

3) A recitativo stromentato or accompagnato is a recitative with orchestral backing. The accompaniment is used to increase the dramatic tension of the words.

CHORUS — A bit where the whole chorus (or choir) sings together. Choruses are usually written for SATB choirs (see previous page), but in Baroque operas the soprano parts would be sung by trebles (boy sopranos).

Oratorios are **Religious** Versions of **Operas**

1) Oratorios often tell Bible stories, or tales with a religious or moral theme — they're a type of sacred music.

2) They're not usually acted out with scenery and costumes (unlike operas).

3) They normally have an instrumental accompaniment.

4) Oratorios have arias, recitatives and choruses just like operas.

COMPOSER	LIVED	FAMOUS ORATORIO
Carissimi	1605-1674	Jephte
Handel	1685-1759	Messiah
Haydn	1732-1809	The Creation
Berlioz	1803-1869	L'Enfance du Christ
Mendelssohn	1809-1847	Elijah
Elgar	1857-1934	The Dream of Gerontius
Tippett	1905-1998	A Child of Our Time

5) The table above gives some composers and their most famous oratorios. Have a listen to them and try to spot the different types of song, as well as listening out for the different musical styles.

Handel

Handel was one of the most important composers in the Baroque period.

Handel was a German Composer

1) George Frideric Handel was born in Germany in 1685. From about 1710, he lived in England. He died in London in 1759 and is buried in Westminster Abbey.

2) He was popular with Queen Anne, George I and George II — he composed 'Zadok the Priest' for the coronation of George II (see below), and it's been played at every coronation since then. He also wrote music for the Calvinist church in Germany and the Church of England.

3) Handel wrote loads of music, including lots of oratorios and operas (see p.86). As well as choral music, he also wrote many orchestral pieces — one of the most famous is the 'Water Music'.

Messiah is a Famous Oratorio by Handel

He also wrote lots of other oratorios — including Solomon, Israel in Egypt and Judas Maccabaeus (which has the famous 'See the Conquering Hero').

1) Messiah tells the story of Jesus' life.

2) It's written for SATB soloists, SATB choir and a full orchestra. At the time Handel wrote it, all the parts would have been sung by men.

3) Handel wrote it for a small choir, but it has since been performed by choirs with hundreds of singers.

4) Much of the Messiah is melismatic (a single syllable of text is sung over a succession of notes). In the chorus 'For Unto Us a Child is Born', the soprano part has a run of 57 notes for the word 'born'.

The opposite of melismatic is syllabic, where every syllable is sung to a single note.

Tenor

Crook - ed

5) Handel also uses word-painting — where the music matches the words. E.g. the word 'crooked' is split over four notes each time it is sung, making it sound crooked.

6) The most famous bit of the Messiah is probably the 'Hallelujah Chorus', but there are lots of other choruses, recitatives and arias (as well as some duets and instrumental sections).

Handel Wrote the Coronation Anthems for George II

1) Handel wrote four anthems (choral pieces performed in Protestant churches) for the coronation of George II and Queen Caroline in October 1727.

2) The anthems are 'Zadok the Priest', 'Let Thy Hand Be Strengthened', 'The King Shall Rejoice' and 'My Heart is Inditing'. Each one is divided into different sections. The lyrics are taken from the Bible.

3) As they were written for a grand occasion, the anthems need a large choir and massive orchestra to perform them, which emphasised the importance of the event.

4) Although the strings are used for most of the accompaniment, Handel frequently uses trumpet fanfares in the most triumphant sections (e.g. when the choir sings 'rejoic'd' in 'Zadok the Priest'), which adds to the ceremonial feel. He also uses oboes, bassoons, timpani and organ (which plays a basso continuo in some sections).

5) Much of the music is in a major key as it was written for a celebration, but there are a couple of sections in a minor key for the more solemn aspects of the coronation.

6) Handel uses a variety of textures to different effects. For example, the repeated line 'God Save the King' in 'Zadok the Priest' is sung homophonically in rich chords to give it more impact. In contrast, the 'Alleluja' section of 'Let Thy Hand Be Strengthened' is polyphonic, with parts weaving in and out of each other in imitation to give it a bright, celebratory feel. There's also parallel harmony (see p.45), with parts moving together in thirds (e.g. in the 'Glory and Worship' section of 'The King Shall Rejoice').

Hallelujah — it's the end of the page...

Have a listen to 'Zadok the Priest' — it's in D major and sounds very triumphant. The last section ends with a plagal cadence (a plagal cadence is chord IV then chord I — see p.43).

From Baroque to Classical

Classical music came from Baroque, so it's <u>similar but not the same</u>...

Tastes Moved Towards a Simpler Sound

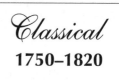

Classical
1750–1820

1) The <u>Classical</u> period of music was from around <u>1750 to 1820</u>. <u>Mozart</u>, <u>Haydn</u> and <u>Beethoven</u> were key composers during this time.

2) The style of music <u>didn't just change overnight</u> — the Classical style <u>developed</u> from the Baroque style as <u>tastes changed</u> and <u>instruments</u> became more <u>versatile</u>.

3) Towards the <u>end</u> of the Baroque era, many composers <u>moved away</u> from the <u>polyphonic</u> sound (see p.45) that had been a key feature of the period. They began to write more <u>homophonic music</u> with a <u>clear melody line</u> and <u>fewer ornaments</u> (see p.84).

4) This development can be seen in the compositions of J.S. Bach's sons, <u>C.P.E. Bach</u> and <u>J.C. Bach</u>. They were influenced by <u>new styles</u> as well as their <u>father's compositions</u>, and they composed much more <u>homophonic</u> music than their father.

5) There was also a move towards more <u>subtle dynamics</u>. Composers began to use <u>crescendos</u> and <u>diminuendos</u> rather than sudden changes in volume — this was partly due to the invention of the <u>piano</u> (see below).

Forms and Structures Developed Too

1) Baroque forms and structures <u>changed over time</u>, and grew into popular Classical <u>structures</u>:

- The <u>solo concerto</u> became <u>more popular</u> than the <u>concerto grosso</u> (see p.81) — it became an <u>important form</u> in the <u>Classical period</u>.

- The <u>Baroque trio sonata</u> consisted of a number of movements played by <u>three instruments</u> plus a <u>harpsichord continuo</u>. This developed into the <u>Classical sonata</u>, a form consisting of three or four movements, usually composed for a <u>solo instrument</u> (see p.91).

- In the <u>Baroque</u> period, operas often began with an '<u>Italian overture</u>' — an <u>orchestral</u> piece consisting of <u>three sections</u> — a <u>fast</u> section followed by a <u>slow</u> section, followed by another <u>fast</u> section. These pieces were often performed <u>independently</u> of the opera. The <u>Classical symphony</u> (see p.92) developed from this (although Classical symphonies tended to have <u>four</u> movements).

2) Other forms that were popular in the Baroque period continued to be used — <u>binary form</u>, <u>ternary form</u> and <u>theme and variation form</u> (see p.81-82) were still <u>important</u> in the <u>Classical era</u>. <u>New structures</u> such as <u>sonata form</u> (p.92) were also developed.

The Invention of the Piano had a Big Impact

1) The <u>piano</u> was invented in about <u>1700</u>. It became more popular than the harpsichord because it was able to create a much <u>greater variety</u> of tones — the notes could be played in a <u>legato</u> or <u>staccato</u> style and the <u>dynamics</u> could be <u>varied</u> depending on how hard the keys were pressed. The full name of the piano is actually '<u>pianoforte</u>', which means '<u>soft-loud</u>'.

2) <u>C.P.E. Bach</u> and <u>J.C. Bach</u> both composed for the <u>piano</u> and were <u>influential</u> in increasing its <u>popularity</u>. The piano became <u>very widely used</u> in Classical music.

3) <u>Other instruments</u> (such as the <u>clarinet</u>) were <u>developed</u>, and this led to important changes in the structure of the <u>orchestra</u> — see the next page.

Souvenir shops suffered terribly as the use of ornaments declined...

Remember, Classical music developed from Baroque music, so many of the features you've come across in Baroque music still make an appearance. But there's lots of new stuff to get to grips with too...

The Classical Orchestra

Orchestras <u>got bigger</u> during the Classical period as new instruments were developed.
The <u>set-up</u> of an orchestra (i.e. what instruments were included) became more <u>standardised</u>.

Orchestral Music was Written for **Wealthy Audiences**

1) At the start of the Classical period, composers worked for <u>royalty</u> and <u>aristocrats</u>.
   They were <u>paid</u> to write music for <u>official events</u>, <u>church services</u> and plain old <u>entertainment</u>.
   Composers had to write music that their <u>patrons</u> (employers) would <u>approve of</u>.

2) <u>Later</u> in the Classical period, society <u>changed</u>. Middle-class people had more <u>money</u> and
   wanted entertainment. <u>Public concert halls</u> were built, where people could go to listen to music.

3) Famous Classical composers like <u>Haydn</u> and <u>Mozart</u> worked for patrons,
   but they also put on concerts in the new concert halls.

4) By the <u>1800s</u>, composers could earn quite a bit of money from ticket sales
   at concert halls. This gave them more <u>freedom</u> — they could write for the
   tastes of <u>concert-goers</u> instead of just pleasing their patrons.

Orchestras **Grew** During the **Classical Period**

1) At the start of the Classical period, composers wrote for <u>smallish</u> orchestras — mainly <u>strings</u>,
   with <u>horns</u>, <u>flutes</u> and <u>oboes</u>. There'd be <u>two</u> horns and <u>one</u> or <u>two</u> woodwind.

2) Later on, the <u>woodwind</u> section <u>grew</u> — <u>clarinets</u> were developed during the Classical period and
   were included in the orchestra. <u>Mozart</u> was the first composer to use the clarinet in a symphony.

3) <u>Brass</u> instruments were used more widely. <u>Horns</u> were developed so
   they could produce <u>more notes</u> and play in a greater <u>variety of keys</u>.

4) The <u>percussion</u> section grew too — <u>timpani</u> became a
   standard fixture, and some orchestras used <u>bass drums</u>,
   <u>snare drums</u>, <u>triangles</u> and <u>cymbals</u> as well.

5) In some <u>early</u> Classical music, there'd be a <u>harpsichord</u> (see p.66),
   but after a while composers <u>stopped</u> using it. The harpsichord was
   there to fill in the <u>harmonies</u>, but it wasn't really needed once the
   extra woodwind had been added.

6) This is a fairly <u>typical layout</u> for a later Classical orchestra:

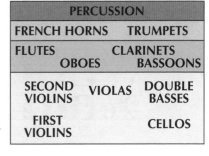

PERCUSSION	
FRENCH HORNS	TRUMPETS
FLUTES	CLARINETS
OBOES	BASSOONS

SECOND VIOLINS	VIOLAS	DOUBLE BASSES
FIRST VIOLINS		CELLOS

Classical Orchestras Mostly Use **String Instruments**

1) The most <u>important</u> section in a Classical orchestra is the <u>strings</u>.
   They're the <u>dominant sound</u> in most Classical music.
   The <u>violins</u> generally play most of the <u>melodies</u>.

2) The <u>wind</u> instruments play extra notes to fill out the <u>harmony</u>.
   When they do get the tune, they mostly <u>double</u> the string parts.

3) You do hear the occasional wind <u>solo</u>. Orchestral pieces called <u>concertos</u> (see p.91)
   feature one or two <u>solo instruments</u> accompanied by an orchestra.

4) In later Classical music, the woodwind section started to have a more <u>independent role</u>.
   They'd sometimes play the melody <u>alone</u>, and there'd be more solos.
   The strings were still really important though.

You need to know what instruments were used in the Classical era...

Orchestras grew in size because composers in the Classical period began to include more parts
for different instruments. This gave rise to a greater variety of music later in the Classical period.

The Classical Style

A whole page about the features of Classical music... enjoy.

Classical Melodies Have a **Clear, Simple Structure**

Classical music sounds <u>clearer</u> and <u>simpler</u> than music from other periods. This is partly because the melodies are structured in a very straightforward way, with <u>short</u>, <u>balanced</u> 2- or 4-bar phrases.

Here's an excerpt from Haydn's *Clock Symphony* (see p.94-96):

And here's the opening of Mozart's *Piano Sonata No. 16 in C major* with two-bar phrases:

Classical **Textures** are Mainly **Melody** and **Chords**

1) Most Classical music has just <u>one melody</u> with <u>accompanying chords</u>. This makes the tune really stand out. It's called <u>homophonic texture</u> (see page 45).

2) These accompanying chords can be played in <u>different ways</u>:

These are <u>block chords</u>...

... and these are <u>broken chords</u>

3) <u>Polyphony</u> (where <u>several tunes</u> weave in and out of each other) is used too, but not as often.

Classical Music Uses **Major** and **Minor Keys**

1) Classical music is always in either a major or minor key — the <u>tonality</u> is major or minor.

2) <u>Bright</u>, <u>cheery</u> bits are in major keys and <u>gloomy</u>, <u>sad</u> bits are in minor keys.

3) Classical harmony is what's known as <u>diatonic</u> — nearly <u>all</u> the notes belong to the <u>main key</u>.

The **Beat** is Obvious and **Easy to Follow**

1) The <u>metre</u> in Classical music is very regular. You can happily <u>tap your foot</u> in time to the music.

2) The <u>tempo</u> stays <u>constant</u> — the speed of the beat stays pretty much the same all the way through, <u>without</u> massively <u>speeding up</u> or <u>slowing down</u>.

Classical style — a wig, tailcoat and breeches...

This is important stuff, so make sure you're happy with the key features of the Classical period. Make a list of them all, then learn it. Keep going over it to check you know them off by heart.

Classical Structures

Concertos, sonatas and symphonies were very popular in the Classical period.
Take your time and make sure that you're familiar with each one of these structures.

Concertos are Played by a Soloist and Orchestra

1) A concerto is a piece for a soloist and orchestra. The soloist has most of the melody, and can really show off. The orchestra does get the melody too — they're not just an accompaniment.

2) A concerto usually has three movements — quick, slow and quick.

3) They often have a bit called a cadenza (p.57), where the orchestra stops and the soloist can show everyone how brilliant they are. A cadenza is sometimes improvised — it's often just indicated by a pause above the music.

4) Piano and violin concertos were the most popular in the Classical period, but some concertos were written for other solo instruments too. Composers used concertos to showcase the new instruments (like the clarinet and the keyed trumpet) and show off their capabilities.

5) Famous examples of Classical concertos include Haydn's Trumpet Concerto in E♭ major (listen out for the cadenza in the first movement) and Mozart's Horn Concerto No. 4 in E♭ major.

A Symphony is Played by a Full Orchestra

1) A symphony is a massive piece. They can last more than an hour and have real impact because they use the full orchestra.

2) Symphonies usually have four movements (but some have three, and they can have more than four). The contrast between the movements is important.

3) At least one of the movements is in sonata form (see next page) — usually the first, and sometimes the last.

4) Examples include Haydn's Surprise Symphony and Beethoven's Eroica Symphony.

Overtures and Suites were also Written for Orchestras

1) An overture is a one-movement piece for orchestra.

2) Overtures are written as introductions to larger works like operas and ballets.

3) They use ideas, moods and musical themes from the main work to prepare the audience. For an example, have a listen to Mozart's overture to his opera *The Magic Flute*.

4) Classical orchestral suites are another offshoot of ballets and operas.

5) In music from this period, a 'suite' is an orchestral arrangement of the music used to accompany the action on stage. It would be put together as a separate piece of music and played at concerts.

Sonatas are for One or Two Instruments

1) Sonatas are mostly written for one instrument, but there are some sonatas for two instruments and a few for two different instruments, with each one playing a different part.

2) A sonata usually has three or four movements, with breaks in between them.

3) A sonata has a similar structure to a symphony — it has one or more movements in sonata form (see next page).

4) Piano sonatas were very popular in the Classical era — Haydn alone wrote 62. Have a listen to Mozart's Piano Sonata in C Major, Haydn's Piano Sonata in C Major and Beethoven's Sonata Pathétique.

Classical Structures

The <u>movements</u> of compositions were usually written in <u>standard forms</u> and arranged in a certain order. <u>Symphonies</u>, <u>sonatas</u> and <u>concertos</u> all follow a <u>similar pattern</u> — now there's a stroke of luck...

Symphonies, Sonatas and Concertos have a Standard Structure

1) The <u>four movements</u> of a <u>symphony</u> have the forms shown in the <u>table</u> below.

2) <u>Sonatas</u> with <u>four movements</u> also follow this structure. If the <u>sonata</u> only has <u>three movements</u>, the <u>minuet</u> (third movement in the table) is <u>left out</u>.

3) <u>Concertos</u> usually have <u>three movements</u> — they have the <u>first</u>, <u>second</u> and <u>fourth</u> movements from the table.

FIRST MOVEMENT	sonata form	brisk and purposeful
SECOND MOVEMENT	ternary or variation form	slower and songlike
THIRD MOVEMENT	minuet or scherzo	fairly fast and dance-like
FOURTH MOVEMENT	rondo, variation or sonata form	fast and cheerful

See page 81 for ternary form and page 82 for variation form. The other forms are explained over the next couple of pages.

Sonata Form has Three Main Sections

The <u>movements</u> of a sonata or symphony are themselves made up of a number of <u>different sections</u>. <u>Sonata form</u> has the following sections:

Exposition → **Development** → **Recapitulation**

Themes are "exposed" — heard for the first time.

Themes go through a number of interesting twists and turns.

Themes are "recapped" — played again.

1) The <u>exposition</u> has a number of <u>contrasting themes</u>. It ends in a <u>different</u> (but related) key to the one it started in.

2) The <u>development</u> keeps the piece <u>interesting</u>. It takes <u>extracts</u> from the exposition <u>themes</u>, explores <u>variations</u> on them, and presents them in <u>different keys</u> — the development often <u>modulates</u> through a number of keys. Completely <u>new</u> material might be introduced too.

3) The <u>recapitulation</u> pulls it all <u>together</u> again — the exposition themes are <u>repeated</u>, generally in the <u>same order</u> as in the exposition. They're usually <u>changed</u> a bit — the composer might add <u>ornaments</u> (see p.84) or <u>shorten</u> them. Some themes are heard in a <u>different key</u> — a theme that was in the <u>relative key</u> in the exposition usually moves to the <u>tonic key</u> in the recapitulation.

4) Composers sometimes use <u>bridge sections</u> between the themes and <u>links</u> between the main sections. They usually add a <u>coda</u> to finish off the piece <u>neatly</u> as well.

Fear not, there are more forms to come...

Make sure you've got <u>sonata form</u> clear in your head — it comes up in sonatas, symphonies and concertos. And don't get confused... sonata form is the structure of the <u>first movement</u> of a sonata, not the whole thing.

Classical Structures

Here's some more detail on the <u>forms</u> that make up the <u>movements</u> of a <u>concerto</u>, <u>sonata</u> or <u>symphony</u>.

Minuets and Scherzos are in Ternary Form

1) In a <u>sonata</u> or <u>symphony</u>, 'minuet' is short for '<u>minuet and trio</u>' and <u>scherzo</u> is short for '<u>scherzo and trio</u>'. The <u>third movement</u> of a four-movement work is either a minuet or a scherzo.

2) A minuet is a <u>French dance</u> with <u>three beats</u> in a bar.

3) The <u>trio</u> is <u>another minuet</u> in a <u>contrasting</u> but <u>related</u> key — often the <u>dominant</u> or <u>relative minor</u>. It's often written for <u>three instruments</u> (which is why it's called a trio).

4) The <u>minuet</u> is played <u>first</u>, <u>followed</u> by the <u>trio</u> section, and then the <u>minuet</u> is played <u>again</u> — this gives the movement <u>ternary form</u> (see p.81).

5) The <u>individual</u> minuet and trio sections often have their <u>own ternary form</u>. A <u>common structure</u> for a minuet and trio is shown below.

6) A <u>scherzo and trio</u> is very <u>similar</u>, but a scherzo is <u>faster</u> and more <u>light-hearted</u> than a minuet — scherzo means '<u>joke</u>' in Italian. <u>Beethoven</u> was one of the first composers to use a scherzo like this.

Rondo Form Can Have Any Number of Sections

1) The <u>final movement</u> of a <u>concerto</u>, <u>sonata</u> or <u>symphony</u> is often a <u>rondo</u>.

2) <u>Rondo</u> means <u>going round</u>. A rondo starts with a main idea in <u>Section A</u>, moves into a <u>new section</u>, goes round again to <u>A</u>, moves into another <u>new section</u>, goes round again to <u>A</u>, etc., etc. The <u>new section</u> after each Section A always <u>contrasts</u> with A.

3) Section A is known as the <u>main theme</u> or <u>refrain</u>. The contrasting sections are called <u>episodes</u>.

4) The main theme is always in the <u>home key</u>. Each <u>episode</u> tends to modulate to a <u>related key</u> for contrast.

Musical Signposts Tell You What's Coming Next

1) You've seen that the <u>movements</u> of a work are themselves made up of a <u>number of sections</u>. The most obvious clue that a new section is starting in Classical music is a <u>change of key</u>.

2) Classical composers were also keen on dropping <u>hints</u> that a new section was about to start. These hints are known as <u>musical signposts</u>. They're not all that easy to spot at first, but with a bit of <u>practice</u> you should get the hang of it:

- <u>Bridge passages</u> lead smoothly into the new theme and also help <u>prepare</u> the new key.
- <u>Cadences</u> (p.42-43) clearly mark the end of a phrase or section, and they come at the <u>end</u> of a piece too. When they do, the <u>chords</u> used in the <u>cadence</u> are repeated several times, to let the audience know it's all over.

ABACADAEAFAGAHA — my rondo got a bit out of hand...

These structures might come in handy for your compositions (OK, writing a full symphony might be a bit over the top, but rondo form or minuet and trio form are a bit more manageable).

Haydn — The Clock Symphony Movement 2

The piece you have to study for Western Classical Tradition 1650-1910 is the second movement of <u>Haydn's Symphony No. 101 in D Major</u>, known as the <u>Clock Symphony</u>, which was written in <u>1793-94</u>.

Haydn was an Austrian Classical Composer

1) <u>Franz Joseph Haydn</u> (known just as <u>Joseph Haydn</u>) was born in <u>Austria</u> in <u>1732</u>. *Haydn's Trumpet Concerto* He was one of the most <u>important</u> composers of the <u>Classical period</u> — *in E♭ Major is one of his* he composed over 100 <u>symphonies</u>, a number of <u>concertos</u>, <u>string quartets</u>, *best-known concertos.* <u>piano trios</u>, <u>oratorios</u>, <u>operas</u> and many other works. He died in <u>1809</u>.

2) For most of his career, Haydn was employed as the <u>Kapellmeister</u> (<u>musical director</u>) for the noble <u>Esterházy family</u> — he <u>composed</u>, <u>conducted</u> and <u>performed</u> music for Prince Esterházy, who was his <u>patron</u>. Haydn worked for <u>four different princes</u> during his employment.

3) During his employment for the family, Haydn travelled to <u>London</u> twice, where he was already <u>popular</u>. He wrote <u>six symphonies</u> on <u>each visit</u> (these 12 symphonies are known as the <u>London symphonies</u>). The <u>Clock Symphony</u> is one of these symphonies.

4) Haydn was known for his <u>sense of humour</u> in his compositions — for example, in his 'Surprise' symphony, there is a <u>sudden loud chord</u> in the middle of a <u>quiet section</u>, supposedly designed to <u>shock</u> any audience members who may have <u>fallen asleep</u>.

The Clock Symphony was Written for a Classical Orchestra

1) <u>Symphony No. 101 in D Major</u> (the <u>Clock Symphony</u>) was written in the <u>later</u> stages of Haydn's career. By this point, the <u>clarinet</u> was becoming more <u>popular</u>, so he used it in many of his final works.

2) This symphony was written for a <u>later Classical orchestra</u> (see p.89). There'd be a <u>string section</u> (first and second <u>violins</u>, <u>violas</u>, <u>cellos</u> and <u>double basses</u>) and <u>2 each</u> of <u>woodwind</u> (<u>flutes</u>, <u>clarinets</u>, <u>oboes</u> and <u>bassoons</u>), <u>brass</u> (<u>trumpets</u> and <u>horns</u>) and <u>timpani</u>.

3) The <u>brass instruments</u> at this time were <u>natural</u> (i.e. they had <u>no valves</u>, so could only play a <u>limited</u> <u>range</u> of notes — just <u>two notes</u> in the <u>lower register</u>, but <u>more</u> in the <u>upper register</u>). To <u>change the</u> <u>key</u> of the instrument, different-length <u>crooks</u> (bits of <u>tubing</u>) were added or removed to alter the pitch.

4) Some of the instruments in a Classical orchestra were <u>transposing instruments</u> — the notes they play <u>sound different</u> to the written notes. The main transposing instruments in this symphony were:

- <u>Clarinets</u> in <u>A</u> (when the clarinet plays a <u>C</u>, it sounds like the <u>A below</u> the written note).
- <u>Trumpets</u> in <u>D</u> (when the trumpet plays a <u>C</u>, it sounds like the <u>D above</u> the written note). The <u>second movement</u> is different — the trumpets are in <u>C</u>, so sound the note that is <u>written</u>.
- <u>Horns</u> in <u>D</u> (when the horn plays a <u>C</u>, it sounds like the <u>D below</u> the written note). In the <u>second movement</u>, the horns are in <u>G</u>, so produce a <u>G</u> when then play a written <u>C</u>.

You Need to Learn About the Second Movement

The <u>Clock Symphony</u> has <u>four movements</u> (this is typical of a symphony — see p.92).

1) The <u>first movement</u> (<u>Adagio-Presto</u>) begins with a <u>slow introduction</u> in <u>D minor</u>, then continues in <u>D major</u> with a <u>lively piece</u> in <u>sonata form</u> (see p.92).

2) The <u>second movement</u> (the one you have to study) is the <u>slow</u> movement and is in <u>G major</u> (the <u>subdominant key</u>). There's more about it on the next two pages.

3) The <u>third movement</u> is a <u>minuet and trio</u> (see p.93) in <u>D major</u> (the <u>tonic key</u>).

4) The <u>fourth</u> and final movement is a bit unusual — it's in <u>sonata rondo form</u>, which, as you might expect, is a <u>combination</u> of <u>rondo form</u> (see p.93) and <u>sonata form</u>. It's also in <u>D major</u>.

What time is it Mr Haydn...

Don't forget — the parts for transposing instruments are written in a different key to the rest of the orchestra.

Haydn — The Clock Symphony Movement 2

Now you know a bit of background about the piece, it's time to look at it in a bit more detail.

The Symphony gets its **Name** from the **Second Movement**

1) Symphony No. 101 is known as the Clock Symphony because of a feature in the second movement — a 'ticking' pattern that continues throughout most of the movement. Each 'tick' is a quaver beat. The ticking occasionally stops for a few bars but always comes back in again.

2) For most of this movement, the ticking alternates between 2 notes (though in a few places a different pattern is played). It's first heard on the bassoons, second violins, cellos and double basses. One or more of these instruments plays this pattern for most of the piece, but in bar 63 (and again in bar 86) the flutes take over the ticking for a few bars, accompanied by the bassoons (but no strings).

3) When the strings have the ticking, they are often playing pizzicato (plucked). When the woodwind have it (or when the strings are playing *con arco*, which means with bow), they are marked staccato. This makes the notes sound even more like the ticking of a clock.

4) The tonic key of the movement is G major (the first section is in this key, with a couple of short modulations — see below). The second part (bars 34-62) is in G minor — the tonic minor. The piece then returns to G major, again with some modulations (including to E♭ major, an unrelated key).

5) This movement is marked andante — it's quite slow and steady throughout.

6) Haydn creates a sense of balance through his use of dynamics, phrasing, sequences and harmony. This was typical of music from the Classical period.

The Movement has **Two Recurring Themes**

1) The two main themes of the movement are repeated, with variations each time — e.g. they might be played on different instruments, in a different key or with extra notes added to decorate the melody.

2) There are a number of similarities between the two themes — both use dotted and double dotted rhythms, acciaccaturas (see p.84), descending demisemiquaver runs and staccato notes.

3) The first theme (which I'm going to call theme A) is first heard in bar 2:

THEME A — bars 2-10

- After one bar of 'ticking', the first theme is heard (the first four bars of it are shown above). It's played by the first violins (marked piano) and accompanied by the ticking motif. The C♯ accidentals in the cello/double bass and first violin parts create a short modulation to D major (the dominant key) before the tune returns to G major. The first 10 bars are then repeated.

- Theme A is next heard from bar 25 to bar 34 (after theme B — see next page). The melody is doubled on the flute, and viola chords are added to the accompaniment — but the dynamic drops to **pp**. It is extended by a bar, and has a slightly different melody in the second half.

- After the minor section (see next page), theme A returns again in bar 63. The melody is identical to the first time it was played, but this time it is pianissimo and accompanied by ticking from the bassoon and flute (but no strings). There's also one bar of oboe quavers.

- The second version of the theme is repeated in bars 87-96 — again the melody is the same but it is accompanied by the flute and bassoon ticking (and a few bars for the oboe).

- The first few bars of the theme are heard from bar 99, but this time in E♭ major. The melody is extended slightly, and there is antiphony (see p.47) between the first violins and the flutes.

- This theme is not heard in full again for the rest of the movement — but there's another variation of it from bar 112. This variation is also mirrored in the final section.

Haydn — The Clock Symphony Movement 2

That's theme A out of the way, now let's have a look at theme B.

Theme B Uses Sequences

THEME B — bars 11-23

- Theme B begins with a <u>dotted rhythm</u> that changes between <u>piano</u> and <u>forte</u>, played by the <u>first violins</u>. The 'ticking' is a bit different here — it's <u>passed</u> between the <u>second violins</u> and the <u>cellos/double basses</u>.

un poco cresc.

A pedal note (see p.39) is called 'inverted' if it's in one of the higher parts.

There's a <u>sequence</u> a few bars later, played in <u>unison</u> by the <u>first</u> and <u>second violins</u>, accompanied by <u>ticking</u> on the <u>lower strings</u> and an <u>inverted pedal note</u> on the <u>oboe</u>. The theme ends with <u>semiquavers</u> and another brief <u>modulation</u> to <u>D major</u>.

- Theme B returns in <u>bar 73</u>. The melody is again played on the <u>violins</u>, but this time it is <u>not</u> accompanied by the lower strings. Here, the <u>bassoon</u> plays the <u>ticking pattern</u>, and the <u>flutes</u> have a <u>high counter-melody</u> and <u>decoration</u> (with occasional interjections from the <u>oboe</u>).

- This <u>flute counter-melody</u> is heard again in <u>bar 121</u> (<u>doubled</u> in <u>octaves</u> by the <u>oboe</u>). However, this time the <u>violins</u> are playing something <u>different</u> — a <u>sextuplet pattern</u> (see below) that loosely follows the <u>original melody</u> of theme B, but with <u>variations</u>. The <u>full orchestra</u> (including the <u>brass</u>) is playing at this point, so the music is <u>louder</u> and has a <u>denser texture</u>.

There's a Dramatic Minor Section

1) In <u>bar 34</u> (for the second time — i.e. after the repeat), there's a <u>dramatic change</u> from a <u>pianissimo</u> section in <u>G major</u> to a <u>forte</u> section in <u>G minor</u> (the <u>tonic minor</u>). The <u>clarinets</u>, <u>trumpets</u>, <u>horns</u> and <u>timpani</u> are heard for the <u>first time</u>, with the <u>brass</u> instruments playing <u>chords</u>.

2) The <u>main feature</u> of this section is a <u>dotted rhythmic pattern</u>, based on the <u>third bar</u> of <u>theme A</u> (see previous page). This pattern is played by the <u>flutes</u>, <u>oboes</u>, <u>bassoons</u> and <u>all string parts</u> at some point.

3) The <u>upper strings</u> play <u>demisemiquavers</u> in this section — there's <u>antiphony</u> between the <u>first violins</u> and the <u>second violins/violas</u> (e.g. <u>bars 40-44</u>), and they also play in <u>unison/octaves</u> (e.g. from <u>bar 48</u>).

4) <u>Bars 50-59</u> introduce a <u>new feature</u> — the <u>woodwind</u> (<u>flutes</u>, <u>oboes</u>, <u>clarinets</u> and <u>bassoons</u>) play the same <u>dotted rhythm</u> as before, but this time in <u>fortissimo chords</u> (rather than changing notes).

5) The music <u>modulates</u> to <u>B♭ major</u> (the <u>relative major</u> of G minor), then goes back to <u>G minor</u> before modulating to <u>G major</u> in preparation for the <u>major section</u> and the return of <u>theme A</u> in <u>bar 63</u>.

There Are Sextuplets Towards the End

1) From <u>bar 112</u> to almost the <u>end</u> of the piece, the <u>first</u> and <u>second violins</u> play <u>semiquaver sextuplets</u> (i.e. <u>6 notes</u> per <u>beat</u>). The <u>woodwind</u> (especially the <u>flutes</u>) occasionally have these sextuplets too.

2) The sextuplets are mainly used as part of the <u>accompaniment</u> (in addition to the <u>ticking</u>), but also form part of the <u>tune</u> (e.g. in the <u>flute</u> part in <u>bar 113</u>), adding more <u>variation</u> to theme A.

3) In the <u>coda</u> (<u>bar 144</u> to the <u>end</u>), there's the <u>ticking bassoon</u>, <u>violin sextuplets</u> and <u>chords</u> on the <u>brass</u>, <u>timpani</u> and <u>lower strings</u>, with a final <u>descending scale</u> on the <u>flutes</u> and <u>oboes</u>. The piece <u>diminuendos</u> to <u>pianissimo</u> and finishes with <u>three final ticks</u> on a <u>G major chord</u>.

Hickory dickory dock — the bassoon sounds like a clock...

It's a good idea to listen to the piece a number of times — and try to follow it on a score as well. Make sure you can identify each of the different sections, and know the key features of each bit.

Orchestral Music of Mozart

Mozart is still considered to be one of the greatest composers that ever lived.

Mozart was an **Austrian Composer**

1) <u>Wolfgang Amadeus Mozart</u> was born in <u>Salzburg</u>, <u>Austria</u> in <u>1756</u> and died in <u>Vienna</u> in <u>1791</u>. He was taught <u>performance</u> and <u>composition</u> by his father, <u>Leopold Mozart</u>, who was also a composer.

2) Wolfgang showed his <u>musical talent</u> at a very <u>young</u> age — he composed his first piece of music when he was just <u>5 years old</u>. By the time he was <u>10</u> he had <u>toured Europe</u>, performed for <u>kings</u> and <u>queens</u> and written his first <u>symphony</u>.

3) He went on to write over <u>600</u> pieces of music, including <u>operas</u>, <u>masses</u>, <u>symphonies</u> and <u>concertos</u>. He also wrote smaller works, like <u>chamber music</u> and <u>string quartets</u>.

He Wrote Lots of **Symphonies...**

See p.91 for more on symphonies.

1) Mozart wrote over <u>40</u> symphonies in his short life. Along with <u>Haydn</u>, Mozart was one of the first composers to introduce <u>sonata form</u> (see p.92) as a <u>standard structure</u> in symphonies.

2) He wrote most of his symphonies before he was <u>25</u>, then took a <u>break</u> from them — he could make <u>more money</u> from composing <u>concertos</u>, and get a <u>better reputation</u> from writing <u>operas</u>. He <u>returned</u> to symphonies later on — <u>Symphony No. 40</u> was written in <u>1788</u>:

- Symphony No. 40 is one of only <u>two</u> of Mozart's symphonies in a <u>minor key</u> (the other is <u>No. 25</u> — they're both in <u>G minor</u>).
- It was written for a <u>fairly small orchestra</u> — there's <u>no percussion</u> at all, and the only brass instruments are the <u>French horns</u>. The <u>original</u> version didn't have <u>clarinets</u> (as they'd only just been invented), but Mozart wrote a <u>later version</u> that included them.
- Like most symphonies, No. 40 has <u>four movements</u>. What's <u>unusual</u> is that he uses <u>sonata form</u> in <u>three</u> of the four movements (instead of just the first movement). The first movement has <u>no introduction</u> — the <u>first theme</u> starts at the end of the <u>first bar</u>.
- Another unusual feature of this symphony is that it <u>finishes</u> on a <u>minor chord</u>.

3) Mozart's works reflect the <u>changing structure</u> of the symphony — most of his <u>early</u> ones have <u>three movements</u> (as was typical of the time), with a <u>quick-slow-quick structure</u> (see p.91). Many of his <u>later</u> symphonies have <u>four movements</u>, with a <u>minuet and trio</u> coming <u>after</u> the slow second movement.

... and Many **Concertos** Too

See p.91 for more on concertos.

1) Mozart wrote <u>concertos</u> for a <u>variety</u> of instruments. Most (nearly 30) were for <u>piano</u>, but he also wrote a number of <u>violin</u> and <u>horn</u> concertos, as well as some for <u>bassoon</u>, <u>flute</u>, <u>oboe</u> and <u>clarinet</u>.

2) The concertos generally followed the three-movement <u>quick-slow-quick structure</u>, with the first movement in <u>sonata form</u>. However, as was typical in many Classical concertos, he tended to use a <u>double exposition</u> section. The <u>orchestra</u> would play <u>first</u> (usually <u>without</u> the soloist), and <u>introduce</u> the <u>main themes</u>. The <u>soloist</u> would then <u>restate</u> these themes (<u>accompanied</u> by the orchestra) — but often with some <u>variation</u> or <u>new ideas</u>.

3) As with all Classical concertos, Mozart's concertos gave the <u>soloist</u> an opportunity to <u>show off</u>. The soloist didn't always have a <u>starring role</u> throughout though — in his <u>Clarinet Concerto in A Major</u>, at one point the clarinet <u>accompanies</u> the orchestra with an <u>Alberti bass</u> (see p.39).

4) Mozart also wrote <u>overtures</u> to his <u>operas</u> (see p.91). These are often played as <u>free-standing orchestral pieces</u> (i.e. not just before the opera). Examples include *The Marriage of Figaro* and *The Magic Flute*.

Mozart's full name was Johannes Chrysostomus Wolfgangus Theophilus Mozart...

Remember — a symphony is a piece for a full orchestra and a concerto is for a soloist and orchestra.

Orchestral Music of Beethoven

Beethoven was a very influential composer whose career bridged the Classical and Romantic periods.

Beethoven was a German Composer

1) Ludwig van Beethoven was born in Germany in 1770 and died in Vienna in 1827.

2) His hearing deteriorated over the course of his life, resulting in almost complete deafness for his last ten years. However, he continued to compose, and produced some of his best pieces despite this (e.g. Symphony No. 9 premiered in 1824).

3) He wrote lots of orchestral music (including symphonies and concertos), as well as sonatas and string quartets.

4) He was a very significant composer in Western classical music — his music is famous for its drama, intensity and emotion. Beethoven was important in developing musical styles — he moved from the stricter forms and harmonies of the Classical period to the freer forms and richer harmonies of the Romantic era. There's more on Romantic music on the next couple of pages.

Some of Beethoven's Nine Symphonies Have Names

1) Symphony No. 3 is known as the *Eroica* symphony — 'eroica' means 'heroic', and it certainly sounds heroic (listen out for the horn fanfares in third movement).

2) No. 5 is the *Fate* symphony — the famous four-note motif (see p.80) that opens the symphony (and appears throughout it) is thought to represent fate knocking at the door.

3) No. 6 is the *Pastoral* symphony:

  • The *Pastoral* symphony is an example of programme music (music that sets a scene or tells a story). It represents a visit to the countryside (which is where the name comes from).

  • Each movement has a description of the scene it portrays — for example, the second movement is 'scene by the brook'. Unusually, this symphony has five movements (there's an additional quick movement after the third movement scherzo).

  • The music is very descriptive — in the second movement, the woodwind imitate bird calls, the third movement represents a folk dance and the fourth movement portrays a violent storm.

4) Symphony No. 9 is the *Choral* symphony — it uses a choir, which sings in the final movement. The words come from a poem called 'Ode to Joy'. Beethoven swapped the order of the second and third movements in this symphony (so the scherzo comes before the slow movement).

Beethoven Pushed the Boundaries of Classical Music

1) Whilst most of his symphonies have the standard four-movement structure (see p.92), Beethoven's early symphonies were already moving away from the strict forms of Classical music. For example, the *Eroica* symphony (No. 3) is nearly twice as long as typical Classical symphonies, and is very emotional (especially the second movement, which is a funeral march).

2) Beethoven made full use of the developments in instruments. His symphonies often used large orchestras, with lots of woodwind instruments (that played an independent role). He was one of the first composers to regularly use trombones, and the first to use a choir in a symphony (No. 9).

3) Beethoven used lots of variation in dynamics — in his Piano Concerto No. 1 in C Minor they range from *pp* to *ff*, with sudden *fp* changes and *sf* accents, plus more gradual crescendos and diminuendos. Dynamics like these are more common in Romantic music than Classical.

I'm going to call my symphony Trevor...

Have a listen to the *Pastoral* symphony and try to pick out the features described above.

The Romantic Period

The Romantic period was about how passionate emotions can be expressed through art and music.

The **Romantic Period** was in the **19th Century**

1) The Romantic period was from about 1820-1910 (though there's always a bit of an overlap between different musical periods).

2) Writers, artists and composers at this time were portraying contrasting emotions and ideas, such as love and hate, happiness and grief, and life and death.

3) They were inspired by the natural world too, and were fascinated by supernatural ideas.

4) Composers wrote programme music — music based on a poem or painting, or that tells a story.

5) Tchaikovsky, Wagner and Chopin were all Romantic composers. Some of Beethoven's later pieces also fitted into the Romantic period.

Romantic Music is More **Dramatic** Than Classical

1) Romantic music used a wide range of dynamics. Sudden changes made the music very dramatic — it could go from *ppp* to *fff* and back again within a bar. Sforzandos and accents added to the drama.

2) To make the music more expressive, composers gave extra instructions — as well as tempo markings, they would include instructions like *dolce* (sweetly), *amoroso* (lovingly) or *agitato* (agitated).

3) There were more tempo changes — a piece might change speeds lots of times within the same section. Musicians in this period used *rubato* as well — it means 'robbed time' and it's when performers speed up a little in one phrase and slow down in another to make up for it. It gives them the freedom to be more expressive.

4) Composers added extra notes to chords to make the harmonies more interesting — they used 7ths, 9ths, 11ths and 13ths (9ths, 11ths and 13ths are just 2nds, 4ths and 6ths but an octave higher). They helped create dissonance (clashing notes), which let them show emotions like pain and misery.

5) There was a lot of virtuoso playing — composers wrote technically difficult music to give performers the chance to show off. It was very exciting to watch and listen to. Rachmaninov and Liszt wrote solo piano music that had to be written on four staves as there were so many notes to play.

6) Lots of Romantic composers were very proud of the countries they came from — they used folk tunes and dance rhythms from their homelands to show their national pride. Tchaikovsky used the French and Russian national anthems in his 1812 Overture.

The Orchestra **Developed** in the **Romantic Period**

1) Orchestras got much bigger — extra instruments were added.

2) The piccolo, bass clarinet and contrabassoon (which plays an octave lower than the bassoon) were added to the woodwind section.

3) Percussion sections grew to include xylophones, glockenspiels, drums, cymbals, bells and triangles as standard. Celestes (keyboard instruments that sound like glockenspiels) and harps were used too.

4) Brass instruments now had valves so were able to play more notes. Trombones and tubas were added.

5) The changes allowed composers to write music with a larger range of texture, timbre and dynamics.

6) The development of the piano (see next page) meant that it became a much more popular and important instrument. Lots of piano music was written in the Romantic period.

If music be the food of love — play on...

Make sure you know all the key features of Romantic music — you might well need to spot them in the exam. You'll need to listen out for dynamic contrasts, variations in tempo and interesting harmonies.

The Romantic Period

The <u>piano</u> was definitely one of the most <u>important</u> instruments in the <u>Romantic period</u>.

The **Piano Developed** in the **Romantic Period**

The piano's been around since the <u>18th century</u>, but the <u>developments</u> in the <u>19th century</u> made it really popular with <u>Romantic</u> composers.

SIZE: the piano <u>changed shape</u> a bit and got <u>bigger</u> (and <u>louder</u>). This meant it had a <u>bigger dynamic range</u>.

KEYS: the number of <u>keys</u> (and <u>notes</u>) <u>increased</u> to just over <u>7 octaves</u>. Composers now had a larger range in <u>pitch</u> to compose for.

PEDALS: both <u>pedals</u> (the <u>sustain</u> pedal that <u>holds notes on</u> and the <u>soft</u> pedal) became more <u>effective</u>. Some <u>modern</u> pianos have <u>three</u> pedals — the third pedal allows some notes to be held on while others are not.

STRINGS: the strings inside were both <u>thicker</u> and <u>longer</u>, making a <u>fuller tone</u>. They were also pulled <u>tighter</u>, so they were more <u>tense</u>.

FRAME: the frame used to be made of <u>wood</u>, but was now made of <u>metal</u> (to cope with the new strings). This made it easier to <u>transport</u> them.

HAMMERS: the hammers were given a <u>felt</u> covering (instead of a <u>leather</u> one). This made the <u>tone softer</u> and more <u>rounded</u>.

Melodies Were the **Focus** of Piano Pieces

1) In Romantic piano pieces, the <u>melody</u> was the most important part. Melodies were often marked *cantabile* — to be played in a <u>singing style</u>.

2) There were lots of <u>virtuosic sections</u> and <u>cadenzas</u> (see p.57) to give the pianist chance to <u>show off</u>.

3) The music had a <u>large range</u> of <u>dynamics</u>, <u>articulation</u> and <u>tone</u>. Pianists had to use the <u>pedals</u> a lot to get the <u>right sounds</u>.

4) The <u>accompaniment</u> was often <u>broken chords</u> (see p.39), but unlike many <u>Classical</u> pieces, the broken chords would be spread across <u>several octaves</u>.

Concertos, Sonatas and **Preludes** Were Written for the **Piano**

1) The piano was popular as the <u>solo</u> instrument in <u>concertos</u> — the pianist was able to really <u>show off</u> in the <u>cadenza</u>. <u>Rachmaninov</u> wrote famous piano concertos.

2) Lots of <u>sonatas</u> (see p.91) were written for the piano — <u>Chopin</u> (see next page), <u>Liszt</u>, <u>Mendelssohn</u> and <u>Schumann</u> (see p.102) all composed piano sonatas.

3) <u>Preludes</u> were originally the bit of music that came <u>before</u> the <u>main piece</u>. During the Romantic period, they became popular as <u>stand-alone pieces</u>. <u>Debussy</u>, <u>Liszt</u>, <u>Rachmaninov</u> and <u>Chopin</u> all wrote preludes for the piano.

I'll have soup as a prelude to my dinner...

Pianos were popular because they were so versatile — with a range of over seven octaves, composers had fewer limitations when they were composing. The newly-developed piano could play a range of dynamics, and the pedals could be used to change the tone of the instrument too. Perfect for Romantics.

Piano Music of Chopin

As you saw on the previous page, the piano was very popular in the Romantic period.
Some composers (like Chopin) just couldn't get enough of it.

Chopin was a **Polish Composer**

1) <u>Frédéric Chopin</u> was born in <u>Poland</u> in <u>1810</u> — lots of his music uses <u>Polish folk tunes</u> and <u>dance rhythms</u>. He died in <u>Paris</u> in <u>1849</u>.

2) He made a name for himself in <u>Vienna</u> before moving to <u>Paris</u>.

3) As well as <u>composing</u>, he also <u>performed</u> and <u>taught</u> music.

4) He composed a lot of <u>piano</u> music, and had a reputation as a '<u>tragic</u>' Romantic composer, because he was <u>ill</u> a lot, and <u>died young</u>.

Chopin Mainly Wrote **Piano Music**

This doesn't cover every single type of Chopin's piano compositions — he wrote loads of others too.

1) The vast majority of Chopin's compositions were <u>solo piano pieces</u> — even his main <u>orchestral</u> works were <u>piano concertos</u>. He also wrote a number of <u>songs</u> for <u>voice</u> and <u>piano</u>.

2) His music was characterised by its <u>expressive melodies</u> and <u>unique treatment</u> of the piano. He came up with new ways of <u>fingering</u> (such as playing the <u>black keys</u> with the <u>thumb</u>) and made extensive use of the <u>pedals</u> to explore the <u>full potential</u> of the piano.

3) Chopin wrote many piano solos based on <u>dances</u> — including <u>mazurkas</u>, <u>polonaises</u> (both types of <u>Polish</u> dance) and <u>waltzes</u>, as well as a few others, such as a <u>bolero</u> and a <u>tarantella</u>.

4) He composed four piano <u>impromptus</u> — compositions with <u>no strict form</u> and an <u>improvised feel</u> that were popular with Romantic composers.

5) Chopin wrote twenty-seven piano <u>études</u> (<u>studies</u>) that <u>developed</u> the style from a set of <u>exercises</u> to <u>concert</u> pieces that had an <u>imaginative melody</u> while still being <u>technically demanding</u>. Most have been given <u>nicknames</u> (e.g. '<u>Revolutionary</u>' or '<u>Waterfall</u>'), though Chopin <u>didn't</u> use these names.

6) A <u>nocturne</u> is a piece meant to represent the <u>night</u>. Chopin wrote <u>twenty-one</u> nocturnes, <u>developing</u> a style established earlier in the Romantic period. <u>Key features</u> of the nocturnes include a <u>melody</u> in the <u>right-hand part</u> above <u>broken chords</u> (see p.39) in the <u>left</u>, a generally <u>sad feel</u> and a <u>slow tempo</u>.

Chopin Wrote a **Prelude** in **Every Key**

He also wrote three other preludes that don't form part of this set.

1) Chopin wrote a set of <u>twenty-four preludes</u> — one in each <u>major</u> and <u>minor key</u>. The <u>order</u> of the preludes <u>alternates</u> between major and minor keys and follows the <u>circle of fifths</u> (see p.26) — No. 1 is in <u>C major</u>, No. 2 is in <u>A minor</u>, No. 3 is in <u>G major</u>, etc. Each prelude is fairly <u>short</u> (the longest is only <u>90 bars</u>), so they're often performed as a <u>set</u> — but each works as a <u>stand-alone piece</u>.

2) Like the études, many of the preludes have been given <u>nicknames</u> that represent <u>features</u> of the piece — e.g. the '<u>Raindrop</u>' prelude (see below). Each prelude has <u>different characteristics</u> (e.g. particular <u>rhythms</u> or distinctive <u>bass parts</u>). They cover a wide range of <u>tempos</u>, from *lento* to *presto*.

3) The preludes demonstrate many <u>key features</u> of <u>Romantic</u> music. For example:

- <u>Prelude No. 15 in D♭ Major</u> is known as the '<u>Raindrop</u>' prelude because of <u>repeated quavers</u> played throughout the piece, in either the right hand (an <u>inverted pedal</u>) or left-hand part (a <u>pedal note</u> — see p.39). The 'raindrops' are occasionally <u>doubled</u> in <u>octaves</u>.

- The piece is marked *sostenuto* ('<u>sustained</u>'), which means it should have a <u>slow</u>, <u>held-back</u> tempo. Chopin uses <u>augmentation</u> (see p.18) to make parts of the prelude feel slow and <u>heavy</u>.

- Chopin also includes many other <u>musical directions</u> — such as *sotto voce* ('<u>in an undertone</u>'), *smorzando* ('<u>dying away</u>'), a range of <u>dynamics</u> and marks to show when to press the <u>pedals</u>.

- The piece is in <u>ternary form</u> (ABA) — section A is in <u>D♭ major</u>, and section B is in <u>C♯ minor</u> (the <u>enharmonic equivalent</u> — see p.11), but both sections explore <u>different keys</u> as well.

Piano Music of Schumann

Schumann mainly wrote piano music and music for voice and piano —
but he did branch out into other genres, including symphonies and an opera.

Schumann was a German Composer

1) <u>Robert Schumann</u> was born in <u>1810</u> and died in <u>1856</u>. He spent most of his life in <u>Germany</u>.

2) He gave up a degree in <u>law</u> with the aim of becoming a <u>concert pianist</u>, but an <u>injury</u> to his <u>hand</u> meant he had to <u>abandon</u> that dream. Instead, he focused on <u>composition</u>.

3) Most of his <u>early</u> work was <u>piano music</u>, but <u>later</u> in his career he composed other works, such as <u>symphonies</u>, <u>Lieder</u> (see below) and an <u>opera</u>.

4) He married <u>Clara Wieck</u>, the daughter of his piano teacher — she was also a talented <u>pianist</u> and <u>composer</u>. Many of Schumann's pieces were <u>written for</u>, or <u>inspired by</u>, his <u>wife</u>.

5) Schumann was an important composer in the <u>Romantic period</u> — he was <u>highly regarded</u> for his ability to combine <u>poetry</u> and <u>music</u>.

Schumann's Piano Pieces Have Descriptive Titles

1) Many of Schumann's <u>piano pieces</u> are examples of <u>programme music</u> (see p.99). Their titles <u>describe</u> what the music <u>represents</u> — examples include *Papillons* ('<u>Butterflies</u>'), *Nachtstücke* ('<u>Night Pieces</u>'), *Waldszenen* ('<u>Forest Scenes</u>') and *Kinderszenen* ('<u>Scenes from Childhood</u>').

> *Kinderszenen* is made up of <u>thirteen pieces</u>, most of which are fairly <u>short</u> (some of them last for less than a minute). Each piece has a <u>name</u> (such as '<u>Blindman's Buff</u>' and '<u>The Poet Speaks</u>'). Some of the pieces are <u>light</u> and <u>playful</u>, while others are more <u>gentle</u> and <u>reflective</u>. Nine are in <u>major keys</u> and the other four are in <u>minor keys</u>. The <u>first</u> and <u>last</u> are in the same key (<u>G major</u>), which provides a sense of <u>unity</u> for the whole set.

2) *Carnaval* is a solo piano piece composed in 1834-35 — it depicts a <u>masked ball</u> at a <u>carnival</u>. It has twenty-two movements — most of which represent <u>characters</u> at the carnival (e.g. a <u>pierrot</u> and a <u>harlequin</u>) or <u>friends</u> of Schumann (including <u>Clara</u> and <u>Chopin</u>).

3) He also wrote a number of <u>variations</u> (see p.82). He based his variations on <u>themes</u> written by composers he <u>admired</u>, such as <u>Beethoven</u>, <u>Paganini</u> and his wife <u>Clara</u>.

Schumann Wrote Lots of Lieder

Other composers of Lieder include Schubert, Beethoven and Brahms.

A <u>Lied</u> (pronounced 'leed') is a <u>song</u> for <u>one singer</u> and a <u>piano</u> (the plural of Lied is <u>Lieder</u>). Lieder were really popular in the <u>Romantic period</u>, especially with <u>German</u> composers.

- Lieder are usually based on <u>German poems</u>. They tell <u>stories</u> — they're often very <u>dramatic</u>.
- The <u>piano part</u> in a Lied is <u>more</u> than just a background accompaniment. It helps with the <u>story-telling</u> and sets the <u>mood</u>.
- Lieder are usually either <u>through-composed</u> or have a <u>strophic</u> structure (see p.56). They often have <u>motifs</u> — little bits of repeated music that represent an <u>idea</u>, <u>character</u> or <u>place</u>.
- A <u>collection</u> of Lieder could be put together in a <u>song cycle</u> (a set of songs with the same <u>theme</u>).

Schumann wrote many of his Lieder in <u>1840</u> (the year he married Clara), including two of his famous <u>song cycles</u>, *Frauenliebe und -leben* and *Dichterliebe*. The first (which means '<u>woman's love and life</u>') is a set of eight Lieder, based on poems by <u>Adelbert von Chamisso</u>. The second (meaning '<u>a poet's love</u>') is a set of sixteen, based on poems by <u>Heinrich Heine</u>. This cycle has themes of <u>love</u>, <u>nature</u> and <u>fairy tales</u>.

Robert Schumann — Lieder of the pack...

When you're listening to piano music by Chopin and Schumann, see if you can pick out the features of the piece that are typical of the Romantic period (see p.99-100 for a reminder).

Requiems

After many pages of orchestral or piano music, I'm going to finish this section with a return to choral music.

A **Mass** is a Type of **Sacred Music**

The term 'mass' can be used in the Church of England too.

1) A mass is a Roman Catholic church service. Parts of it are often set to music, and sung by a choir and soloists. These parts include:

2) The words of a mass were traditionally in Latin.

3) Masses were originally written to be used in church, but they're now often performed in concerts too.

4) Famous settings of the mass include J.S. Bach's Mass in B Minor and Beethoven's Mass in C Major. There are also modern masses, such as The Armed Man: A Mass for Peace by Karl Jenkins.

- *Kyrie* ('Lord have mercy...')
- *Gloria* ('Glory be to God...')
- *Credo* ('I believe in one God...')
- *Sanctus* ('Holy, holy, holy...')
- *Benedictus* ('Blessed is He...')
- *Agnus Dei* ('O Lamb of God...')

A **Requiem** is a **Mass** for the **Dead**

1) A mass for the dead is called a requiem. Requiems use some parts of the normal mass (such as the *Kyrie*, *Sanctus* and *Agnus Dei*), but miss out the happier sections (e.g. the *Gloria* and the *Credo*).

2) These sections are replaced by more solemn bits. These include the *Introit*, which begins 'Requiem aeternam' ('Grant them eternal rest'), the *Dies Irae* (which means 'Day of Wrath') and the *Pie Jesu* (which is taken from the last couple of lines of the *Dies Irae* and means 'Merciful Jesus').

Requiems were **Popular** with **Romantic Composers**

1) Although there had been earlier requiems (such as the well-known Requiem Mass in D Minor by Mozart), it was during the Romantic period that requiems became popular as a form of large-scale composition for performance in concert rather than a church service.

2) The text of the requiem is very dramatic and emotional (especially the *Dies Irae*), so it's easy to see why Romantic composers chose to set it to music.

3) Requiems are usually in a minor key to match the grave nature of the lyrics. Romantic requiems were often written for a large choir and massive orchestra to add drama and tension to the music.

Verdi's Requiem was written in 1873-74 in memory of the writer Alessandro Manzoni. It was sung by four soloists (soprano, mezzo-soprano, tenor and bass) and a full choir. The singers are accompanied by a huge orchestra — including 2 flutes, a piccolo, 4 bassoons and a large brass section with a whopping 8 trumpets. There's also a prominent percussion section, which has timpani, a bass drum and crash cymbals. This made it very dramatic — the *Dies Irae* in particular, which starts with loud orchestral chords (with bass drum off-beats) and a wide range of pitch from the choir. The trumpet fanfare after the *Dies Irae* starts with one trumpet and builds up to all eight before the choir enters, creating a rich polyphonic texture. There are gentler sections to provide contrast (such as the *Agnus Dei*), where the soloists sing above a light orchestral accompaniment.

In contrast to Verdi's operatic style, Fauré's Requiem (which he started in 1887 and revised several times before the final version was completed in 1900) is gentle and serene. The vocal parts are for a choir and just two soloists (a soprano and a baritone). The orchestra is joined by an organ. Instead of the exciting *Dies Irae*, Fauré includes a tranquil *Pie Jesu*, sung by the soprano soloist with a quiet orchestral accompaniment. Some sections are in a major key and sound calm and peaceful, though there are more emotional sections with rich harmonies and dramatic crescendos.

Be prepared for a dies irae if you don't revise...

There are later requiems too — a famous 20th century example is the War Requiem by Benjamin Britten (see p.154-155), which uses Latin words from the Requiem Mass and war poems by Wilfred Owen.

Warm-up and Exam Questions

Before you have a go at the exam questions, give these warm-up questions a whirl — they'll get your brain in gear and give you a fighting chance when you get onto the harder ones.

Warm-up Questions

1) Describe how dynamics were used in the Baroque period.

2) In a concerto grosso, what is: a) the concertino?   b) the ripieno?

3) Describe ground bass form.

4) What is an appoggiatura?

5) What were the four different types of voice in a Baroque choir?

6) What is an aria?

7) Who wrote Messiah?

8) Name an instrument that was included in the Classical orchestra but was not used in orchestras of the Baroque period.

9) What is the standard structure of a Classical concerto?

10) What are the three main sections of a piece in sonata form?

11) What is Haydn's Symphony No. 101 also known as?

12) Name two other Classical composers.

13) Give the approximate dates of the Romantic period.

14) What does *sotto voce* mean?

15) What is a Lied?

16) Name one section of a requiem that doesn't appear in a mass.

Exam Questions

Have a go at these exam-style questions.

Track 32 is an excerpt from the 2nd Movement of Haydn's Clock Symphony.

Play the excerpt **four** times, leaving a short pause for writing time between each playing.

 Track 32

a)   In the third bar of this excerpt, the ornament below is played.
     What is the name of this ornament?

....

[1 mark]

b)   Name the two different instruments playing the melody at the start of the excerpt.

....

....
[2 marks]

c)   This movement is in $\frac{2}{4}$. Suggest a suitable tempo for this excerpt.

....
[1 mark]

d)   Identify two features of this excerpt that are typical of the Classical period.

....

....

....

....
[2 marks]

e)   About halfway through the excerpt, the mood changes.
     Describe the similarities and differences between the two sections.

....

....

....

....

....

....
[4 marks]

f)   Which of the words below best describes the texture created by the first
     and second violins towards the end of the excerpt? Circle your answer.

unison   antiphony   counterpoint   monophony
[1 mark]

Exam Questions

Track 33 is an excerpt from 'Dies Irae' by Verdi.
Play the excerpt **four** times. Leave a short pause between each playing.

Track 33

a) i) What larger work does this movement come from?

....
[1 mark]

ii) What does 'Dies Irae' mean? Circle your answer.

Lord have mercy   **Eternal rest**   **Day of wrath**   **Merciful Jesus**
[1 mark]

b) Tick one box for each statement below to indicate whether it is true or false.

	True	False
The excerpt opens with homophonic chords.	☐	☐
The bass drum plays on the off-beats.	☐	☐
The choir sing in unison.	☐	☐
The strings play ascending runs between the choral sections.	☐	☐

[4 marks]

c) Describe the texture of this excerpt.

....

....

....

....

....
[3 marks]

Exam Questions

d)   This piece is marked *allegro agitato*. Explain what this means.

....

....

[1 mark]

e) i) During which period of Western classical music history was this piece composed?

....

[1 mark]

    ii) Identify the features of this piece that are typical of that period
      and explain why they were used. You might want to comment on
      musical elements such as instrumentation, dynamics and harmony,
      as well as any other elements you think appropriate.

....

....

....

....

....

....

....

....

....

....

....

[8 marks]

Revision Summary for Section Six

What you need to take away from this section are the facts about Baroque, Classical and Romantic music — it's really important that you know how they were different from each other. You also need to be up to speed on the study piece too (Haydn's Clock Symphony). You know what to do — keep going through these questions until you can answer them all without needing to look back at the section.

1) Give the approximate dates of the Baroque period.

2) What is a basso continuo and what instruments would normally play it?

3) What is a concerto grosso?

4) Which Baroque structure can be described as ABA?

5) What was the function of a prelude in the Baroque period?

6) In theme and variation form, what is the theme?

7) What is the main difference between theme and variation form and ground bass form?

8) Explain what each of these terms means:
   a) melodic inversion   b) retrograde   c) ostinato.

9) Name three different ornaments used by Baroque composers and explain what they are.

10) What is a falsetto voice?

11) What are the four different voices in an SATB choir?

12) What is a baritone voice?

13) What is an opera?

14) Name the three types of song in an opera.

15) What is an oratorio?

16) Name a famous oratorio by Handel.

17) Give a brief definition of word-painting.

18) Name two of Handel's coronation anthems.

19) Give the approximate dates of the Classical period.

20) Why did the piano become increasingly popular in the Classical period?

21) What was the most important section in a Classical orchestra?

22) Classical music usually has a homophonic texture. What does this mean?

23) What is a symphony?

24) How many instruments are sonatas usually composed for?

25) What is the structure of a symphony with 4 movements?

26) Briefly describe rondo form.

27) Name two transposing instruments used in Haydn's Symphony No. 101.

28) Why is Symphony No. 101 known as the Clock Symphony?

29) What key does the second movement of this symphony start in?

30) How did Mozart's symphonies reflect the changes in style of Classical music?

31) What is programme music?

32) Name a symphony by Beethoven that is an example of programme music.

33) Name three techniques that Romantic composers used to show drama and emotion in their work.

34) Describe three ways in which the piano developed in the Romantic period.

35) What instrument was most of Chopin's music written for?

36) Why is Chopin's Prelude No. 15 known as the Raindrop prelude?

37) Describe Schumann's *Carnaval*.

38) What is a song cycle?

39) What is a requiem?

40) What instruments and voices are needed to perform Verdi's Requiem?

Voices in Pop

This section starts by looking at some general things that are relevant to most pop music — first up, vocals.

The **Lead Singer** Sings the **Main Melody**

The lead singer (or <u>vocalist</u>) sings the main melody of a song. They're the <u>soloist</u>, and if they're part of a <u>band</u>, they're often the most <u>famous</u> member (e.g. <u>Freddie Mercury</u> in <u>Queen</u>, <u>Jon Bon Jovi</u> in <u>Bon Jovi</u> and <u>Axl Rose</u> in <u>Guns N' Roses</u>). If you get a pop song in the Listening Exam, say something about the lead vocalist's <u>style</u>. It's even worth mentioning obvious stuff like whether the singer's <u>male</u> or <u>female</u>.

Backing Singers Sing the **Harmonies**

The backing vocalists are the ones who sing the <u>harmonies</u>. These are the main ways backing singers do their thing:

Listen out for the backing vocals in 'Surfin' USA' by The Beach Boys.

IN HARMONY	**IN UNISON**	**DESCANT**	**CALL AND RESPONSE**
all singing <u>different notes</u>	all singing the <u>same notes</u>	singing a <u>higher</u> part in time with the main tune	<u>repeating</u> whatever the lead vocalist sings or <u>answering</u> the lead with another tune

Singers Can Do All Sorts of **Fancy Stuff**

There are different ways to sing. Make sure you can <u>describe</u> exactly what you're hearing. Listen out for:

1) **A CAPPELLA** — singing with <u>no instrumental backing</u>.
2) **VIBRATO** — when singers <u>quiver up and down</u> slightly in pitch. It makes the voice sound <u>warmer</u> and <u>more expressive</u>.

   Vocal parts can be <u>syllabic</u> (one note per syllable) or <u>melismatic</u> (multiple notes per syllable).

3) **FALSETTO** — when men (or occasionally women) make their voices go <u>really high</u>. <u>Sam Smith</u>, <u>The Bee Gees</u> and <u>Michael Jackson</u> are all famous for their falsetto voices.
4) **PORTAMENTO** — when a singer <u>slides</u> from one note to another.
5) **SCAT** — <u>improvising</u> using syllables like '<u>doo</u>' and '<u>dat</u>'. Scat comes from <u>jazz music</u>.
6) **RIFFING** — when singers <u>decorate</u> and add bits to the tune. They often go up and down a scale before coming to rest on one note. Riffing usually comes at the <u>end of a phrase</u>, <u>between sections</u> or to <u>finish the song</u>. <u>Whitney Houston</u>, <u>Mariah Carey</u> and <u>Celine Dion</u> are famous for riffing.
7) **BELTING** — when a singer sings notes from their <u>higher register</u> at a <u>louder volume</u> than normal. It's often used for the <u>emotional climax</u> in <u>musical theatre</u> songs (see p.119-120).
8) **RAPPING** — when <u>rhyming lyrics</u> are <u>spoken</u> or <u>chanted</u> to a <u>rhythmic beat</u>.
9) **BEATBOXING** — using the <u>voice</u> to make <u>percussive sounds</u>, imitating a <u>drum kit</u> or <u>DJ equipment</u>.

Electronic Effects Can Be Added to Vocal Parts

There's more on these effects on p.72-73 and p.75.

Another way to make the vocals on a pop song sound interesting is to add <u>electronic effects</u>.

1) **REVERB** (short for <u>reverberation</u>) adds an <u>echo</u> to a sound.
2) **MULTI-TRACKING** (or <u>layering</u>) is when <u>each part</u> is recorded on its own <u>track</u>, and all the tracks are played back together. It means <u>one singer</u> can record <u>all</u> the parts in a song — for example, in some <u>Queen</u> songs, <u>Freddie Mercury</u> sings the <u>solo part</u> and the <u>backing vocals</u> at the <u>same time</u>.
3) **SAMPLING** is when you use a <u>short recording</u> (a <u>sample</u>) of someone else's voice in your song.
4) A **VOCODER** (a type of <u>synthesizer</u>) <u>electronically alters</u> a voice recording and creates <u>weird effects</u>. Similar technology is used with <u>auto-tuning</u> — adjusting notes on a recording so that they're in tune.

I'm singing in the shower, just singing in the shower...

Next time you're listening to pop music, pay close attention to the techniques the singers use.

Instruments of Pop

Pop songs can use any instruments at all — but there are some common instruments that are often used.

Most Pop Songs Use **Electric Guitars**

The **Lead Guitar** Plays **Tunes**, the **Rhythm Guitar** Plays **Chords**

The lead guitar plays the melody, as well as improvised solos in the instrumental sections (Brian May from Queen and Slash from Guns N' Roses are famous for their guitar solos). The lead guitar also adds in fancy bits all the way through to decorate the tune.

The rhythm guitar fills in the harmony all the way through. They either strum the chords or pick out broken (arpeggiated) chords (see p.39) and often play rhythmic riffs (see p.58). Some artists (e.g. Bob Dylan and Ed Sheeran) play rhythms on acoustic guitars instead.

The **Bass Guitar** Plays the **Bass Lines**

See p.65 for more about guitars.

The bass guitar plays the lowest notes. The bass guitarist picks out individual notes (not chords) to form the bass line. As well as picking, bass guitarists sometimes play glissandos by sliding their finger up and down the string (this is easier on a fretless bass).

Electric Guitars Can Play **Effects**

By plugging an electric guitar into an effects box or using different pedals you can get all sorts of effects:

1) **DISTORTION** — a grungy, dirty sound.
2) **FUZZ** — fuzzy-sounding distortion.
3) **CHORUS** — makes it sound like more than one instrument is playing.
4) **FLANGER** and **PHASER** — create a 'whooshing' noise.
5) **WAH WAH** — makes the guitar go, er... "wah wah".
6) **COMPRESSION** — evens out variations in volume.
7) **PANNING** — sends different sounds through different speakers. If you've got two guitarists trading solos, one could be panned left and one right to separate the sounds.

You can also produce reverb (echo) on a guitar as well. There's more about guitar effects on p.75.

The **Drums** Add the **Rhythm**

1) The drummer sets the tempo and plays rhythms to fit the style of the song (like the rhythm guitar).
2) The main instruments of a drum kit are snare drum, bass drum, hi-hat, tom-toms and cymbals. There are different playing techniques — e.g. for a rim shot, you hit both the rim and head of the snare drum.
3) Drum pads and drum machines can replace acoustic drums, or sometimes play alongside them.

The **Piano** or **Keyboard** Provides **Melody** and **Harmony**

The piano or keyboard can play the melody (and instrumental solos) or chords to fill out the harmony. Not all pop songs will have a piano, but some only have a piano accompaniment (e.g. Bob Dylan's 'Make You Feel My Love' and Adele's 'Someone Like You'). These songs tend to be gentler than other pop songs.

Synthesizers Can Do Lots of Jobs

There's more about synthesizers on p.72.

Synthesizers (synths) can play any part — they can make the sound of virtually any instrument you want, e.g. a full string section or brass section (although some bands have live strings or brass). They can play rhythmic chords, solos or hooks (short, catchy, memorable bits).

Rock 'n' Roll

Rock 'n' roll is sometimes used to mean rock music in general — but for these two pages, it means the particular style of music that developed in the USA in the 1950s and '60s and spread across the world.

Rock 'n' Roll Came from the United States in the 1950s

1) Rock 'n' roll developed in the southern states of America in the late 1940s and early 1950s. African Americans moved to urban areas, which meant that black and white people were living closer together than ever before. Their styles of music mixed and evolved, creating new genres of music.

2) Rock 'n' roll was a mix of rhythm 'n' blues (which itself came from blues — see p.129-130) and country and western music, but also had influences of gospel, folk and jazz. Typical songs were a faster version of the 12-bar blues with the distinctive twang of country and western singing.

3) It might seem pretty tame today, but rock 'n' roll caused a massive uproar in the 1950s. Teenagers loved it, but their parents' generation hated it — they thought it was tasteless and immoral, and some even went as far as to say it was evil. Teenagers could afford to buy their own records though, so rock 'n' roll was extremely successful, and made superstars out of its biggest artists (e.g. Elvis Presley). It was used in films and TV programmes, which made it even more popular.

4) Rock 'n' roll continued to develop throughout the '50s and '60s, leading to rock music itself from the mid 1960s (see p.112-113).

Cleveland DJ Alan Freed made the term 'rock 'n' roll' popular.

Rock 'n' Roll Songs Were Lively With a Strong Beat

1) Rock 'n' roll songs were generally up-tempo, with a clear beat (most of them were in $\frac{4}{4}$). This made them ideal for dancing — dances in high school gyms were popular (like in *Grease*), and popular TV shows featured teenagers dancing to current hits.

2) The general line-up for a rock 'n' roll band was a lead singer, electric guitars, a bass guitar, a drum kit and sometimes a piano. In earlier bands, the piano played more of a lead role and some had a saxophone as well. A double bass was used before the bass guitar became more common.

3) The lyrics appealed to teenagers because they were about teenage issues, such as love, school, cars and summer holidays. Key lines were repeated throughout the song, which made them memorable.

4) The structure of the songs was fairly simple — most were either strophic (all verses had the same tune — see p.56) or had a verse-chorus structure (see p.58). Some had an AABA structure (four sections, three with the same melody and one that contrasts). A lot of hits featured at least one instrumental section, where a soloist (usually the lead guitarist) would improvise.

5) The verses and choruses themselves were often based on a 12-bar blues. There was a lot of call and response between the lead singer and the band, and most songs had a catchy hook.

Early Rock 'n' Roll Stars Included Bill Haley and Elvis Presley

- One of the first rock 'n' roll hits was 'Rock Around the Clock' by Bill Haley & His Comets.
- Elvis Presley was a huge star — his early hits included 'Hound Dog', 'Heartbreak Hotel' and 'Jailhouse Rock'. Elvis also acted and sang in films, which made him even more popular. He was adored by teenage girls — at his concerts, his gyrating hips caused a commotion.
- Bill Haley, Elvis Presley, Jerry Lee Lewis (who sang 'Great Balls of Fire') and Buddy Holly ('That'll Be The Day') were all rockabilly singers (a sub-genre of rock 'n' roll).
- Britain produced some rock 'n' roll stars as well, who were heavily influenced by American rock 'n' roll. The Beatles started out in rock 'n' roll (there's more about them on p.114-116).

You ain't nothin' but a revision dog...

In a nutshell, rock 'n' roll took the African American rhythm 'n' blues and made it accessible to young people of all backgrounds. Rock 'n' roll was more than just a type of music — it was an entire culture.

Rock Music

Rock music is <u>developing</u> all the time — but you need to know about rock music from the '<u>60s</u> and '<u>70s</u>.

Rock Music Developed in the 1960s

1) During the <u>1960s</u>, rock 'n' roll <u>evolved</u> into more <u>guitar-dominated</u> music known simply as <u>rock</u>.

2) Like the <u>12-bar blues</u> (see p.130), rock songs tend to be based around the chords <u>I</u>, <u>IV</u> and <u>V</u> (and sometimes <u>VI</u>). Songs are often in $\frac{4}{4}$ with a <u>steady drum rhythm</u> and follow a <u>verse-chorus structure</u>.

3) Rock music often uses <u>power chords</u> (chords made up of the <u>tonic</u> and <u>fifth</u>).

4) Many rock bands were <u>formed</u> in the 1960s — though most <u>continued</u> into the following decades. These were bands such as <u>The Beatles</u> (see p.114-116), <u>The Rolling Stones</u> (whose '60s hits included '<u>(I Can't Get No) Satisfaction</u>' and '<u>Get Off Of My Cloud</u>'), <u>The Kinks</u> ('<u>You Really Got Me</u>'), <u>The Who</u> ('<u>My Generation</u>'), <u>The Doors</u> ('<u>Light My Fire</u>') and <u>Led Zeppelin</u> (their most famous song, '<u>Stairway to Heaven</u>' — see below, was released in <u>1971</u>, but the band was formed in the late '60s).

The Instrumentation Varies

1) A <u>rock band</u> was originally made up of a <u>lead electric guitar</u>, a <u>rhythm electric guitar</u>, a <u>lead singer</u>, a <u>bass guitar</u> and a <u>drummer</u>.

2) As rock developed, <u>more instruments</u> were added. In some songs, bands might use a <u>string section</u> (with <u>violins</u> and <u>cellos</u>), a <u>brass section</u> (<u>trumpets</u> and <u>trombones</u>) or a <u>wind section</u> (<u>flutes</u>, <u>clarinets</u>, <u>saxophones</u> and <u>oboes</u>). They also brought in <u>pianos</u> or <u>keyboards</u> and <u>synthesizers</u>.

3) Musicians used the <u>effects</u> on <u>electric guitars</u> to produce new sounds — like <u>distortion</u>, <u>feedback</u> (the noise you get when a guitar or microphone is too close to a speaker) and <u>reverberation</u> (echo).

4) Rock bands use lots of other <u>techniques</u> to get <u>unusual sounds</u> — <u>Led Zeppelin</u> often used a <u>pounding beat</u> turned up really loud as their main rhythm. They sometimes used <u>violin bows</u> on their <u>guitar strings</u> to get a <u>sustained note</u>.

Developments in technology have played an important part in rock music.

Rock Songs Are a Way of Expressing Yourself

1) Lots of rock bands write their <u>own lyrics</u> to songs (as well as the music). They use things like <u>religious themes</u>, <u>political causes</u> and <u>personal experiences of love</u> and some told <u>stories</u>.

2) <u>Led Zeppelin</u>, <u>David Bowie</u> and <u>Bob Dylan</u> all use the influences of <u>folk music</u> — they've written whole albums in a folky style (often described as <u>folk rock</u>).

3) <u>Costumes</u> were used to help the music along — David Bowie's <u>jumpsuits</u> and <u>make-up</u> (such as his famous <u>lightning bolt</u> make-up) really helped to <u>set the scene</u> for the <u>characters</u> that appeared in Bowie's songs (e.g. <u>Major Tom</u> and <u>Ziggy Stardust</u>).

Songs Became Longer and Albums Had Themes

- Queen's '<u>Bohemian Rhapsody</u>' (released in 1975) lasts for a whopping <u>6 minutes</u>. It <u>doesn't</u> have a <u>chorus</u> — it's made up of <u>unrelated sections</u>, including a <u>slow ballad</u>, a <u>guitar solo</u>, an <u>operatic</u> section and a <u>heavy rock</u> section. The song is <u>through-composed</u> (see p.56).

- '<u>Stairway to Heaven</u>' (1971) by <u>Led Zeppelin</u> lasts for an even more whopping <u>8 minutes</u>. It has different sections — the first is <u>gentle</u>, with a <u>recorder</u> and <u>acoustic guitar</u> accompaniment. The next section is a little <u>faster</u>, with <u>electric guitars</u>, and is followed by a long <u>electric guitar solo</u>. The final section is <u>fast</u>, <u>hard rock</u> (see next page).

- *Sgt. Pepper's Lonely Hearts Club Band* (1967) by <u>The Beatles</u> (see p.114) was one of the first rock <u>concept albums</u> — an album with a <u>theme</u> that <u>links</u> all the tracks.

- <u>Pink Floyd's</u> 1973 album *The Dark Side of the Moon* is another example of a concept album.

Rock Music

Don't worry, you don't need to know masses of detail about the different types of rock music below. Make sure you're happy with their common features though, such as the importance of the guitar.

There Are Lots of **Types** of Rock

Over time, rock has branched out into lots of different sub-genres. Here are some of the most popular:

HARD ROCK

- Loud and aggressive, dominated by a distorted electric guitar — solos and power chords were key features.
- Bands include Led Zeppelin and The Who.

HEAVY METAL

- Harder and more distorted than hard rock, with even longer guitar solos.
- Bands include Black Sabbath and Iron Maiden.

GLAM ROCK

- Theatrical and glitzy.
- Easier to listen to than hard rock, with a more rock 'n' roll feel and catchy hooks.
- Performers dressed up in spangly catsuits and wore lots of make-up.
- Artists include David Bowie and Kiss.

PUNK ROCK

- Harsh and angry music from the '70s — it's all about anarchy and rebellion. Lyrics were often shouted.
- Bands include The Sex Pistols and Blondie.

PROGRESSIVE (PROG) ROCK

- Songs were experimental and complicated, and albums often had a theme.
- Features long instrumentals, electronic effects and mythological or nonsensical lyrics.
- Bands include Yes and Pink Floyd.

PSYCHEDELIC ROCK

- From the '60s artistic movement psychedelia — it tried to recreate the surreal images and sounds experienced with hallucinogenic drugs like LSD.
- The music used lots of guitar effects and unusual electronic instruments and effects. It took inspiration from other cultures (including Eastern music). Lyrics were weird and dreamlike.
- Bands include The Beatles and The Doors.

Classic Rock Songs are Known as **Anthems**

1) Because of the powerful nature of the music and lyrics, a lot of rock songs can be described as anthems. They usually have memorable, singable (or shoutable) choruses. Here are a few examples:

   - 'Born to Be Wild' by Steppenwolf was released in 1968 — it was one of the first songs to be described as 'heavy metal' (see above), and even uses the words 'heavy metal thunder'. It has distorted electric guitars and the repeated line 'born to be wild' is simple and memorable.
   - 'We Will Rock You' by Queen was released in 1977. The only accompaniment to the vocals is the instantly-recognizable 'stamp stamp clap' rhythm that continues throughout the song (go on, you know you want to). The chorus is just one repeated line, almost like a chant. An electric guitar comes in right at the end and plays a solo.

2) Arena rock (or stadium rock) came about in the middle of the 1970s — developments in technology meant that rock bands could be amplified more. This allowed them to perform in larger spaces, such as arenas and stadiums (hence the name).

   Rock anthems were perfect for arena performances.

3) Technology also meant that special effects (such as pyrotechnics and light shows) could be used. Arena performances were about the effects and experience as much as the music.

Born to revise for GCSE Music...

'We Will Rock You' features in the 2001 film *A Knight's Tale*, where it's played at a jousting tournament. Perhaps not the most historically-accurate choice of song, but you can't beat a classic rock anthem.

The Beatles

Your study pieces for popular music are three tracks by The Beatles from the album *Sgt. Pepper's Lonely Hearts Club Band*, which was recorded at the Abbey Road studios and released in 1967.

The Beatles Were From Liverpool

THE BEATLES

- The members of the band were John Lennon, Paul McCartney, George Harrison and Ringo Starr. They were all from Liverpool.

Their producer George Martin was often known as 'the fifth Beatle'.

- Their standard line-up was Lennon on rhythm guitar, McCartney on bass guitar, Harrison on lead guitar and Starr on drums, although there was some variation. All four members provided vocals, and Lennon and McCartney were the main songwriters. In later songs, they used a variety of other instruments, including the piano and sitar.

- Their early songs (such as 'I Saw Her Standing There' and 'She Loves You') were influenced by Elvis Presley, Chuck Berry and other rock 'n' roll stars.

- Although they're usually classed as a rock band, their style changed so much over the years that it's almost impossible to put them into one category. As well as rock 'n' roll, they used musical ideas from rhythm 'n' blues, folk, classical music and non-Western cultures (such as Indian music). They also used pioneering recording techniques such as sampling.

- These different styles can be heard on their albums — for example, *Please Please Me* is rock 'n' roll, whereas *Help* has more of a rock sound.

- They had loads of hits — some of their most famous songs include 'Yesterday', 'Hey Jude', 'All You Need is Love', 'A Hard Day's Night' and 'I Want to Hold Your Hand'.

In the mid-60s, bands like The Beatles, The Rolling Stones and The Who became really popular in the USA. This was known as the British Invasion. The excitement The Beatles inspired was known as Beatlemania.

Sgt. Pepper's Lonely Hearts Club Band is a Concept Album

1) The Beatles stopped touring in 1966 for a number of reasons — including being tired and fed up of it, and threats to the band in Japan, the Philippines, the USA and Canada. Not being able to be heard above the screaming fans and the limitations of performing live (such as only being able to use a few instruments, and being unable to use technology) were also important factors.

2) *Sgt. Pepper's Lonely Hearts Club Band* was the first album to be recorded after they stopped touring. The name of the album is the name of the fictional band that The Beatles used as their alter ego — pretending to be someone else gave them the chance to experiment with different styles of music.

3) This allowed them to create a concept album (see p.112) — the idea was that the whole album was a live performance by Sgt. Pepper's Lonely Hearts Club Band, so should be played in one go, with the tracks in the order that they appeared. This idea was reinforced by features such as noises of an orchestra tuning up before the start of the first track and audience applause during the song.

4) The songs on the album use a wide variety of instruments — including a 40-piece orchestra who play a long, dissonant crescendo in the middle of 'A Day In The Life', a French horn quartet on the title track and classical Indian instruments on 'Within You Without You' (see next page).

5) The overall genre of the album is psychedelic rock — see previous page.

6) The three Beatles tracks you have to study all come from this album — they are 'With A Little Help From My Friends', 'Lucy in the Sky With Diamonds' and 'Within You Without You'. These pieces are covered in more detail over the next two pages.

Yesterday — wish my music exam was yesterday...

The Beatles broke up in 1970 and the members went their separate ways, continuing to record and perform their own projects. However, the music they created together has had a lasting impact on the world of pop.

The Beatles

Now it's time to have a look at your study pieces in a bit more detail...

Within You Without You Has Indian Influences

1) 'Within You Without You' is the eighth track on the album (on the original record, it was the first track on the second side). It was written by George Harrison who sang lead vocals and played the guitar, sitar and tambura (see below). None of the other Beatles were involved with this track.

2) Harrison was inspired by Indian classical music (he'd taken sitar lessons with the famous sitar player Ravi Shankar) — this track has many Indian influences:

INDIAN MUSIC

- Indian classical music is based on a raga (a set of notes, usually between 5 and 8). Ragas are very different from Western scales. By using microtones (intervals between notes that are smaller than a semitone), they often include notes that aren't heard in Western music. Ragas are meant to create different moods, representing times of the day and seasons.

- Raga performances are improvised (see p.132) using the notes of the raga and rhythm patterns known as talas. The melody is played over a drone (a simple rhythmic pattern of 2 notes), which creates harmony.

The sitar

- Traditional Indian instruments are the sitar (a large, long-necked string instrument, often with 7 strings), the tambura (similar to a sitar but usually has 4 strings) and the tabla (a pair of drums). There are many other instruments too, including the dilruba and esraj — bowed string instruments with frets.

- The sitar, dilruba and esraj have strings underneath the main strings known as 'sympathetic' strings. These strings vibrate when the main strings are played, creating a thick, shimmery sound. Playing techniques include pitch bends and glissandos (stretching a string slightly or sliding a finger along the string, producing a sound called meend).

- The melody is improvised on the sitar, the tambura plays a drone and the tabla plays the rhythm.

3) As well as the sitar, 'Within You Without You' features the dilruba, tambura and tabla, as well as the swarmandal (also known as the Indian harp — a type of zither). It also has Western instruments, including an acoustic guitar, violins and cellos.

4) The song has quite a mournful feel and sounds a bit like a chant — with spiritual lyrics influenced by Eastern philosophies. They talk of how life carries on 'within you and without you'.

With A Little Help From My Friends is the Second Track

1) 'With A Little Help From My Friends' was written by John Lennon and Paul McCartney for Ringo Starr to sing. The other Beatles sing backing vocals and play electric guitar, bass, cowbell and piano (George Martin plays the Hammond organ in this piece too). Starr also plays the drums.

2) It's the second track on the album — it follows directly on from 'Sgt. Pepper's Lonely Hearts Club Band'. The tracks have been cross-faded together (where one track merges into the next, so there's no gap) with pre-recorded applause — this reinforces the idea that the album was a live recording.

3) Ringo Starr sings it in the character of Billy Shears, his alter ego in the fictional band. Billy Shears is introduced by the backing singers at the start (following a longer introduction in the previous track).

4) The melody has quite a limited range (the verses stay within a perfect fifth), and is generally conjunct (except for the first two notes of each line of the chorus and an octave leap to the final note).

5) Starr sings lead vocals throughout, and Lennon and McCartney provide harmony with their backing vocals. There's also call and response in the second verse — Starr asks a question, and Lennon and McCartney answer it (and vice versa in the third verse).

I'll get by with a little help from my revision notes...

If you're wondering when I'm going to run out of song lyrics about revision, the answer is NOT YET.

The Beatles

With A Little Help From My Friends Has Swung Rhythms

1) 'With A Little Help From My Friends' has swinging, syncopated rhythms (see p.129), which gives it a relaxed, lilting feel. There are also triplets (some tied to quavers) in the chorus.

2) The song is in $\frac{4}{4}$, and has a moderate tempo. It's in a major key throughout.

3) The texture is homophonic (melody with accompaniment) all the way through. There's a drum fill before the second verse, where everything stops apart from the drum kit.

Lucy in the Sky With Diamonds Was Sung By John Lennon

1) 'Lucy in the Sky With Diamonds' is the third track on the album. It was mainly written by John Lennon (who also sang lead vocals), with input from Paul McCartney. As well as the standard rock band instruments, the song also has an acoustic guitar, tambura and Lowrey organ.

2) The song is said to have been inspired by a painting done by Lennon's four-year-old son, with lyrical influences from the surreal ideas in *Alice's Adventures in Wonderland* and *Through the Looking Glass* by Lewis Carroll. This is evident in the psychedelic imagery — e.g. 'marmalade skies' and 'kaleidoscope eyes'. There is speculation that the song references the drug LSD, though The Beatles have denied this.

3) The verses of the song are in a steady $\frac{3}{4}$, while the choruses are in $\frac{4}{4}$. Its tonality is mainly major — the verses are in A major, the bridge sections are in B♭ major and the choruses are in G major.

4) The melodies are generally conjunct, and the chorus is the same line repeated three times.

The Album Used New Technology

As it was never intended to be performed live, the album uses lots of different types of technology, including some that were invented just for The Beatles. These techniques are particularly noticeable on 'Lucy in the Sky With Diamonds'. The technology they used included:

1) The album was recorded using 4-track tape machines (an early form of multi-tracking). Up to four different tracks could be recorded (sometimes a couple of instruments on the same track), then combined into a single track (known as 'bouncing' or 'reduction mixing') on another 4-track machine. This track could then be mixed with other tracks, allowing The Beatles to use lots of instruments.

2) Double tracking is when the same part is recorded twice and both takes are played back at the same time — it's often used on vocal parts to produce a bigger sound. To avoid Lennon having to keep recording the same parts, an Abbey Road technician invented automatic double tracking (ADT — also called artificial double tracking), which copies the track and plays it back with a small delay.

3) A direct input transformer (DIT or DI) is used to plug an electronic instrument into a mixing desk (without a microphone). This improves the sound quality and reduces background noise or feedback.

4) Close-miking (putting the microphone close to the instrument) creates an intense timbre. It means other instruments are less likely to be picked up, which makes panning easier. Panning is where different tracks are heard through different speakers — listen out for it at the start of 'Lucy in the Sky...'. To pan, you need stereo sound, which uses two or more speakers (rather than mono, which uses one).

5) Various effects are used on the vocal and guitar parts, such as echo, delay, distortion and flanging (see p.110) — this adds to the surreal sound. Some effects were created using a Leslie speaker.

6) 'Lucy in the Sky...' also makes use of electronic instruments, such as a Lowrey organ, which is used here to mimic the sound of a celeste. Other tracks use a Hammond organ (another electric organ).

7) To alter the pitch and tone of some of the tracks, the playback speed was changed (i.e. the tracks were played back at a different speed from how they were recorded).

Lucy, sitting at home — doing some revision...

Even though you only have to study these three tracks, it's well worth listening to the whole album.

Pop Music — 1990s-Today

The next two pages are going to look at pop music from 1990 onwards — both bands and solo artists.

Girl Bands and Boy Bands Were Popular in the 1990s

1) As the name suggests, boy bands are groups with all male members and girl bands are all female. There are usually four or five members in the group, and they're generally quite young — i.e. in their late teens or early twenties. The bands tend to focus on singing (rather than playing instruments).

2) Although there have been boy and girl bands around for years (e.g. the Jackson 5 formed in the 1960s), they became really popular in the 1990s. British and Irish groups included Boyzone, Westlife, Take That, the Spice Girls and All Saints, while the USA had the Backstreet Boys, *NSYNC and Destiny's Child.

3) These bands particularly appealed to teenage girls, who fell in love with the boy bands, and wanted to be like the girl bands. The songs were written for this target audience — they ranged from ballads (songs that tell stories, often slow and emotional, where the voice is the main feature) to up-tempo dance numbers (which the bands would dance to themselves). Songs were often about love.

Britpop Came About in the Mid '90s

1) Britpop was a reaction to American grunge music (a fusion of punk rock and heavy metal — like the music of Nirvana), which was popular in the early '90s. Britpop was influenced by British bands from the '60s, '70s and '80s — such as The Beatles (see p.114-116), the Sex Pistols, and The Smiths. It had elements of glam rock, punk rock (see p.113) and indie rock.

2) Key Britpop bands include Pulp, Blur, Oasis and Suede — there was a rivalry between Blur and Oasis. Blur's album *Parklife* and *Definitely Maybe* by Oasis were important early Britpop albums.

3) Britpop music tended to be quite up-tempo and was played by a typical rock band (see p.112), with a focus on the guitar (rather than synthesized instruments). The lyrics were important — they were often quite witty and about everyday things, and the singers' British accents were noticeable.

4) Later bands described as post-Britpop include Coldplay, Radiohead and the Stereophonics.

A Solo Artist's Voice and Personality are Key Features

1) Solo artists have been popular throughout the '90s and '00s, but today's charts in particular are dominated by solo artists. Many solo artists have instantly recognisable vocal features.

- Michael Jackson was well known for his high (sometimes falsetto) singing voice. He also used 'vocal hiccups' (a short intake of breath) and vowel sounds (such as "ah" and "hee hee").
- Whitney Houston had an impressive vocal range and was capable of producing big sounds. She was famous for her use of melisma and riffing (see p.109).
- Adele's rich, soulful voice is capable of producing a range of timbres, from a gentle, raspy sound (like at the start of 'Turning Tables') to a big, powerful sound (like the chorus of 'Skyfall').
- Lana Del Rey has a sultry, dreamy voice. George Ezra, Amy Winehouse, Robbie Williams and Paloma Faith all have voices that are easy to recognise.

2) Image is important to all pop musicians, but solo artists really need their personalities to come across. Personality can help sell a song — charismatic solo artists can engage with an audience on a more personal level than a band. This can be particularly effective in live performances.

Adele's emotional live performance of 'Someone Like You' at the 2011 Brit Awards made both her and her music really popular. The song was about a break-up, and the personal experience evident in the song resonated with the audience. Her personality and emotions are clear in many of her songs (most of which she writes herself), which makes it easy for the audience to relate to her.

People of the world — spice up your revision...

More recent boy/girl bands include One Direction, The Wanted, Girls Aloud, The Saturdays and Little Mix.

Pop Music — 1990s-Today

There have been so many different pop artists from the 1990s onwards — this page covers a few examples.

The Accompaniment and Structure Varies

Pop artists use different accompaniments and structures depending on the style and purpose of the song.

1990s

- 'Black or White' by Michael Jackson (released in 1991) has a typical rock band accompaniment (see p.112). The song has a number of different sections, including an intro featuring Jackson's distinctive falsetto 'ow's, verses that end with a mini chorus ('it don't matter if you're black or white'), a half-chanted section, a rap section and an outro, with guitar interludes in between.

- Bryan Adams' '(Everything I Do) I Do It For You' (also released in 1991) starts with a simple piano accompaniment, before the rest of the rock band comes in, building up the texture. This song also has a guitar solo in the middle.

- Westlife's 1999 hit 'Flying Without Wings' is a typical pop ballad. It's fairly slow, and opens with a solo voice before a gentle guitar comes in. The accompaniment builds up, adding a drum kit, strings, piano and backing vocals as the song reaches its emotional climax.

2000s

- 'Can't Get You Out Of My Head' by Kylie Minogue (released in 2001) has two memorable hooks — the repeated 'la la la' and the first line of the chorus ('I just can't get you out of my head'). The song doesn't follow a standard structure — the choruses and sections with long, held-on notes are broken up by the 'la la la' sections. The song uses synthesized instruments and has a strong drumbeat, which makes it ideal to dance to in a nightclub.

- Busted play their own electric guitars on their 2002 song 'What I Go To School For'. It follows a standard verse-chorus structure, and has a bridge with different lyrics and melody.

- Britney Spears' hit 'Toxic' (2003) also uses synthesized instruments, distorted guitars and wailing strings to create a futuristic sound. It has a strong, driving beat.

2010s

- 'Someone Like You' by Adele (released in 2011) has a simple accompaniment of a piano playing broken chords (see p.39). The song has a rough verse-chorus structure, but with some variations — the verses are different lengths, and one repeated verse has a different melody. There is a bridge with backing vocals sung by Adele herself (see below).

- For his 2014 single 'Sing', Ed Sheeran accompanies himself on the acoustic guitar, but the song also has electric guitars, percussion and backing vocals. There are several different sections to the song — including falsetto sections, repeated 'oh's and a half-sung, half-rap verse.

Artists Use Technology to Create Vocal Effects

As well as synthesized instruments, many pop artists use different forms of technology and vocal effects to add variety. Here are a few examples:

- 'Can't Get You Out Of My Head' was recorded using MIDI technology (see p.72).

- 'Someone Like You' uses overdubbing in the bridge section. A separate track of Adele singing in harmony with the melody is recorded and then mixed in.

- 'Telephone' by Lady Gaga (featuring Beyoncé) uses different vocal effects such as delay, reverb and pitch bends, as well as samples (see p.73) of a telephone ringing and a telephone operator speaking.

Keep revising until you can't get it out of your head...

It's hard to make generalisations about pop music as it's so varied. You might be asked about the vocals, the accompaniment, technology or style — try and pick out the key features.

Musicals

Musical theatre is a lighter, more modern version of opera. It's been developing since the 19th century. You need to know about Broadway musicals from the 1950s-1990s.

Musicals Have **Songs, Dialogue** and **Dances**

1) Musicals came from less serious versions of opera, like opéra comique and operetta (see p.86). Towards the end of the 19th century, Gilbert and Sullivan wrote lots of popular comic operas.

2) The type of musicals that are around today started in the 1920s, and developed throughout the rest of the 20th and into the 21st century. They started out on Broadway, a famous theatre street in New York. Some started in London's West End.

3) Musicals use singing, dancing and talking to tell stories.

4) They usually have an orchestra to accompany the singers and play incidental (background) music.

5) Some musicals that started out on the stage have been made into really popular musical films — like *Grease*, *West Side Story* and *Sweeney Todd*. Sometimes, a film is adapted into a musical performed on stage — like *Spamalot* (based on Monty Python and the Holy Grail) and *Billy Elliot*.

6) Some musicals are based on novels — like *Les Misérables*, *Oliver!* and *Jekyll & Hyde*.

Musical Styles are Always **Changing**

Musicals are generally written in the style of the popular music that's around at the time — so musicals from different times sound very different. Earlier musicals were influenced by jazz and swing music (see p.131-132), while lots of musicals from the 1970s onwards used rock music (see p.112-113). Have a listen to some of these musicals to hear the different styles they use:

1920s-1950s	**COLE PORTER**:	*Paris, Anything Goes, Kiss Me, Kate, Silk Stockings*
1940s-1950s	**RODGERS & HAMMERSTEIN**:	*Oklahoma!, South Pacific, The King and I, The Sound of Music*
1950s-2010s	**STEPHEN SONDHEIM**:	*Follies, Sweeney Todd* and lyrics for *West Side Story*
1960s-1990s	**KANDER & EBB**:	*Cabaret, Chicago, Kiss of the Spider Woman*
1970s-2010s	**ANDREW LLOYD WEBBER**:	*Joseph and the Amazing Technicolour Dreamcoat, Jesus Christ Superstar, Evita, Cats, Phantom of the Opera, School of Rock*
1970s-2000s	**SCHÖNBERG & BOUBLIL**:	*Les Misérables, Miss Saigon*

Some Musicals Contain **Pop Songs**

1) Songs from musicals sometimes hit the charts. In the UK, musicals by Andrew Lloyd Webber and Tim Rice have spawned a few chart hits, such as 'Don't Cry For Me Argentina' from *Evita*, 'Memory' from *Cats* and 'No Matter What' from *Whistle Down the Wind* (sung by Boyzone).

2) Sometimes chart hits find their way into musicals — *Mamma Mia!* was written around a collection of ABBA hits. The plots of these musicals often have nothing to do with the band, but use their songs to tell a story. Others tell the story of the band or singer (e.g. *Buddy — The Buddy Holly Story*).

Musicals Can Be About **Any Topic**

1) Some musicals deal with very serious subject matter — *Miss Saigon* is set during and after the Vietnam War, and *Cabaret* is set in Nazi Germany. These musicals are often tragic and emotional.

2) Other musicals are based on Shakespeare's plays — *West Side Story* is based on *Romeo and Juliet*, but set in 1950s New York. The two rival gangs are the Jets (Americans) and the Sharks (Puerto Rican immigrants). The music has lots of jazz elements, a number of dance scenes and looked at social problems in America, which made it quite different to other musicals at the time.

3) In contrast, some musicals have quite bizarre plots, such as *Little Shop of Horrors* (which is about a man-eating plant) and *Starlight Express* (which is about a train set, with the cast on rollerskates).

Musicals

Here's how to create that Broadway sound...

Most Musical Songs are **Easy on the Ear**

Musicals are meant to be <u>entertaining</u> and <u>easy to listen to</u>. This is how they do it...

1) The melodies are easy to <u>sing</u> — audiences tend to prefer songs they can sing along to.

2) The harmony is <u>diatonic</u> — it'll be in either a major or a minor key.

3) The song <u>structure</u> is often <u>simple</u>, with alternating verses and choruses and a middle eight (similar to the structure of a <u>pop song</u>).

Intro	Chorus Verse Chorus Verse	Middle 8 Chorus Verse Chorus Verse	Chorus Outro

Grabs the audience's attention and sets the mood for the song.

Has new chords and new lyrics — a change of mood to keep the audience interested.

Ties the song off — either loud and brassy or sad and quiet.

4) The chorus is often in <u>32-bar song</u> form. The 32 bars break down into 4 sections of 8 bars each. Sections 1, 2 and 4 use the <u>main theme</u> (sometimes with slight variations). Section 3 has a <u>contrasting theme</u> (middle eight).

5) The chorus has a <u>hook</u> — a catchy bit of lyrics and melody that makes the song memorable, e.g. '<u>I like to be in America</u>' (*West Side Story*), '<u>It's the hard-knock life</u>' (*Annie*) or '<u>And all that jazz</u>' (*Chicago*). The hook is the bit that gets stuck in the audience's head (so they want to order a CD when they get home) and often becomes the title of the song.

There are **Four Basic Types** of Musical Song

When you hear a musical song you should be able to identify what <u>type</u> of song it is:

1) **SOLO CHARACTER SONG** — a character sings about how they're <u>feeling</u> — in <u>love</u>, full of <u>hate</u>, over the moon with <u>happiness</u>, etc. '<u>Maria</u>' from *West Side Story* and '<u>Maybe This Time</u>' from *Cabaret* are both solo character songs.

2) **DUET** — duets are basically the same as solo character songs, except there are <u>two people</u> singing so you get <u>two different reactions</u> to a situation. '<u>I Know Him So Well</u>' from *Chess* is a great example.

3) **ACTION SONG** — the words of the song tell you what's going on in the <u>plot</u> — they lead you into the next bit of the story.

4) **CHORUS NUMBER** — the whole <u>ensemble</u> get together and have a <u>big old sing-song</u>. Like at the end of *Grease* — 'We go together like ramma lamma lamma ka dinga da dinga dong...' and '<u>Food, Glorious Food</u>' at the beginning of *Oliver!*.

You can also get trios, quartets etc. (i.e. more than one character singing, but not a chorus number).

All these styles of song developed from opera — solo songs are like <u>arias</u>, action songs are like <u>recitatives</u>.

The lyrics in a musical song tell part of the story. They're usually <u>written first</u>, so the composer has to fit the music around them.

It's showtime — let's see those jazz hands...

Listen to the quintet version of 'Tonight' from *West Side Story* — it features Tony, Maria, Anita and the two rival gangs. At one point, all five different parts are sung at the same time.

Film Music

SPOILER ALERT: the next three pages may contain spoilers. Consider yourself warned.
<u>Composers</u> who write <u>film music</u> have to write music to <u>fit</u> with the <u>action</u> already set by the <u>film makers</u>.

Look Out for **Leitmotifs** in Most Film Music

'Leitmotif' can also be spelt 'leitmotiv'.

1) A <u>leitmotif</u> is a <u>tune</u> that <u>returns</u> throughout the film (there's often <u>more than one</u>).

2) It <u>represents</u> a particular <u>object</u>, <u>idea</u> or <u>character</u> in the <u>story</u>, and often returns in the <u>background</u> or in an <u>altered</u> form.

3) Leitmotifs are used throughout the *Lord of the Rings* films (see p.123). 'Hedwig's Theme' is the main leitmotif in the *Harry Potter* films — it's repeated in <u>all the films</u> and played by <u>different instruments</u>. It's associated with the world of <u>magic</u> and <u>wizards</u>.

4) Sometimes the leitmotifs give you a <u>hint</u> as to what will happen <u>later</u> in the film — if a character turns out to be a bad guy, their theme might have <u>menacing chords</u> being played in the background.

> In the final few bars of '<u>Anakin's Theme</u>' from *Star Wars: Episode I — The Phantom Menace* (1999), you can hear echoes of '<u>Darth Vader's Theme</u>' from *Episode V* (also by <u>John Williams</u>). This is a <u>subtle hint</u> that Anakin (who's good in this film) will <u>become</u> Darth Vader.

Composers Use Lots of **Repetition** in Film Music

1) <u>Repeated sections</u> of music can be used to <u>link</u> different parts of the film together — it can <u>remind</u> you of something that happened <u>earlier</u> in the film.

2) A <u>leitmotif</u> can be repeated throughout the film, but might be <u>transformed</u> to <u>reflect</u> what's going on. The <u>instrumentation</u> can be changed, or it can be repeated in a <u>different key</u> (e.g. it might come back in a <u>minor key</u> to show that things have started to <u>go wrong</u>). Sometimes just the <u>rhythm</u> of the leitmotif is played in the <u>background</u> — it might be so quiet it's hardly noticeable, but it all adds to the <u>drama</u>.

3) Often at the end of the film there's a <u>triumphant modulation</u> of the main theme (as long as the film has a <u>happy ending</u>). It ends in a <u>happy</u>, <u>uplifting</u> key with a <u>drawn-out cadence</u> (see p.42-43), to show that the story of the film has been <u>resolved</u>.

4) Of course, if the film <u>doesn't</u> have a happy ending (or if there's going to be a <u>sequel</u>), the theme may be left <u>unresolved</u>, giving the film a more <u>open</u> or <u>darker</u> ending.

5) Repetition can be used to create <u>tension</u> and <u>suspense</u> — a repeated sequence that's getting <u>louder</u> and <u>louder</u> can really have you on the <u>edge of your seat</u>.

Some Films Use **Pop Songs** to Get **Publicity**

1) Lots of films have <u>pop songs</u> as part of their soundtrack — they're usually <u>released</u> in the <u>charts</u> to generate <u>publicity</u>. They're often performed by <u>famous pop stars</u> — like <u>Pharrell Williams</u>' song '<u>Happy</u>' for the film *Despicable Me 2* (2013).

2) Some films have <u>pop songs</u> over the <u>opening</u> or <u>closing credits</u>. These songs aren't always in the same <u>style</u> of music as the rest of the film, and often <u>don't</u> appear anywhere else in the film (e.g. Take That's 'Rule The World' is <u>only</u> heard over the <u>closing credits</u> of the 2007 film *Stardust*).

3) A song used as the <u>title track</u> might <u>return</u> in the <u>background</u> later. For example, the song '<u>My Heart Will Go On</u>' by <u>Celine Dion</u> pops up many times in the film *Titanic* (1997).

A good excuse to watch some films...

Film music is written to create a certain <u>atmosphere</u>. Composers use it to set the <u>scene</u>, create a <u>mood</u> or describe a <u>character</u>. It should help the overall effect of the film and add to the <u>drama</u> of the story.

Film Music

Film composers use music to <u>set the scene</u> — it helps you believe it's in a <u>different country</u> or <u>time</u>.

Traditional Instruments Give You a Feel for Time and Place

1) Music can be used to create the mood of a different <u>time</u> or <u>place</u>.

2) <u>Westerns</u> are set in 19th century North America. They generally tell a simple story and they can often be very <u>dramatic</u> and <u>violent</u>.

3) Westerns use music <u>from the time</u> to <u>set the scene</u>. For example, <u>Ennio Morricone</u> composed some of the music for <u>Django Unchained</u> (2012). He used elements of <u>traditional music</u>, with <u>instruments</u> including the Spanish guitar, banjo, tin whistle, trumpet and percussion.

4) Films set in the <u>70s</u> or <u>80s</u> might use <u>pop songs</u> from the time to set the scene. People will <u>recognise</u> the songs and it'll <u>remind</u> them of that decade.

5) <u>Tim Rice</u> and <u>Elton John</u> composed the songs for Disney's <u>The Lion King</u> (1994). The songs have a lot of <u>African influences</u> (including <u>drumming</u>, <u>traditional instruments</u> and <u>isicathamiya singing</u> — see p.133), which helps the audience <u>imagine</u> the film's setting. <u>Hans Zimmer</u> composed the <u>orchestral</u> music for the film, and also used <u>traditional African music</u> and <u>singing</u>.

The Music in War Films Creates the Atmosphere

1) The music in war films needs to create an <u>atmosphere</u> for the <u>time</u> and <u>place</u> of the war, as well as showing the <u>action</u> and <u>emotion</u> of the plot. For example, the battle scenes of <u>Gladiator</u> (2000) are accompanied by <u>threatening music</u> (by <u>Hans Zimmer</u>), which creates tension.

2) <u>Sound effects</u> (like <u>explosions</u> and <u>gunfire</u>) can be incorporated into the music to suggest <u>war</u>.

3) <u>Saving Private Ryan</u> (1998) is set in the <u>Second World War</u>. The music (by <u>John Williams</u>) is only heard <u>between</u> the battle scenes (the battles have no musical accompaniment). However, the frequent use of the <u>snare drum</u> is a <u>constant reminder</u> of the fighting (it sounds like a <u>military march</u>). The music is generally quite <u>mournful</u> and <u>reflective</u>, focusing on the <u>cost</u> to life, rather than the <u>heroism</u> of war.

Unnatural Sounds Make Strange Places Seem Even Stranger

<u>Horror</u>, <u>science fiction</u> or <u>fantasy</u> films are often set in <u>strange places</u> or on other <u>planets</u>. Composers need to <u>transport</u> the audience to a <u>weird reality</u>, where nothing is quite what you'd expect.

1) <u>Unusual harmonies</u> and <u>time signatures</u> are used when things are a bit <u>weird</u> — they're not what you're expecting, so they sound odd.

2) <u>Synthesizers</u> and <u>samples</u> of bizarre <u>sounds</u> often have no relation to what's happening on-screen, but make the audience wonder what's going on and set their imagination racing.

3) <u>Instruments</u> or <u>voices</u> can be <u>distorted</u> using <u>computers</u>.

4) There's often no clear <u>structure</u> so it's hard to predict what's going to happen.

5) <u>Discords</u> and <u>diminished</u> chords make it difficult to listen to.

6) <u>Rapid scalic patterns</u> (going up and down scales) and <u>interrupted cadences</u> (see p.43) can make <u>pulse-raising</u> scenes feel more frantic.

7) In the famous <u>shower scene</u> in <u>Psycho</u> (1960), the <u>stabbing</u> of the <u>knife</u> is accompanied by (and emphasised by) the <u>violins</u> also <u>stabbing</u> out a <u>high-pitched tritone</u> (p.29). Each chord goes right through you, and makes what you're seeing on-screen feel much more <u>real</u>.

8) <u>James Horner's</u> music for <u>Avatar</u> (2009) combines <u>instruments</u>, <u>timbres</u> and <u>textures</u> from music from all over the world to create the <u>music</u> and <u>culture</u> of the <u>Na'vi people</u>.

Music revision can be used to put you in a mood...

There are loads of little tricks that film composers can use to help set the scene and create an atmosphere.

Film Music

Sometimes, film music helps you understand what's happening. It can also help to build tension.

The **Style** of Music **Changes** With the **Mood** of the Scene

1) The soundtracks for the three _Lord of the Rings_ films (2001-2003) were written by Howard Shore.

2) Shore created different leitmotifs (see p.121) to represent the different places and characters in the films. For example, the one that represents the group of characters who make up the Fellowship of the Ring is heroic — it appears less frequently after the Fellowship falls apart.

3) The Shire (the home of the Hobbits) is represented by a happy melody in a major key — the theme first appears in the piece 'Concerning Hobbits'. It's first played on a solo Irish tin whistle then solo violin. It's light and playful, and reflects the comfort and safety of the Shire.

4) During fight scenes, the mood is tense and dramatic — the music is played by low brass instruments. There are lots of crescendos to accompany the escalating action.

5) Shore uses a large choir throughout the films to create a sense of mystery and drama. The choir often sings in the (made-up) languages of Middle Earth.

Composers Can Keep You on the **Edge** of Your Seat

1) Ostinati keep the audience on edge. For example, in _The Thomas Crown Affair_ (1999) an ostinato made up of clapping and a piano motif from Nina Simone's 'Sinnerman' is used to accompany a heist in an art museum.

2) In some sci-fi films there's background music with just drums and bass, generated on computers. It's played throughout the film to let the audience know that the danger is always there.

3) A good example of this is in _Tron: Legacy_ (2010), which has music written by Daft Punk. They use computer-generated noises to mimic the sound of high-intensity computer games from the '80s, which helps create the virtual-reality setting.

4) Sustained notes create suspense (e.g. tremolo strings), and minor or dissonant chords make the audience feel uneasy. Suspensions that don't resolve (see p.41) are another good way of doing this.

5) Composers know how to build the tension and make you feel like something bad is going to happen:

> • Dynamics get louder.
> • Tempo gets faster — like the two-note motif in _Jaws_ (1975), which speeds up (and gets louder) as the shark gets closer.
> • Pitch gets higher.
> • A tune played earlier in a scary bit sometimes comes back to remind you.
> • Sometimes they use silence before a loud bit just to make you jump.

Diegetic Music is Music the Characters Can **Hear**

1) In most films, the music is extra-diegetic — it's not actually part of the story. It's put 'over the top' of the action to increase the effect of the film. It's for the audience's benefit only.

2) Sometimes film-makers want to include music in the story for the characters (as well as the audience) to hear — this is diegetic music.

> • In _The Hunger Games: Mockingjay — Part 1_ (2014), Katniss sings a song for one of her companions. It is recorded and turned into a propaganda video by the rebels, and used as their battle song.
> • In _Inception_ (2010), the song 'Non, je ne regrette rien' by Édith Piaf is used diegetically as a plot device. The song helps wake a character up from a dream. Characters in a dream can hear a slowed-down version of the song, while in the real world it's heard at the original tempo. In fact, much of the soundtrack to the film is based on an extremely slowed-down version of the original.

Game Music

From fairly basic origins, video game music has developed into a pretty important genre in its own right.

Early Video Game Music Was Very Simple

1) Due to limited technology, the music for early video games was very simple — it could only have a couple of different instruments or parts, so was often monophonic (or very basic polyphony).

2) The music wasn't usually played throughout the game — it would sometimes just be used as a theme tune at the start, or played in response to something happening in the game (e.g. completing a level).

> Space Invaders (created by Tomohiro Nishikado in 1978) was one of the first games to have music playing continuously throughout the game — it was based on a loop of four descending notes in the bass part, which changed speed to match the movements on screen.

3) Early video game music would often use synthesizers (see p.72), which could be integrated into the video game hardware to create and manipulate synthetic sounds (rather than recording real instruments).

4) MIDI (Musical Instrument Digital Interface) allowed composers to write for a range of instruments that played back consistently on different pieces of equipment (and different types of computer).

5) From the 1990s, video games were able to use higher quality music with more realistic instrumental timbres because of the technological advances in CD audio. Nowadays, soundtracks can be created very effectively using DAW (digital audio workstation) software like Logic Pro or Cubase.

Recent Game Music is More Like a Film Score

1) In modern video games, better technology has led to games with a more intricate plot or complicated mission for the player to complete. Better audio technology has enabled game music to become more like a film score. As well as synthesizers, it frequently uses orchestral and choral elements.

2) As there are often different locations within a game, composers will create music to go with each place or time — using similar methods to film composers (see p.122).

3) Games often use motifs (short melodic ideas), which can be developed to reflect the changing actions. Some ways of altering motifs include sequencing, playing inversions or retrograde versions (see p.83), augmentation and diminution (lengthening or shortening all note values or intervals — see p.18). These changes have different effects — e.g. diminution of the note values makes it sound more urgent.

4) Like films, there are different genres of game — e.g. sci-fi, fantasy, war or racing. The techniques that film composers use for these types of film can be used in game music too (see p.122).

5) Some well-known film composers have also written music for games — e.g. Harry Gregson-Williams. (who composed some of the music for the *Metal Gear Solid*® series of games, the *Shrek* films and *The Martian*) As a result, some games have full soundtracks.

- In *Halo*®, the player takes on the role of the supersoldier Master Chief in a fight against an alien religious group called the Covenant. It is set on a range of planets in the 26th century.

- There have been a number of different composers for the games in the series, including Martin O'Donnell (the lead composer), Michael Salvatori, Stephen Rippy and Neil Davidge.

- The main theme opens with male voices singing (like monks chanting — this represents the Covenant), which sounds eerie and mysterious. A driving syncopated drum rhythm (playing an ostinato) builds up the intensity and creates a sense of excitement. Low strings enter playing the melody, which is based on the same rhythmic pattern over increasing intervals (the first time, it's a perfect octave, then a major ninth and so on) — it sounds a bit like a fanfare. Other string parts are introduced, creating a complex layering of orchestral parts and giving the music energy.

I didn't know there was a video game version of Master Chef...

Next time you're playing a video game, pay attention to the music and see what effect it has. Careful not to get too distracted though — you don't want to fail your mission (or your exam).

Warm-up and Exam Questions

Before you get stuck into the exam-style questions, have a go at these warm-up questions first.

Warm-up Questions

1) What does a cappella mean?
2) Name one singer who sings falsetto.
3) When did rock 'n' roll become popular in the USA?
4) What is a concept album?
5) Describe four different sub-genres of rock music.
6) Name the four members of the Beatles.
7) What is a meend?
8) Who sang lead vocals on 'Lucy in the Sky With Diamonds'?
9) What does ADT stand for?
10) How can personality help a solo artist become popular?
11) Name two songs that were hits in the 2010s.
12) What is a musical?
13) Describe 32-bar song form.
14) Name the **four** main types of songs found in musicals.
15) What is a leitmotif?
16) How is repetition used in film music?
17) Why are instruments from a particular time or place sometimes used in film music?
18) What is DAW software?

Exam Questions

To make sure you really know your stuff, here are a couple of exam questions.

Track 34 is an excerpt from 'Something's Coming' from *West Side Story*.
Play the excerpt **four** times. Leave a short pause between each playing.

Track 34

a) Name the woodwind instrument that can be heard at the start of this excerpt.

....
[1 mark]

b) The trumpets in this excerpt sometimes play *con sordino*.
Explain what this means and how it affects the sound of the instruments.

....

....
[2 marks]

Exam Questions

c)   What is the interval between the two notes for the opening words 'could be'?
Circle the correct answer.

      major third   **perfect fourth**   **perfect fifth**   **major sixth**

[1 mark]

d)   Describe the dynamics in the first half of this excerpt (up to 'bright as a rose').

....

....

....

[3 marks]

e)   This song is sung by the character Tony.
Circle the word that correctly describes his voice.

      bass   **baritone**   **tenor**   **treble**

[1 mark]

f)   How does the composer create a sense of anticipation and excitement?
Try to comment on rhythm, tempo, tonality, melody and lyrics.

....

....

....

....

....

....

....

....

....

....

....

[8 marks]

Exam Questions

These questions are about 'With A Little Help From My Friends',
from the album *Sgt. Pepper's Lonely Hearts Club Band* by The Beatles.

Unfortunately, we were unable to get permission to include this track on our audio CD.

However, it's readily available to listen to online —
you just need to listen to the first 1 minute of the recording.

Play the excerpt **three** times. Leave a short pause between each playing.

a) What is the tonality of this excerpt?

....
[1 mark]

b) What cadence is used on the phrase 'walk out on me'?

....
[1 mark]

c) Identify two types of recording or production technology used in this excerpt
that are typical of this style of music.

....

....
[2 marks]

d) The last line of the chorus ('...try with a little help from my friends') uses two chords.
Circle the correct pair of chords.

IV and I   **V and I**   **IV and V**   **VI and I**
[1 mark]

e) Describe the use of backing vocals in this excerpt.

....

....

....

....

....

....
[3 marks]

Revision Summary for Section Seven

That section was a bit of a whizz through the 20th century — with a bit of the 21st century too. Just have a go at these revision questions, then you can stop to catch your breath and work out which decade you're in. You know the drill — try and answer them without looking back at the section, then go back over any bits you're not sure about.

1) Describe four different ways backing vocals can be sung.

2) Describe: a) scat   b) riffing

3) Name two electronic effects that can be added to vocal parts.

4) Describe typical lead guitar, rhythm guitar and bass guitar parts in pop music.

5) What were the two main influences on rock 'n' roll music?

6) Who made the term 'rock 'n' roll' popular?

7) Write down three things that rock 'n' roll songs were often about.

8) Name three early rock 'n' roll stars.

9) Describe punk rock.

10) Name two rock anthems.

11) What is arena rock?

12) Name three songs by The Beatles.

13) Name three bands who were part of the British Invasion.

14) Give one reason why The Beatles stopped touring.

15) What genre does the album *Sgt. Pepper's Lonely Hearts Club Band* belong to?

16) Name three Indian instruments used in 'Within You Without You'.

17) Who is Billy Shears?

18) Describe one inspiration for 'Lucy in the Sky With Diamonds'.

19) Name three different types of technology used on the album
Sgt. Pepper's Lonely Hearts Club Band.

20) Name one boy band and one girl band.

21) Briefly describe Britpop.

22) Name three solo artists who have distinctive voices.

23) Describe two different solo artists from the 1990s.

24) Describe the accompaniment of Adele's 'Someone Like You'.

25) Describe one effect used on Lady Gaga's 'Telephone'.

26) Give one example of a musical that was based on a book.

27) Name four different composers who wrote musicals.

28) In musical terms, what is a hook?

29) What does an action song in a musical do?

30) How did Tim Rice and Elton John create the African setting of *The Lion King*?

31) What type of films might use music with unusual harmonies or weird time signatures?

32) Describe how the music in *The Lord of the Rings* films illustrates the different places and characters.

33) How are ostinati used in film music?

34) How do composers create suspense?

35) What is diegetic music?

36) Give three ways that motifs in game music can be altered.

The Blues

You might not associate the blues with 'traditional music', but it took influences from traditional sources and reinterpreted them. It still has an <u>influence</u> on jazz, pop and rock 'n' roll music today.

African Slaves in America Started Off the Blues

1) In the <u>1600s</u> and <u>1700s</u>, millions of Africans were captured and sold as <u>slaves</u>. Many were taken to work on plantations in <u>North America</u>.

2) To take their minds off their work, which was often brutally hard, they sang <u>work songs</u>, using their tools to give the music a <u>beat</u>. The lyrics were often about the <u>hardship</u> and <u>misery</u> of being a slave.

3) Over the years, <u>African musical styles</u>, such as <u>call and response</u> singing (p.55), blended with features of <u>European music</u>, especially <u>chords</u>. This combination was the beginning of the <u>blues</u>.

4) Even after slavery was finally <u>abolished</u> in the <u>1860s</u>, life remained hard for ex-slaves living in the <u>southern states</u>. The <u>lyrics</u> and <u>tone</u> of their songs carried on being <u>sad</u> and '<u>blue</u>'.

5) The traditional blues instruments are the <u>harmonica</u>, <u>guitar</u>, <u>banjo</u>, <u>violin</u>, <u>piano</u>, <u>double bass</u> and <u>voice</u>. They're all <u>acoustic</u> — electric instruments hadn't been invented when blues began.

6) In the <u>early twentieth century</u>, black Americans began to play the blues in bars <u>beyond</u> the southern states. By the <u>1920s</u>, blues was popular all over America with both white and black audiences.

7) In the <u>1940s</u> and <u>1950s</u> a style called <u>rhythm'n'blues</u> (R'n'B) was developed. It's a <u>speeded-up</u> version of blues played on <u>electric guitar</u> and <u>bass</u>.

Blues has its Own Scale

1) You get a blues scale by <u>flattening</u> the <u>3rd</u>, <u>5th</u> and <u>7th</u> of any major scale. The unflattened <u>5th</u> is played too.

2) The flattened notes are called <u>blue notes</u>. They're not always lowered by a <u>full semitone</u> — sometimes they're flattened by a <u>microtone</u> instead (see p.134).

3) Singers and players often <u>slide</u> up or down to blue notes — this is known as <u>pitch bend</u>. This feature comes from the '<u>bent</u>' notes used in African singing.

4) The <u>2nd</u> and <u>6th</u> notes are often left out.

Blues scale on C

Blues Melodies have Swinging, Offbeat Rhythms

1) In normal '<u>straight</u>' rhythm the beats split up into <u>equal halves</u>.

I want chips and egg

I want <u>chips</u> and <u>egg</u>

2) In <u>swung</u> rhythm, the first bit of the beat is <u>longer</u>, as it <u>steals</u> time from the second bit to give the music a <u>swinging</u> feel. The rhythm shown on the left is a special type of swung rhythm called '<u>shuffle</u>'.

3) <u>Syncopation</u> creates an <u>offbeat sound</u> by avoiding the <u>strong beats</u> — it puts the <u>oomph</u> in <u>unexpected places</u>.

4) A <u>backbeat</u> is when beats <u>2</u> and <u>4</u> are emphasised.

Please don't make me beg

The blues have influenced almost all forms of popular music...

The blues doesn't have to be mournful, sad and depressing — it just sounds better that way...

The Blues

There are lots of different types of blues, but the most popular song structure is the 12-bar blues.

Twelve-bar Blues has a **Repeated Twelve-Bar Structure**

12-bar blues uses a set chord pattern that is 12 bars long. Singers like Bessie Smith and Robert Johnson made the 12-bar blues structure really popular in the 1920s. It's still one of the most popular styles today.

Chord I	Chord I	Chord I	Chord I
Chord IV	Chord IV	Chord I	Chord I
Chord V	Chord IV	Chord I	Chord I (V)

If the 12-bar structure is repeated, chord V is played in bar 12 instead of chord I, to lead back to Bar 1.

1) The only chords are I, IV and V.

2) The 12-bar pattern is repeated throughout the song.

3) You can make the chords even more bluesy by adding minor 7ths (see p.29).

12-bar blues has had a huge influence on other musical styles including ragtime, jazz, rock and roll and R&B. Loads of pop songs today still use the standard 12-bar structure.

Twelve Bars Break Nicely into **Three Lines of 4 Bars**

The lyrics of a 12-bar blues song usually stick to three lines for each verse of the song.

Lines 1 and 2 are usually the same. → *Woke up this morning feeling blue.*
Woke up this morning feeling blue.

Line 3 is different, but rhymes with lines 1 and 2. → *Feeling sad and lonesome without you.*

The words are usually pretty gloomy.

Each line of music lasts for 4 bars, but the words don't always fill up the whole line. The singer's part (the call) is followed by an instrument playing an answer (the response) in the gap before the next line.

There are **Sixteen-Bar Patterns** too

1) Blues doesn't have to use a 12-bar pattern. 16-bar patterns, based on the 12-bar structure, can be used.

2) There are a few different versions of the 16-bar pattern. Sometimes the first line of the 12-bar blues is repeated to make a 16-bar pattern. The rest of the pattern then follows the 12-bar structure.

3) This variation is the same as the 12-bar pattern, except bars 9 and 10 are repeated twice. →

Chord I	Chord I	Chord I	Chord I
Chord IV	Chord IV	Chord I	Chord I
Chord V	Chord IV	Chord V	Chord IV
Chord V	Chord IV	Chord I	Chord I

'Hoochie Coochie Man', performed by Muddy Waters, uses the 16-bar blues.

4) 12-bar and 16-bar patterns can be used in the same piece, for example 16-bar verses with a 12-bar chorus. The 16-bar patterns are also divided into 4-bar lines, so it's easy to switch between the two.

Jazz

Jazz developed from a fusion of African and European influences.

Jazz has its **Roots** in **African American Blues** and **Ragtime**

1) <u>Jazz</u> is a type of music that developed in the <u>USA</u> in the <u>early 20th century</u>. It's a <u>fusion</u> of <u>African</u> and <u>European</u> influences that came from the music of the <u>newly-freed slaves</u>.

2) It started off as <u>Dixieland jazz</u> in <u>New Orleans</u> in the early 1900s. Dixieland jazz is a mix of <u>brass band marches</u>, <u>ragtime</u> (music with lots of <u>syncopated melodies</u> that was often played on the <u>piano</u>) and <u>blues</u> (see p.129-130). Dixieland jazz is <u>polyphonic</u> (different parts move at different times).

3) It was played in <u>bars</u> — one of the few places <u>black musicians</u> were allowed to perform because of <u>segregation</u> (<u>black people</u> weren't allowed to use the same <u>places</u> as <u>white people</u>).

4) In <u>1920</u>, jazz moved to <u>Chicago</u>. This was the era of the <u>Prohibition</u> (from <u>1920-1933</u>, <u>alcohol</u> was <u>banned</u> in the United States). <u>Illegal bars</u> (called <u>speakeasies</u>) often had jazz bands playing. Jazz started to get a <u>bad reputation</u>. Some people thought it was <u>immoral</u>.

5) The <u>1920s</u> were known as '<u>the Jazz Age</u>' or the '<u>Roaring Twenties</u>'.

Jazz has **Developed Over Time**

1) <u>Swing music</u> is a type of jazz that can be <u>danced</u> to. It's played by a big band (see below).

2) It's usually quite <u>fast</u>, and rhythms are <u>swung</u> (see p.129). Most pieces are in $\frac{4}{4}$ time. It has <u>regular phrases</u> and an <u>emphasis</u> on the <u>first</u> and <u>third</u> beats of the bar to make it easier to dance to.

3) It was popular because it was played on the <u>radio</u>, which was more <u>accessible</u> and <u>acceptable</u> than going to illegal bars. The radio introduced swing to a <u>wider audience</u>.

4) In the 1940s, <u>bebop</u> (or just <u>bop</u>) developed from swing music. Bebop is <u>fast</u> with lots of <u>improvisation</u>. It has <u>complex harmonies</u>, exciting <u>syncopated rhythms</u> and <u>irregular phrase lengths</u>. Bebop is <u>much less structured</u> than swing.

5) <u>Free jazz</u> developed in the <u>1950s</u> and <u>1960s</u> as a <u>reaction</u> against the <u>limits</u> of swing and bebop.

6) It didn't follow the normal rules of <u>tempo</u> and <u>rhythm</u> — players <u>within the same band</u> would play at <u>different speeds</u> to each other. There wasn't a <u>regular</u> rhythm.

7) It involves lots of <u>improvisation</u> (see p.132). Soloists <u>don't follow</u> the chords or structure of the band.

> Jazz didn't stop developing in the 60s. There are even more <u>experimental</u> forms of jazz, such as <u>avant-garde jazz</u>, which <u>pushes the boundaries</u> of what's considered "<u>normal</u>".

Trumpets, Trombones and Clarinets are Used in Jazz

1) A typical <u>jazz band</u> has a <u>trumpet</u>, a <u>trombone</u> and a <u>clarinet</u> on the <u>front row</u>. Later, <u>saxophones</u> were included too. The <u>front row instruments</u> play <u>improvised solos</u>.

2) There's also a <u>rhythm section</u> with <u>piano</u>, <u>drums</u>, a <u>double bass</u> and sometimes a <u>guitar</u>.

3) Big bands are made up of <u>saxophones</u>, <u>trumpets</u>, <u>trombones</u> and a <u>rhythm section</u>. The saxophone section has <u>alto</u>, <u>tenor</u> and <u>baritone saxophones</u> and sometimes <u>clarinets</u>. Some big bands have a <u>singer</u> too.

4) A typical big band has <u>5 saxophones</u> (2 altos, 2 tenors and a baritone), <u>4 trumpets</u>, <u>4 trombones</u> and a <u>4-piece rhythm section</u> (piano, bass, guitar and drums).

Mmmmmm Jaaazz...

There's loads of different types of jazz out there — the best thing you can do to appreciate it is to listen to as much as you can get your hands on. You might discover that you're a massive jazz enthusiast...

Jazz

Jazz has lots of features that mean you'll <u>recognise</u> it when you hear it — for example, it has a <u>swing</u> to it.

Jazz is **Swung** and **Syncopated**

1) Early jazz music was based on a <u>12-bar blues</u> structure (see p.130).
2) The <u>rhythm section</u> played the chords, and the <u>front row</u> instruments would <u>improvise</u> over them.
3) Jazz musicians use <u>call and response</u> and <u>blue notes</u> (see p.129) — key features of jazz and blues.
4) <u>Syncopated</u> and <u>swung rhythms</u> are common in jazz.

Jazz Often **Isn't Written Down**

1) <u>Improvisation</u> is where a performer <u>makes up</u> music on the spot. There are often <u>improvised</u> <u>solo sections</u> in <u>jazz</u> pieces. This means the same piece can be played in radically <u>different</u> ways — even if a piece is played twice by the same people, it <u>won't</u> sound the same.
2) The improvisations <u>aren't totally random</u> though — the soloist will know which <u>chords</u> to improvise over. This is often a <u>12-bar blues</u> chord pattern (see p.130). Some improvisations use a <u>mode</u> (see page 27) instead of a chord pattern.
3) There are lots of different <u>devices</u> a soloist can use to make their solo <u>interesting</u>:

   - <u>Triplets</u> and <u>dotted rhythms</u> help the tune flow (see p.17).
   - <u>Blue notes</u> (see p.129) are often used in jazz improvisations.
   - <u>Ornaments</u> (like <u>passing notes</u> and <u>appoggiaturas</u>) make the tunes more lively (see p.41).
   - A range of <u>dynamics</u> and <u>accents</u> (see p.20) also bring variety to a solo.
   - <u>Dissonant</u> notes keep the solo <u>interesting</u>.
   - Some performers <u>pinch</u> bits of <u>other tunes</u> in their solos
     — it keeps the audience entertained when they spot them.

4) Jazz <u>songs</u> are a bit different — the singer has <u>less chance</u> to improvise, but they can use <u>scat</u> (a type of <u>improvised singing</u> with <u>nonsense words</u> and <u>syllables</u>).
5) In early jazz (and some today) the music wasn't written down.
6) The band follows the <u>band leader</u>, so they know when a new section's starting, or the piece is ending.
7) Jazz involves lots of <u>interaction</u> between the soloist and the band, such as <u>call and response</u> — the soloist plays a phrase (the <u>call</u>) and the band answers it (the <u>response</u>), or the other way around.

Jazz is Used in **Lots** of **Fusion Genres**

1) Jazz fusions take <u>any element</u> of jazz and add it to elements of other (often quite <u>different</u>) genres.
2) The elements of jazz that are often used in fusions are the <u>instruments</u>, <u>free rhythms</u>, <u>chords</u> and <u>chord patterns</u>, <u>improvisation</u> and <u>call and response</u>.

   - <u>Salsa</u> is a fusion of <u>Cuban son</u> music with <u>big-band jazz</u>. It uses son <u>rhythms</u> with jazz <u>instruments</u> such as the trumpet and trombone (see p.131).
   - <u>Ska</u> uses jazz instruments and elements such as a <u>walking bass line</u> with rhythms from <u>Jamaican mento</u> music and <u>calypso</u> from Trinidad and Tobago (see p.135).

Improvisation is important in jazz...

...and other genres as well. Make sure you learn the ways a soloist can make their solo exciting and that you can pick them out when you're listening. Oh, and learn everything else too...

African Music

This page is about music in <u>sub-Saharan Africa</u>. It's different from North African music (see next page).

Drums Play a Big Part

1) Drums are one of the most <u>most widely-played instruments</u> in sub-Saharan Africa. They're used to play an <u>accompaniment</u> for <u>singing</u>, <u>dancing</u> and even <u>working</u>.

2) Drums can also be used to <u>call people together</u> for important <u>community events</u> like weddings and funerals — a bit like church bells in Europe. There are <u>different drumbeats</u> for different events.

3) Here are some of the main types of drum from West Africa:

- The <u>djembe</u> is played with the <u>hands</u>. It comes in different sizes. The <u>size</u> of the drum affects its <u>pitch</u> — <u>smaller</u> drums are <u>higher-pitched</u>.
- Dunduns are <u>cylindrical drums</u> played with <u>sticks</u>. They have a drum skin at each end. There are three types: the <u>kenkeni</u> (a high-pitched drum that keeps the beat), the <u>sangban</u> (a mid-pitched drum) and the <u>dundunba</u> (a large, low-pitched drum).

- The <u>donno</u> from Ghana is also known as the <u>talking</u> drum. It's played with a stick. The <u>strings</u> round the sides attach to the drumhead. The player can <u>squeeze</u> and <u>release</u> the strings as they play to change the <u>pitch</u> of the drum.

4) Most African music is passed on through <u>aural tradition</u> — it's not written down.

The Rhythms are Complex

1) The music is structured using <u>rhythmic cycles</u> of varying lengths, with <u>accents</u> on particular beats.

2) Rhythmic cycles with <u>accents</u> in <u>different places</u> are often played at the <u>same time</u> — this creates <u>polyrhythm</u> and <u>cross-rhythm</u> (see p.14), and adds <u>tension</u> to the music.

3) Notes that don't fall on a strong beat can be emphasised, giving a <u>syncopated</u> effect.

4) Although the music is based on repeated cycles, individual players introduce <u>small variations</u>. These gradually <u>develop</u> the basic patterns throughout the performance.

This means 'repeat the previous bar'.

A Cappella Singing is a Feature of Some African Music

1) <u>South African</u> all-male choirs (such as <u>Ladysmith Black Mambazo</u>) sing <u>a cappella</u>.

2) There are two main types of South African Zulu a cappella singing:

- mbube — <u>loud</u>, <u>powerful</u> singing, with <u>high-pitched</u> <u>lead vocals</u> over a <u>four-part harmony bass line</u>.
- <u>isicathamiya</u> — <u>softer</u> and <u>gentler</u> singing, with <u>four-part harmonies</u> singing <u>call and response</u>.

3) <u>Techniques</u> such as <u>glissandos</u> (slides in pitch, also called <u>portamento</u>), whistles and yodels are used.

African Music

Let's have a look at some more sub-Saharan instruments, before getting onto North African music.

The **Thumb Piano**, **Balafon** and **Kora** are Popular

These are some of the most popular instruments in sub-Saharan Africa.

A balafon is a wooden xylophone. The lumpy things hanging under the keys are dried gourds. They create a warm, mellow sound.

The kora is made and played by the Mandingo people. It's got 21 strings and you play it by plucking — a bit like a harp.

The mbira or thumb piano is really popular — partly because it's pocket-sized. It makes a liquid, twangy sound.

← These two are mostly played in West Africa. →

The thumb piano is played all over sub-Saharan Africa.

1) In West Africa, the balafon, kora and ngoni (a lute with 4-7 strings) are played by griots.

2) The griots have been around for centuries. They use music to tell stories about the history of the village and region they live in, including recording births, deaths and marriages.

3) They go through years of training to memorise the stories and master their instruments.

4) Senegalese griots play a type of drum called a sabar (a bit like a djembe) at weddings and naming ceremonies. Different rhythms have different meanings in sabar music.

North African Music is Influenced by Arabic Music

1) North African music is different to music from sub-Saharan Africa.

2) It's strongly influenced by Arabic and Andalusian music. Muslim Arabs came to North Africa from the Middle East and Al-Andalus (Spain and Portugal's name when they were part of the Islamic empire).

3) Arabic and Arab-influenced music is characterised by an emphasis on rhythm and melody, rather than harmony as in Western music. Musicians often improvise over a drone — a continuous bass note.

4) Microtones are also an important feature — they're any size of interval smaller than a semitone.

5) Andalusian classical music has a precise structure — it is performed in nubas (sets of different pieces), which each have a certain mode.

6) Each nuba is performed in five 'movements', called mizan, which each have a different time signature.

A Libyan nuba mode. The flat sign with a line through it means the note is a quartertone flat — it's a microtone.

7) Improvisation is key in North African music — musicians use the modes as a basis for improvising.

Some North African instruments

The ney is a flute made from a type of cane. It has a breathy sound.

The oud is similar to a lute. It tends to have 5 or 6 pairs of strings, with each pair tuned to the same pitch. It has a rich, resonant sound.

The rabab is a bowed string instrument with a small body and long neck. It tends to only have 1-3 strings, so it has been partially replaced by the violin, which has a greater range.

It's worth listening to what these instruments sound like...

Have a listen to some African music and try to see if you can pick out the instruments described above. Make sure you learn to recognise features such as call and response.

Caribbean Music

Caribbean music has indigenous, Latin American, African and European influences.
Different styles have developed on different islands, based on what the mix of influences has been.

Caribbean Music is Rich in Variation

1) Caribbean music's <u>diversity</u> is due to its <u>history</u>. People inhabited the islands for centuries before they were colonised by <u>Spain</u>, <u>France</u>, <u>Britain</u> and the <u>Netherlands</u>. The European nations brought millions of <u>Africans</u> to the Caribbean as slaves. Each of these people had <u>different influences</u> on the <u>music</u>.

2) <u>Steel pans</u> are well-known Caribbean instruments. They were originally made from large oil drums, and produce a <u>bright</u>, <u>ringing</u> sound. They're played using <u>sticks</u> with rubber heads.

3) Modern pans are often made from sheet metal. They come in <u>various sizes</u> and are named in line with their <u>range</u>, e.g. a <u>bass</u> pan plays the <u>lowest</u> notes. <u>Oval-shaped dents</u> in the pans give different notes.

4) The instruments reflect the <u>diversity</u> of the music.

Caribbean instruments

<u>Percussion</u> (especially <u>drums</u>) is important in Caribbean music due to the <u>African</u> influence.

The <u>guiro</u> makes a scrapy noise.

<u>Maracas</u> come from the Caribbean.

Types of <u>guitar</u> introduced by the Spanish are common. The <u>tres</u> has 3 sets of 2 or 3 strings, while the <u>cuatro</u> can have 4 or 5 pairs of strings.

 <u>Bongos</u> are paired drums played with the hands. <u>Congas</u> and <u>timbales</u> are also paired drums.

 <u>Claves</u> (wooden sticks) are often used to beat out a rhythm to <u>set the tempo</u> (see p.136 and p.139).

Calypso comes from Trinidad

1) <u>Calypso</u> music has its origins with <u>African slaves</u> who were brought to Trinidad. They used music to <u>communicate</u> with each other. The <u>lyrics</u> had a big role in <u>traditional</u> calypso songs — the songs had <u>funny</u> or <u>mocking lyrics</u> that the plantation owners couldn't understand. They told <u>stories</u> about important topics such as <u>social issues</u> or <u>relationships</u>, and were often <u>improvised</u>.

2) Over the centuries, the island came under the rule of <u>Spain</u>, <u>France</u> and <u>Britain</u>. Calypso music was <u>influenced</u> by the cultures of those countries, in addition to its <u>African roots</u>.

3) The <u>French</u> introduced <u>carnival</u> — it's still held <u>each year</u>, just before the start of <u>Lent</u> (the period before Easter). <u>Calypso</u> plays a big part, and <u>steel pan bands</u> and <u>singers</u> compete for <u>prizes</u>.

4) Calypso bands use a <u>wide range</u> of instruments, mixing the percussion mentioned above with instruments such as guitars, brass and woodwind instruments. <u>Steel pans</u> are important in calypso.

- Calypso music is usually in $\frac{2}{2}$ or $\frac{4}{4}$ time.
- The rhythms are <u>syncopated</u> (see p.129), and mostly follow a <u>3-3-2 pattern</u>. Each bar has <u>three beats</u>, but the final beat is <u>shorter</u> than the others.
- The songs can have a <u>verse-chorus</u> or <u>strophic</u> structure.
- The texture can be <u>homophonic</u>, with a main melody and accompaniment, or <u>polyphonic</u> with melodies and countermelodies (see p.47).

These are two calypso rhythms. The square brackets show how the beats are divided.

Cooking with steel pans is not recommended...

Have a listen to some calypso — listening to it will help you remember what the key features of it are.
Try picking out the rhythms and the 3-3-2 pattern, as well as the distinctive sound of the steel pans.

Caribbean Music

You may not be familiar with the styles of music on this page, but they influenced some genres that you've probably heard of — reggae and salsa, among others.

Mento is a Type of Jamaican Folk Music

1) Mento is similar to calypso, and was very popular in Jamaica in the first half of the 20th century.

2) It draws on musical traditions brought by West African slaves, as well as European influences.

3) It usually features acoustic instruments, including:

- acoustic guitar
- banjo — a plucked string instrument with a long neck and small body
- drums
- a rhumba box — a type of large mbira (see p.134) that can be sat on while it's being played

4) The lyrics were often lighthearted and witty, dealing with everyday life as well as political issues.

5) It's in strophic form — all the verses have the same melody (but different lyrics). See p.56 for more.

Son is Music from Cuba

Son is a type of dance music from Cuba. These are its key features:

1) A basic repeated rhythm pattern called a clave (pronounced *clah-vey*) is played on claves (*clayves*).

2) Other rhythmic patterns are played on instruments such as the maracas and bongos. These parts are often syncopated and form complicated cross-rhythms and polyrhythms against the clave part.

3) The melody is played by brass instruments, such as trumpets.

4) Call and response between the lead singer (called the sonero) and the chorus (the choro).

5) The lyrics in son music often talk about love, or comment on life in Cuba.

Salsa (see p.139) is a mix of son and big-band jazz (see p.131).

Merengue and Zouk are also Types of Dance Music

Merengue is from the Dominican Republic (there's a similar form called méringue from Haiti). It has African and Spanish influences. Caribbean instruments such as the cuatro and tambora (a double-headed drum) and 'Western' ones such as the accordion and saxophone are used to play it. It has a fast $\frac{2}{4}$ or $\frac{4}{4}$ beat, and uses catchy melodies with a simple harmony. It's sung in Spanish.

Zouk comes from the French Antilles

1) The French Antilles are a group of eastern Caribbean islands that were colonised by France.

2) Zouk is a mix of African styles, Caribbean music such as cadence (Haitian pop) and calypso, and American funk (a mix of soul, jazz and R'n'B).

3) It uses gwo ka — a name for both drums from Guadeloupe and the rhythms played on them — as well as the use of synthesizers and backing singers. It tends to have a fast beat.

4) Its modern sound has helped it become popular worldwide, especially in France.

Don't mix up clave and clave...

Phew, there were a lot of different styles on that page. Make sure you're clear on which one is which, and what the key features of each one are. You'll need to know about some of them for the fusions pages.

Fusions

Fusions are a combination of two or more styles of music. Ska and reggae are two types of fusion.

Styles Can Be Combined to Create Fusions

1) Fusion is when two or more styles of music are merged to create a new style.
2) It can happen gradually and naturally over time as two cultures become mingled, or it can be done deliberately when musicians experiment with different styles.
3) There are different ways of combining styles — e.g. you can mix the rhythms of one with the melodies of another, or use the instruments of one culture to play the melodies of another.
4) Some fusion styles have since been fused again to create even more new types of music.

Ska is a Fusion of R'n'B and Mento

Ska is a type of dance music that combines rhythm 'n' blues (R'n'B — see p.129) from the United States with rhythms from mento and calypso. It emerged in the 1950s. Here are some of its key features:

1) It uses jazz instruments such as trumpets and saxophones with electric guitars, percussion and piano or keyboard — this lineup is influenced by R'n'B.
2) There's a walking bass line — usually in crotchets, a walking bass line is improvised by the bassist around the notes of the chords being played. It's common in jazz and the blues.
3) It's usually in $\frac{4}{4}$ time with offbeat rhythms, an influence of mento. There's often a drumbeat on the 2nd and 4th beats, and the rhythm guitar plays offbeat 'skank' rhythms (see below).
4) Ska hits include purely instrumental music as well as songs with lyrics.

Reggae Came After Ska

Rocksteady is like a much slower version of ska. Reggae developed from this by mixing rocksteady with new effects and a slightly faster beat, driven by the bass guitar. Reggae tracks tend to have singers.

1) Electric and bass guitars, drum kit and keyboard or an electric organ are usually used. The bass guitar plays riffs — repeated patterns only a few bars long.
2) The lyrics are often political. The songs are usually in verse and chorus form.
3) Simple chord sequences are used. Reggae's played in $\frac{4}{4}$ time:

'Skank' rhythm, played by the rhythm guitar.

The rhythm guitar plays an offbeat pattern.
It has a 'choppy' sound created by the guitarist strumming
upwards rather than down — known as 'upstroke'.

'Bubble' rhythm, played by the keyboard.

The keyboard plays repeated offbeat
chords, alternating between left and right
hands. The rhythm above is often used.

- Reggae uses a fair amount of music technology and effects.
- The bass guitar sound is adjusted so that higher frequencies are less prominent and lower frequencies are emphasised, giving it a characteristic heavy sound.
- Remixing techniques are often used, particularly delay. A delay is a bit like an echo — it's a short recording of a bit of music which is then repeated over the top of the piece.
- Reggae musicians began to release versions of their tracks with added effects, in which they used 'toasting' — speaking over the top of the music. Hip-hop and rap followed on from this.

4) Reggaeton is an urban style of music similar to hip-hop or rap. It's dance music, popular in clubs. It's a blend of reggae and dub (a DJ rapping over bass guitar and drums) with American R'n'B, rap and hip-hop, as well as Latin American influences.

Fusions

Here are some fusions of Western popular music with genres of music from Africa.

Mbalax comes from Senegal and the Gambia

1) Mbalax is a form of <u>dance</u> music from <u>Senegal</u> and <u>the Gambia</u>.

2) It developed from a fusion of the drumming tradition of <u>sabar</u>, played by Senegalese <u>griots</u> (see p.134), <u>Western</u> popular music and <u>Afro-Caribbean</u> influences. Mbalax is also the name for the <u>rhythms</u> used in sabar music.

3) It's characterised by the <u>complex rhythms</u> and the <u>percussion</u> instruments used in sabar music.

4) 'Western' instruments such as <u>electric guitars</u> are used, as well as <u>synthesizers</u>.

5) The lyrics are usually in <u>Wolof</u> (spoken by the Wolof people of Senegal), <u>French</u> or <u>English</u>.

6) <u>Youssou N'Dour</u> made the genre famous with his 1994 duet with Neneh Cherry, '7 Seconds'.

Raï is Pop Music from Algeria

1) Some Algerian musicians wanted to create something <u>different</u> to North African classical music (p.134) — <u>raï</u> was the result. It developed over time from the <u>early 20th century</u>, but became more <u>popular</u> in the <u>1980s</u>. Eventually, it got fused with <u>pop</u>, <u>rock</u> and <u>jazz</u> to create a form of popular <u>dance</u> music.

2) <u>Trumpets</u>, <u>saxophones</u> and <u>accordions</u> are used alongside <u>North African</u> instruments (see p.134).

3) Some Western instruments used in raï are <u>fixed-pitch</u>, so they can't produce the <u>microtones</u> common in North African music. This makes the <u>tonality</u> a bit different to the classical music raï comes from.

4) <u>Rock instruments</u> such as <u>electric guitars</u> and <u>drum kit</u> are used as well. <u>Synthesizers</u>, <u>drum machines</u> and techniques such as <u>reverb</u> (an echo effect) are used in raï to create a <u>modern</u> sound.

5) Raï lyrics often discuss <u>everyday life</u> and <u>political issues</u>.

6) Raï is popular in <u>France</u>, which is home to many people with a North African background.

Fusions can be Quite Specific

Fusions can be the work of just one <u>band</u>, or a single <u>track</u> or <u>album</u>.

Afro Celt Sound System

1) The band <u>Afro Celt Sound System</u> play a fusion of <u>sub-Saharan African</u> and <u>Celtic</u> music.

2) They use traditional <u>Irish</u> and <u>African musical styles</u> (e.g. an <u>Irish air</u> with an <u>African drumbeat</u>).

3) They play a mixture of <u>Irish</u> and <u>African instruments</u> (e.g. a <u>tin whistle</u> and a <u>djembe</u>).

4) The music's based on <u>pentatonic scales</u> (a Celtic influence) and complex African rhythms.

5) An <u>electronic dance beat</u> ties the music together.

Graceland

1) *Graceland* was an album created by the American singer <u>Paul Simon</u> and the South African all-male choir <u>Ladysmith Black Mambazo</u>.

2) The songs are a fusion of <u>pop</u>, <u>rock</u> and <u>folk music</u> with <u>a cappella singing</u> (see p.133).

3) For example, the song 'Diamonds on the Soles of her Shoes' has <u>isicathamiya</u> singing at the start before the choir is joined by a <u>Western rock band</u> and <u>African drums</u>.

I hope you're not fused out after all that...

With fusions, it's important you know which genres of music were combined to make them and what the main features of these genres are. Then you can spot which bits have been used to make the fusion...

Salsa

Salsa is a popular form of dance music, particularly in Latin America and the Caribbean.

Salsa Grew Out of Son and Big-Band Jazz

1) Latin American musicians living in New York combined <u>Cuban son</u>
   (see p.136) with <u>big-band jazz</u> to create <u>salsa</u> in the 1960s and 1970s.

2) Taking the basic structure of son, <u>salsa bands</u> added the harsher,
   brass-based arrangements of <u>big band jazz</u>. The <u>trombone</u> was a big focus.

3) Salsa also took inspiration from <u>Puerto Rican</u>, <u>Brazilian</u> and <u>African</u> music.
   It soon became popular throughout <u>Latin America</u> and <u>beyond</u>.

Clave is the Rhythm of Salsa

1) The <u>clave</u> is the <u>basic rhythm</u> of a piece of salsa music. The most common rhythm is the <u>son</u> clave.

2) The son clave rhythm has a group of <u>three</u> notes and a group of <u>two</u>.

It goes like this...   ...or like this...

3) A salsa piece doesn't have to use the same clave <u>throughout</u>.
   It might switch to a <u>different clave</u> half-way through.

4) All the other parts are <u>built around</u> the clave — the clave is the <u>foundation</u> of the piece.

The Structure of Salsa is Flexible

There are <u>three main chunks</u> in a salsa tune. The three different chunks
can appear in <u>any order</u>, and they can all be used <u>more than once</u>.

1) In the <u>verse</u>, you hear the <u>main tune</u>, usually sung by the <u>sonero</u> or played by an instrumentalist.

2) The <u>montuno</u> is a kind of <u>chorus</u> where the sonero or lead instrumentalist <u>improvises</u>
   and the choro or other instrumentalists <u>answer</u>.

3) There is a <u>break</u> between choruses, called the <u>mambo</u>, with new musical material —
   e.g. different chords or a different tune. It's often played by the <u>horn section</u>.

4) There's usually an <u>introduction</u> and <u>ending</u>.

5) There could also be a 'break' — a bit where the main tune <u>stops</u> and just the rhythm section plays.

Here's a fairly <u>typical</u> salsa structure:

Another genre named after food...

...'salsa' means 'sauce' in Spanish. I guess you can just think of it as a mix of different foods, to remind you it's a fusion. Make sure you're clear on the clave rhythms and the structure — they're pretty important.

Samba

Samba is one of the most popular forms of dance music in South America, and around the world.

Samba Comes from **Brazil**

1) Samba is a Brazilian <u>street carnival dance</u>. Some of the <u>famous</u> Brazilian carnivals, such as the <u>Rio Carnival</u>, have made samba <u>popular</u> all over the world.

2) It's usually in either $\frac{2}{4}$ or $\frac{4}{4}$. It sounds <u>cheery</u> and is played at a <u>fast tempo</u> in a <u>major</u> key.

3) Samba instruments include a big variety of <u>percussion</u>, <u>Portuguese guitar</u> (a bright-sounding guitar with 12 strings), <u>keyboards</u>, <u>whistles</u> and, in larger street bands, <u>saxophones</u> and <u>trumpets</u>.

4) Samba is played by huge bands at carnivals, and by smaller bands for dancing <u>samba-salão</u> in ballrooms, or to accompany <u>samba-canção</u> (samba songs).

The **Samba Beat** Sounds like **Footsteps**

1) The main <u>samba beat</u> is played by a pair of loud, resonant <u>bass drums</u> called <u>surdo drums</u>.

2) The basic surdo rhythm sounds like steady marching <u>footsteps</u>. The surdo players alternately <u>hit</u> the drum with a stick then <u>damp</u> it with the hand. This <u>muting and unmuting</u> gives the effect of offbeat <u>springy</u> notes in between the main beats.

3) Over the basic surdo beat you hear many other complex <u>syncopated</u>, <u>ostinato</u> rhythms, such as this <u>agogo bells</u> rhythm:

4) Other <u>common</u> percussion instruments include: <u>shakers</u> (known as <u>ganzás</u>, <u>caxixis</u>, or <u>shekeres</u>), <u>scrapers</u> (the <u>reco-reco</u>) and <u>tambourines</u> (<u>pandeiros</u>).

The **Whistle Player** is **In Charge** of a Samba Band

1) Large samba bands are <u>controlled</u> by a leader playing a two-toned <u>samba whistle</u> and a <u>drum</u>.

2) The whistle sets the <u>tempo</u> and signals <u>call and response</u> sections. In the call and response bits, the leader plays a <u>rhythm</u> (usually on a drum called a <u>repinique</u>) and is <u>answered</u> by the rest of the band.

3) The call and response sections <u>contrast</u> with the sections where everyone plays repeated rhythms.

4) Sometimes the whole band <u>stops</u> and then starts again. This is called a <u>break</u>.

5) Samba <u>melodies</u> are usually very <u>catchy</u> and <u>repetitive</u>. They also <u>build up</u> — parts get <u>added</u> on top.

Samba has been **Fused** to Make **New Styles**

1) Because of its popularity, samba has led to many <u>new</u> musical styles.

2) Samba is often mixed with <u>other dance</u> styles, e.g. <u>tango</u> and <u>rumba</u> (see next page).

3) In the 1950s, samba was fused with <u>jazz</u> to make a style called <u>bossa nova</u>, which has <u>syncopated rhythms</u> and usually features a <u>guitar</u> and <u>vocals</u>.

4) It has also been mixed with <u>soul</u>, <u>funk</u>, <u>rock</u> and <u>disco</u> to create a wide range of <u>subgenres</u> and <u>fusions</u>.

Put 2nd December in your diaries — it's Brazil's National Samba Day...

Just like any type of music, the typical rhythms of samba can be changed or added to, so that it doesn't become too boring and repetitive. The rhythms on this page are common, but there are loads of others.

Contemporary Latin American Music

Lots of Latin American music is intended to be danced to, much the same as salsa and samba...

The **Cuban Habanera** Influenced Many Types of Dance Music

1) The <u>habanera</u> is a <u>Cuban dance</u> from the <u>19th century</u>. It has Spanish and African influences, as well as origins in a <u>European country dance</u> called the <u>contradanza</u>, brought via <u>Haiti</u>.

2) The habanera is usually in $\frac{2}{4}$ and has a distinctive <u>dotted rhythm</u>: ⟶ It's quite <u>slow</u> and <u>deliberate</u>.

3) Lots of other styles of <u>Latin American dance music</u> have <u>developed</u> from the habanera, including:

   - <u>Danzón</u> — a type of dance for <u>pairs</u>, with <u>set steps</u>. The music was traditionally played by an <u>orquesta tipica</u> — a band made up of <u>wind</u> and <u>brass instruments</u>, with a few <u>string instruments</u> as well. The danzón is usually <u>slow</u> and <u>elegant</u>.
   - <u>Cha-cha-cha</u> — a dance style that evolved from danzón in the 1950s. It's a <u>mid-tempo</u> dance (so is slightly faster than the danzón or habanera), in $\frac{4}{4}$ with the 'cha-cha-cha' on beats <u>3 and 4</u>.
   - <u>Tango</u> — see below.

4) The <u>Cuban rumba</u> is an <u>Afro-Cuban dance</u>, accompanied by <u>percussion</u> (including <u>maracas</u>) and <u>voices</u>. There are a few different <u>types</u> of rumba, each with <u>different rhythms</u>.

Tango is **Dance Music** from **Argentina**

1) Tango has a mix of African, Latin American and European influences, including <u>Italian</u> melodies, <u>Cuban habanera</u> rhythms (see above), <u>milonga</u> (syncopated music from <u>Argentina</u> and <u>Uruguay</u>) and <u>candombe</u> (<u>Uruguayan</u> music with African rhythms).

2) Tango instruments include <u>flute</u>, <u>violin</u> and <u>guitar</u>, accompanied by <u>bandoneons</u> (a type of accordion made in Germany) and a rhythm section of <u>piano</u>, <u>double bass</u> and <u>percussion</u>.

3) Tangos have <u>2</u> or <u>4</u> beats in the bar. These are some of the <u>basic rhythms</u>:

4) The main melody often uses a <u>slow rhythmic pace</u> with <u>triplets</u> and <u>syncopation</u> (see p.129).

5) <u>Staccato</u> notes (see p.19) give the music <u>precision</u>.

6) Tango has <u>simple harmonies</u>, often in a <u>minor key</u>, based on the <u>tonic</u> and <u>dominant</u> chords (for example A minor and E major).

7) Prominent and repeating <u>dotted rhythms</u> in the bass often move between the <u>tonic</u> and the <u>dominant</u> notes, as shown below:

The red notes are the tonic, the blue notes the dominant.

This is an habanera rhythm used in early tango music.

Latin Ballads are **Romantic Songs**

1) Latin ballads are <u>sentimental</u> songs that are very popular in Latin America.

2) Ballads are usually <u>narrative</u> songs — Latin ballads often cover the subject of <u>romance</u>.

3) They feature a <u>solo singer</u>, often accompanied by the guitar, a pop band or by a full-scale orchestra.

4) The ballads take influences from the <u>bolero</u> (a slow Cuban or Spanish dance), <u>Italian ballads</u> and <u>American pop</u>. The <u>harmony</u> is often quite <u>simple</u>.

5) Synthesizers and drum machines are used to <u>modernise</u> the sound.

Santana

Carlos Santana is a Mexican-American musician known for his blend of Latin American and rock music. Three of his band's songs are study pieces for the exam, so read these pages carefully and learn them.

Santana is a **Band** Named After **Carlos Santana**

1) Carlos Santana was born in <u>Mexico</u>, but he moved to the <u>United States</u>. This <u>influenced</u> his music, which is a <u>fusion</u> of Latin American styles with North American genres such as blues and rock music.

2) Carlos Santana is known for his virtuosic <u>guitar</u> playing.

3) He began playing with his band <u>Santana</u>, which is named after him, in <u>1966</u>.

4) They had one of their <u>greatest hits</u> in the late <u>1990s</u>, with their album *Supernatural*. *Supernatural* sold more than <u>25 million</u> copies worldwide and received <u>nine</u> Grammy awards.

- Many musicians, including Eric Clapton and CeeLo Green, played with Santana on *Supernatural*.
- The tracks are <u>varied</u>, with <u>jazz</u>, <u>hip-hop</u> and <u>rock</u> influences They have a <u>Latin American</u> sound.
- '<u>Smooth</u>' is the most famous track on *Supernatural*.

5) The band includes <u>rock</u> instruments alongside <u>trumpets</u> and <u>trombones</u> — a nod to its <u>Latin</u> influences.

6) Santana often use music from <u>other genres</u> and give it a <u>Latin twist</u>, as in 'Migra' and 'Love of my Life'. '<u>Jingo</u>' from their first album was a <u>cover</u> of a song by <u>Nigerian</u> percussionist <u>Babatunde Olatunji</u>.

'Migra' is About **Immigration**

1) 'Migra' is a <u>cover</u> of the song '<u>Kelma</u>' by the <u>rock/raï</u> musician (see p.134) <u>Rachid Taha</u> from his album *Olé Olé*. The <u>lyrics</u> are <u>different</u> from the original, but the <u>music</u> is <u>similar</u>.

2) Most of the lyrics are in <u>Spanish</u>. 'Migra' is a <u>slang name</u> for the US <u>immigration authorities</u>. The lyrics <u>protest</u> against the authorities' raids on immigrants who don't have the right documents.

3) The song also <u>sounds like</u> a <u>protest</u> — there are two voices singing in <u>unison</u> and the lines are <u>repeated</u>, which gives a <u>chant-like</u> feel to the song.

4) <u>Call and response</u> is used. Carlos Santana plays <u>guitar</u> phrases in response to <u>each line</u> of the verse.

5) There are lots of <u>instrumental sections</u> in 'Migra', most of which are <u>accompanied</u> by the <u>guitar</u>. Here's its <u>structure</u>:

The accordion is an influence from 'Kelma'.

Intro (drums)	Intro (guitar)	Verse 1	Chorus	Instrumental (accordion)	Verse 2	Instrumental (trumpets)

This sounds Latin American.

Instrumental (bass guitar)	Guitar solo	Chorus	Verse 3	Instrumental (trumpets)	Guitar solo	Instrumental (accordion)

This is dissonant and has atonal tendencies.

6) 'Migra' is based on a '<u>Bo Diddley beat</u>', which originates from the <u>son clave</u> rhythm (see p.139).

This is the 'Bo Diddley beat'.

This is the version used in 'Migra'.

- Carlos Santana uses lots of <u>rock guitar effects</u> in 'Migra'.
- Some are playing techniques, e.g. <u>vibrato</u> (see p.64), <u>glissando</u> (p.20) and <u>pitch bend</u> (p.129).
- Some are <u>technological</u> effects, such as <u>distortion</u> and a 'crying effect', called '<u>wah wah</u>' or '<u>cry baby</u>', which can be heard in the solo and rhythm guitar (see p.110).

Listen out for the Latin American influences...

When you're writing about these pieces in your exam, make sure you've made it clear whether you're talking about Carlos Santana or the band Santana — it could get pretty confusing for the examiner.

Santana

'Love of my Life' and 'Smooth' are influenced by lots of genres, from rap to jazz to Western classical music.

'Love of my Life' was Inspired by Brahms

1) 'Love of my Life' is a <u>collaboration</u> between Santana and Dave Matthews, a <u>rock</u> guitarist and singer.

2) It has <u>hip-hop</u> influences — at the start a <u>rapper</u> introduces the band over a drum kit and bass <u>riff</u>.

3) The <u>main theme</u> is similar to the third movement of <u>Symphony No. 3</u> by <u>Brahms</u>:

Santana changed the time signature from 3/8 to 4/4.

The original is written in tenor clef.

4) The <u>harmony</u> is generally <u>consonant</u> (see p.34) which helps give the song a <u>relaxed</u> feel.

5) The song has <u>two parts</u>. The first half is in a <u>steady tempo</u> and a <u>minor key</u>, with <u>quiet dynamics</u>. This gives it a soft, <u>subdued</u> mood.

6) The <u>legato</u> guitar playing, which is created by having a long <u>decay</u> on the note to <u>lengthen</u> it, adds to the mood of the song. <u>Pitch bend</u> and <u>vibrato</u> also give the guitar a <u>mournful</u> sound.

7) There's <u>call and response</u> between the singer and the guitar, giving a conversational feel.

8) Only electric and bass guitars, vocals, drum kit and <u>congas</u> (see p.135) are used in the first section. It <u>transitions</u> into the second part with a <u>vocal solo</u> accompanied by the piano.

- The <u>second part</u> of the song is <u>influenced</u> by <u>salsa</u>. The tempo <u>increases</u> and the <u>piano</u> enters with more <u>Latin percussion</u>, such as <u>bongos</u> (see p.135) and <u>cowbells</u>. The singer <u>doesn't sing</u> in the second part, so the song becomes <u>instrumental</u> — a common <u>feature</u> of <u>dance music</u>.

- Carlos Santana improvises a <u>solo</u> over this accompaniment. It uses a <u>wide</u> pitch range, fast <u>repetition</u> of notes and <u>pitch bend</u>. He uses bits of the <u>melody</u> from the first section in his solo.

- The piano plays a repeated <u>syncopated</u> rhythm. This is similar to a <u>montuno</u> pattern, which is a type of <u>ostinato</u> that accompanies salsa montuno sections (see p.139). This creates <u>polyphony</u> with Carlos Santana's guitar solo.

- 'Love of my Life' ends with a <u>fade-out</u> — the music gradually gets <u>quieter</u> until it can't be heard.

'Smooth' is Influenced by Rock and Latin American Music

1) 'Smooth' was a <u>hit single</u> — it's one of the most successful chart songs ever.

2) It's in $\frac{4}{4}$ time and has lots of <u>syncopation</u>. <u>Rob Thomas</u> wrote the lyrics and sings the <u>lead vocals</u>.

3) 'Smooth' has a <u>standard rock line up</u> of electric and bass guitars, drum kit, piano and vocals.

4) But it has a <u>Latin-influenced</u> sound, created by the use of Latin percussion such as the <u>guiro</u>, <u>congas</u> and <u>timbales</u> (see p.135), and <u>syncopated</u> rhythms. The use of <u>trumpet</u> and <u>trombone</u> adds a <u>salsa</u> (see p.139) and <u>jazz</u> feel. It has catchy, memorable <u>riffs</u>.

5) The lyrics include some <u>Spanish</u> words, such as 'muñequita' (*little doll*) and 'barrio' (*neighbourhood*).

6) The <u>bass line</u> often moves between the <u>tonic</u> and <u>dominant</u>, like in <u>tango</u> (see p.141).

7) 'Smooth' is <u>strophic</u>. There are two verses, with a <u>chorus</u> and <u>bridge</u> (that comes <u>before</u> the chorus). There are a couple more <u>instrumentals</u> and <u>choruses</u>, before ending with a <u>guitar solo</u>, which <u>fades out</u>.

8) The texture's mostly <u>homophonic</u>, but it's <u>polyphonic</u> when the guitar and vocals have different tunes.

- <u>Distortion</u> is used on the vocals and the guitar line.

- There's <u>panning</u> (see p.110) on the vocals, for example in the <u>second verse</u>.

- <u>Layering</u> is also used — the vocal parts have been recorded <u>separately</u> and then <u>layered</u> on top of each other, so it sounds like <u>several</u> people are singing when it's just one.

- The lyrics 'Or else forget about it' are sung <u>without</u> any <u>accompaniment</u> or <u>layering</u> — a bit like a <u>salsa break</u> (see p.139). This makes the line <u>stand out</u> from the rest of the song.

Celtic Music

Every country has its own type of folk music, which uses local languages, dialects and instruments.

Folk Music was Played by **Ordinary People**

1) Folk music's still around nowadays but it used to be <u>much more popular</u>. In olden times, before radios and record players, the <u>only</u> music ordinary people had was music they played themselves.

2) The tunes tend to be quite <u>simple</u> and work with just a <u>few</u> instruments or voices. This made them <u>easier</u> for people in the <u>pub</u>, <u>field</u> or <u>factory</u> to learn and play.

3) Folk music was hardly ever <u>written down</u>. It survived through the <u>aural tradition</u> — people <u>heard</u> a song or tune they liked and <u>memorised</u> it.

4) Folk music changes over time as people add <u>new ideas</u>. Sometimes they're being deliberately <u>creative</u>, sometimes they <u>can't remember</u> exactly what they've heard and make up a new bit.

5) The <u>instruments</u> used to play along with folk songs and dances tend to be <u>small</u> and <u>easy to carry</u>. The most popular ones are the <u>pipe and tabor</u> (a three-holed recorder and a drum, played together for a one-man band effect), the <u>fiddle</u>, the <u>hurdy-gurdy</u>, the <u>bagpipes</u>, the <u>accordion</u> and the <u>concertina</u>.

6) The main types of folk music are <u>work songs</u> (sung by <u>labourers</u> to help them to work as a <u>team</u> and take their <u>minds</u> off their work), <u>ballads</u> (they tell <u>stories</u> of <u>love</u>, <u>real-life events</u> or <u>legends</u>) and <u>dance</u> music (see next page).

Folk Tunes are Fairly **Simple**

1) A lot of folk melodies are based on <u>pentatonic scales</u> (see p.27). They've only got five notes, which makes writing tunes with them a lot easier.

2) A <u>major pentatonic</u> scale uses notes <u>1</u>, <u>2</u>, <u>3</u>, <u>5</u> and <u>6</u> of an ordinary <u>major scale</u>.

3) A <u>minor pentatonic</u> scale uses notes <u>1</u>, <u>3</u>, <u>4</u>, <u>5</u> and <u>7</u> of a <u>natural minor scale</u>.

4) There are <u>no semitone intervals</u> in pentatonic scales. It makes it much easier to add a <u>harmony</u> because the notes don't clash. It also makes them <u>easy to sing</u>.

> The <u>structure</u> in folk tunes tends to be pretty simple too. <u>Songs</u> are often <u>strophic</u> — the tune stays the same for each verse. Strophic songs can either be a number of <u>musically identical</u> verses (with different words), or can have a <u>chorus</u> that's just a <u>slight variation</u> on the verse (so the structure is A A' A A' A...). Phrases have even numbers of bars — usually <u>four</u>. Often each phrase begins with an <u>anacrusis</u> (upbeat).

Lots of **Celtic Folk Music** Comes From **Scotland** and **Ireland**

1) Lots of places in <u>Western Europe</u> have traditional Celtic folk music — like <u>Wales</u>, <u>Cornwall</u> and <u>Brittany</u> in France.

2) Celtic folk music also includes <u>traditional Scottish</u> and <u>Irish</u> music.

3) The songs are often sung in <u>Gaelic</u> — Celtic languages spoken in Scotland and Ireland. The two most common forms are <u>Scots Gaelic</u> and <u>Irish Gaelic</u>.

4) Traditional Celtic instruments include <u>fiddles</u> (violins), <u>bagpipes</u>, <u>tin whistles</u> and <u>accordions</u>. An Irish framed drum called the <u>bodhrán</u> is also used.

5) <u>English</u> folk is a bit separate from <u>Celtic</u> folk. English folk uses instruments such as the <u>recorder</u> and <u>Northumbrian pipes</u> (a kind of <u>bagpipe</u>) as well as many of those mentioned above.

Folk songs were often just passed from person to person...

Folk music is often about simplicity — pentatonic scales, simple structure and instrumentation. This made it easier to pass on. The use of pentatonic scales gives folk music a pretty distinctive sound.

Contemporary British Folk

This page focuses on folk music that's been mixed with different kinds of popular music to create various fusions. However, there's still a lot of 'traditional' folk around today as well.

Some **Folk** Music is Influenced by **Popular** Music...

1) <u>Modern</u> Irish dance music combines <u>folk rhythms</u> with <u>contemporary beats</u>. It uses both <u>live instruments</u> and <u>MIDI sequencers</u>.

2) A good example of this is the music from <u>Riverdance</u>. It's a sell-out show featuring <u>Irish dancers</u>, a <u>choir</u> and a band using <u>folk instruments</u> alongside others such as the <u>drum kit</u>. It uses techniques such as <u>reverb</u> to enhance the music.

3) Some bands turn folk music into a more <u>modern</u> style by adding a <u>bass line</u> and <u>drum kit</u>.

- The Scottish band <u>Capercaillie</u> combine folk music and instruments with <u>funk</u> bass lines, <u>synthesizers</u> and electric and bass guitars to create a <u>fusion</u>. Capercaillie's album *Beautiful Wasteland* is a good example of Celtic folk rock music.

- Another Scottish band, <u>Runrig</u>, is well-known for its mix of <u>Gaelic folk</u> with <u>rock</u> music. They also use folk instruments with electric and bass guitars and drum kit to create a <u>rock</u> sound. Their lyrics are sung in <u>English</u> and <u>Scots Gaelic</u>. Their rock cover of the song 'Loch Lomond' is very popular.

...and Some **Popular** Music is Influenced by **Folk** Music

1) Irish pop artists like <u>The Corrs</u>, <u>Westlife</u> and <u>Van Morrison</u> sometimes use <u>elements</u> of Irish music.

2) For example, The Corrs use <u>traditional Irish instruments</u> in some of their songs, but their use of <u>music technology</u>, particularly synthesizers, and <u>pop instruments</u> (such as electric guitar) gives their songs a mostly pop music sound.

3) Westlife used the <u>Irish</u> tune '<u>The Londonderry Air</u>' (also used in the song <u>Danny Boy</u>) in their hit single '<u>You Raise Me Up</u>'.

4) Some of <u>Van Morrison's</u> albums were influenced by Irish music — particularly *Astral Weeks* (his second album) and *Irish Heartbeat*, a collaboration with the traditional Irish group <u>The Chieftains</u>.

English Folk is **Less Well-Known**

1) English folk has often had a <u>lower profile</u> than Scottish or Irish folk. However, there are a few examples of it around in <u>mainstream music</u>. This form of modern folk is often known as '<u>nu-folk</u>'.

2) <u>Mumford & Sons'</u> first two albums are known for their folk-influenced sound, created by their use of instruments such as the <u>banjo</u> and <u>double bass</u>. Their lyrics sometimes reference rural topics such as the <u>harvest</u> and <u>owning land</u>. Many of their songs are <u>ballads</u>, a song format often used in folk.

3) They used to play as the backing band to <u>Laura Marling</u>, a folk-influenced singer. Her music, along with that of the band <u>Noah and the Whale</u>, represented a '<u>folk revival</u>' in British music. They brought folk music to a new <u>generation</u> of listeners.

The group <u>The Imagined Village</u> aims to revive interest in English folk. They bring together a diverse group of musicians, such as <u>Afro Celt Sound System</u> band members (see p.138) and a <u>sitar</u> player. The group takes old folk songs and makes them <u>current</u> — for example, they turned a song about the <u>Napoleonic wars</u> into one about the war in <u>Afghanistan</u>.

Folk fusions usually use folk instruments and melodies...

Have a listen to a traditional recording of 'Loch Lomond' and Runrig's version so you can hear how they've fused the folk melody with rock. It's well worth listening to the other bands too.

Warm-up and Exam Questions

Phew, what a long section. Now it's time to see how much you've remembered. Have a go at the warm-up questions to get yourself in the swing of things, and then try the exam questions...

Warm-up Questions

1) Who first created blues music?

2) What is syncopation?

3) Write out the chord pattern used for 12-bar blues.

4) Name four instruments commonly played by jazz musicians.

5) What is scat?

6) What is a kora?

7) What is a microtone?

8) Which two time signatures are usually used in calypso?

9) Where does mento come from?

10) What is a fusion?

11) What styles of music does ska come from?

12) What technique does the rhythm guitar use in reggae?

13) Where does samba come from?

14) What rhythm does Migra use?

15) Name a Santana song that is influenced by hip-hop.

16) What kind of scale is often used in folk music?

17) What is a bodhrán?

Exam Questions

Have a go at these exam-style questions.

Track 35 is an excerpt from 'Migra' by Santana.

Play the excerpt **four** times. Leave a short pause between each playing.

a) Which word best describes the bass guitar line at the start of the excerpt?

Circle your answer.

Drone   **Alberti bass**   **Ground bass**   **Riff**

[1 mark]

Exam Questions

b)   Decide whether each of the statements below is true or false. Write T or F in the boxes.

The hi-hat cymbals play on the beat in the 'bass guitar' section.

An echo effect is used on the whispering in the 'bass guitar' section.

The bass guitar line changes when the electric guitar solo starts.

The rhythm guitar plays during Carlos Santana's guitar solo.

[4 marks]

c)   Describe the guitar techniques Carlos Santana uses in his solo.

....

....

....

....

....

....

....

....

....

....

[6 marks]

d)   Which musical device is used in the final section of the excerpt, after the guitar solo?
     Circle your answer.

   canon   **call and response**   **continuous repetition**   **falsetto**

[1 mark]

e)   Which part of the song's structure is the final section of the excerpt?

....

[1 mark]

Exam Questions

Track 36 is an excerpt from 'Gin-Go-Lo-Ba' by Olatunji.

Play the excerpt **three** times. Leave a short pause between each playing.

Track 36

a) Name the family of instruments used at the start of the excerpt.

....

[1 mark]

b) Tick the rhythm played by the first drum you hear at the start of the excerpt.

[1 mark]

c) Which phrase below correctly describes the device used in the vocal section?
Circle your answer.

   a cappella   **singing in unison**   **polyphony**   **scat**

[1 mark]

d) Name the region of the world this music comes from.

....

[1 mark]

e) Some of the percussion rhythms don't fit perfectly into the $\frac{4}{4}$ bars.
What is the technical term for such a combination of rhythms?

....

[1 mark]

Revision Summary for Section Eight

Go through these questions and make sure you know the answer to all of them. If there are any you don't know, go back through the section and learn the answer. Then go through the questions again, to make sure you're completely comfortable with the material.

1) What are blues lyrics like?
2) What is the blues scale?
3) Explain the difference between straight and swung rhythms.
4) Why is it easy to switch between the twelve-bar and sixteen-bar blues patterns?
5) Name two different types of jazz.
6) List five devices that could be used in improvisation.
7) What is call and response?
8) Name three types of African drum.
9) Describe mbube and isicathamiya singing.
10) What is a griot?
11) Name two features of North African music.
12) What is an oud?
13) Name two types of Caribbean percussion instrument.
14) Write down one calypso rhythm.
15) Give the two definitions of the word 'clave' in Cuban son.
16) What is: i) a sonero? ii) a choro?
17) Which genres does zouk come from?
18) What is a walking bass line?
19) How is the heavy bass guitar sound created in reggae?
20) Name two features of mbalax.
21) How is a modern sound created in raï music? Give two details.
22) Write out a 2-3 son clave.
23) What is a mambo?
24) What are the typical time signatures of samba?
25) What is the role of the whistle player in a samba band?
26) What two styles make up bossa nova?
27) Describe the origins of the habanera.
28) Give two features of the harmony in tango.
29) What is a Latin ballad?
30) Give two guitar techniques used in 'Migra'.
31) Give two features of the first section of 'Love of my Life', and two of the second.
32) What is layering?
33) Which notes of a natural minor scale does a minor pentatonic scale use?
34) What is strophic form?
35) List three bands that play folk fusions.

Aaron Copland

Aaron Copland was a twentieth-century American composer. Two movements of his ballet *Rodeo* are the study pieces for Area of Study 4, so if you've chosen to learn about them, have a good read of these pages.

Copland Wrote Several **Well-Known Pieces**

1) Aaron Copland was an American composer who lived from 1900-1990. He studied composition in France for a few years, before returning to America to work as a composer, conductor and lecturer.

2) Although he used different styles in his compositions during his lifetime, such as jazz and serialism (see p.153), he's most well-known for his American-influenced music.

3) He wrote for different ensembles and purposes, including symphonies, ballet music and film scores. His most famous pieces include his third symphony, the ballets *Billy the Kid*, *Appalachian Spring* and *Rodeo*, several film scores (including *Of Mice and Men*) and 'Fanfare for the Common Man'.

> 'Fanfare for the Common Man' is often used for ceremonial occasions in America, such as at the celebrations for the inaugurations of the presidents Bill Clinton and Barack Obama and the opening of the museum commemorating the 9/11 attacks. It's written for a brass and percussion ensemble.

Copland Created Music that Sounded **American**

Copland wanted to create music that had an American sound. It had a more traditional feel than the music of some other 20th century composers, such as Stravinsky or Schoenberg.

1) Copland's music is tonal — it's in a major or minor key. Other music at the time was more atonal.

2) He makes use of simple melodic and rhythmic material, such as American folk tunes.

3) His pieces often celebrate American history and culture. For example, 'Lincoln Portrait' is about the American president Abraham Lincoln, and includes quotes from his speeches alongside the music.

4) Some of his music captures the spirit of the Wild West and America's landscapes. For example, *Appalachian Spring* portrays life in the Appalachian Mountains.

Rodeo is a **Ballet** About **Life on a Ranch**

> A rodeo is when cattle are rounded up, or a competition in which people show off their horseriding and animal-handling skills.

1) *Rodeo* is a ballet by Copland, first performed in 1942.

2) Unusually for a ballet, it's set in the Wild West (as was Copland's earlier ballet, *Billy the Kid*).

3) *Rodeo* is set on a ranch — a farm where cattle are raised. It's about a Cowgirl who's in love with the Head Wrangler (head cowboy). He isn't interested — he likes the Rancher's Daughter, who's less of a tomboy. Eventually, the Cowgirl falls in love with the Champion Roper, who likes her for who she is.

4) The ballet is in five sections:

- Buckaroo Holiday
- Ranch House Party
- Corral Nocturne
- Saturday Night Waltz
- Hoe-Down

> You can see the influence of the cowboy theme in the names. 'Buckaroo' is another word for cowboy, while a 'corral' is a pen for cattle or horses.

> 'Saturday Night Waltz' and 'Hoe-Down' are the study pieces.

5) Copland used a large orchestra, with lots of brass, woodwind and percussion — though he uses fewer instruments in the slower movements, such as 'Corral Nocturne'.

6) He often uses American folk tunes in *Rodeo* — 'Buckaroo Holiday' uses two different folk melodies.

People liked Rodeo so much it got 22 curtain calls at its premiere...

Copland wrote *Rodeo* for Agnes de Mille, a choreographer and dancer. He also made an orchestral version (without dancers). He removed the second section, 'Ranch House Party', from the version for orchestra.

Aaron Copland

'Saturday Night Waltz' is the fourth movement of *Rodeo*. It's a slow movement.

'Saturday Night Waltz' is Based on an American Folk Song

1) A <u>waltz</u> is a dance that's always in $\frac{3}{4}$ time — it's often danced in the <u>ballroom</u>.
   'Saturday Night Waltz' is <u>waltz-like</u> — it's a <u>slow</u> movement in $\frac{3}{4}$ time. Most of it is marked ♩ = <u>72</u>.

2) However, the movement isn't a <u>typical</u> waltz — it <u>avoids</u> the usual <u>oom-pah-pah</u> waltz rhythm, which
   has a heavy stress on the <u>downbeat</u>, and instead includes lots of <u>syncopation</u> to maintain interest.

3) Its <u>main theme</u> is based on the American folk song '<u>I Ride an Old Paint</u>' (a paint is a type of <u>horse</u>).
   Have a look at the melody below and compare it to the <u>main theme</u> in 'Saturday Night Waltz'.

The Structure is Quite Complex

1) The first few bars of the piece sound like an orchestra <u>tuning</u> up. It's just the <u>string section</u> playing,
   and they're only using <u>open strings</u> — none of the notes are <u>stopped</u>, which gives an open sound.
   They're playing <u>two</u> or <u>three</u> strings at once (<u>double-</u> or <u>triple-stopping</u>), as they often do when tuning.

2) They play <u>open fifths</u> — the <u>tonic</u> and <u>dominant</u> played without the <u>third</u>.
   This makes the tonality <u>ambiguous</u> — it's <u>not clear</u> whether it's in a <u>major</u> or <u>minor</u> key.

3) The <u>whole</u> orchestra then plays a <u>fanfare-like theme</u>. It's as if they're telling the dancers to take their
   places for the waltz. The tempo gradually <u>slows</u> and the note values <u>increase</u>, giving a <u>slower</u> feel.

4) The waltz is roughly in <u>ABA</u> form. It <u>begins</u> with the main theme in E♭ <u>major</u> (<u>section A</u>). The tempo's
   <u>slower</u> at ♩ = <u>72</u> (it began at ♩ = <u>152</u>). Another tune, played by the <u>violas</u>, enters after the main theme's
   been played <u>twice</u>. It <u>mirrors</u> the main theme with its use of <u>dotted rhythms</u> and <u>frequent quavers</u>.

5) Then a <u>transition</u> section <u>unexpectedly</u> modulates to <u>E major</u>, an <u>unrelated</u> key. The tempo <u>doubles</u>.

6) The transition section leads into <u>section B</u>, which is a bit <u>slower</u> (*meno mosso*).
   A new <u>viola</u> melody is accompanied by an <u>arpeggio-like melody</u> played by a <u>clarinet</u> and a <u>flute</u>.

7) Section A <u>returns</u> with a <u>modulation</u> back to E♭ major. It goes back to ♩ = <u>72</u>.

The Instrumentation is Fairly Simple

1) The texture is mostly <u>homophonic</u>, with a <u>main melody</u> and <u>orchestral accompaniment</u>.

2) The use of lots of <u>solo</u> instruments creates a <u>thin texture</u> throughout most of the movement.
   For example, the <u>main theme</u> is introduced by a <u>single oboe</u>, rather than by lots of instruments.

3) The instrumentation in 'Saturday Night Waltz' is <u>simple</u> in comparison to 'Hoe-Down' (see p.152):

   - There are <u>two clarinets</u> and a <u>bass clarinet</u>, but only <u>one flute</u>, <u>oboe</u> and <u>bassoon</u>.
   - The flute part is quite <u>ornamental</u> — it plays lots of <u>acciaccaturas</u> (see p.84).
   - The <u>brass</u> section consists of <u>horns</u> and <u>trumpets</u> but only <u>one trombone</u> and <u>no tuba</u>.
   - The <u>strings</u> and a <u>harp</u> play, but there's <u>no piano</u> or any of the <u>percussion</u> used in 'Hoe-Down'.

4) The <u>harmony</u> is simple, which creates a sense of <u>space</u> in the music. The use of <u>open fifths</u> helps this.

5) The start is <u>dramatic</u>, with the open fifths played <u>forte</u>. The fanfare starts <u>fortissimo</u>, but <u>decreases</u>
   to <u>piano</u> when the main theme enters. The music is mostly <u>quiet</u> and <u>soft</u> from then on.

Saturday Night Waltzing — those cowboys sure knew how to party...

Try comparing 'Saturday Night Waltz' with 'Hoe-Down' — the contrast will help you remember the details.

Aaron Copland

'Hoe-Down' is the final movement of *Rodeo*. It's an upbeat dance, reflecting *Rodeo*'s happy ending.

'Hoe-Down' has Lots of Dance Features

1) A <u>hoe-down</u> is a <u>lively</u> American-style <u>barn dance</u> used to celebrate the end of <u>hay-making</u> or other work. It's in <u>duple metre</u> (usually $\frac{2}{4}$) with a <u>fast</u> tempo. Copland's 'Hoe-Down' shares these features.

2) 'Hoe-Down' centres around two American <u>folk tunes</u>, '<u>Bonaparte's Retreat</u>' and '<u>McLeod's Reel</u>'.

The second part of 'Bonaparte's Retreat'.

The start of 'McLeod's Reel'.

Compare these folk versions with the melodies in 'Hoe-Down'.

3) The instrumentation in 'Hoe-Down' is <u>complex</u>. There's a <u>piano</u> and lots of <u>percussion</u> — <u>timpani</u>, <u>xylophone</u>, <u>snare drum</u>, <u>woodblock</u>, <u>bass drum</u> and <u>cymbals</u>, which help give a <u>strong beat</u>.

4) There are <u>two trombones</u>, a <u>bass trombone</u> and a <u>tuba</u>, as well as a full <u>woodwind section</u>. Changes in <u>instrumentation</u> help <u>signal</u> to the dancers when a <u>new section</u> has <u>begun</u>.

5) The use of a <u>homophonic</u> texture with a <u>clear melody</u> and the <u>repetition</u> of some of the sections also helps to make the music <u>easy</u> for the dancers to <u>follow</u>.

'Hoe-Down' has Several Different Sections

The piece is basically in <u>ternary form</u> (ABA). <u>Section A</u> is a '<u>woodblock</u>' section and '<u>Bonaparte's Retreat</u>'. <u>Section B</u> is '<u>McLeod's Reel</u>' with a bit of an Irish tune named '<u>Gilderoy</u>' in the middle. The sections are <u>different</u> so the dancers know which is which — they're in <u>different keys</u>, with <u>contrasting melodies</u>.

Intro	A		B			A		Coda
Intro	Woodblock section	Bonaparte's Retreat	McLeod's Reel	Gilderoy	McLeod's Reel	Woodblock section	Bonaparte's Retreat	Coda

Intro — D minor

The orchestra plays a <u>fast rhythm</u> from the <u>first half</u> of the '<u>Bonaparte</u>' tune. The strings echo 'Saturday Night Waltz' by playing <u>open fifths</u>. A <u>fanfare-like</u> melody is passed between the trumpets and strings. The <u>pulse</u> gradually <u>shifts</u> from 2 to 3 beats in a bar. After <u>one bar</u> in $\frac{3}{4}$ time, the fast rhythm <u>returns</u> to end the section. It's <u>fortissimo</u> throughout.

Woodblock section — D major

The texture is <u>thin</u> and it's <u>quieter</u> (***mf***). The <u>style</u> of the <u>accompaniment</u> is typical of <u>American fiddle tunes</u>. The <u>piano</u> and strings play a simple chord <u>vamp</u> (a <u>repeated</u> bit). The <u>woodblock</u> sounds like <u>horses</u> trotting. The <u>second</u> time, it's followed by a <u>bridge section</u> with a <u>diminuendo</u> and <u>ritenuto</u> to a ***p*** chord.

Bonaparte's Retreat — D major

This has two parts. The first part has a <u>quaver/semiquaver</u> rhythm with <u>triplet flourishes</u>, and the second has a <u>semiquaver</u> tune (see above). Near the end of the section, this is played against <u>syncopated</u> open fifths to create <u>polyrhythm</u>. The <u>xylophone</u> adds <u>emphasis</u> in the first part.

McLeod's Reel — G major

This <u>disjunct</u> melody is shared between two <u>trumpets</u> before the <u>strings</u> join in. It has <u>strong accents</u>, emphasised by the <u>snare drum</u>. There's a <u>fanfare</u> before Section A returns.

Gilderoy — A minor

The <u>oboe</u> and then the <u>strings</u> play this. The mostly <u>scalic</u>, quiet melody <u>contrasts</u> with 'McLeod's Reel'.

Serialism

Serialism is a twentieth century method of composition — one of the main composers who developed and used this system was Arnold Schoenberg (1874-1951). He invented the 12-tone system in the 1920s.

The 12-Tone System Arranges Notes in a Certain Order

1) To use the 12-tone system, start by arranging the 12 chromatic notes of an octave into a set order (any order you like), written out horizontally — this is called a tone row.

The initial arrangement is called the prime order:

2) Now rearrange the prime order. There are a few different ways of doing this — the first is to play the notes in reverse order (or retrograde).

3) Take the prime order again and turn the intervals between the notes upside down — this is known as an inversion. E.g. if the prime order goes up a semitone, in the inversion you go down a semitone.

4) For the last type of arrangement, take your inversion and play the notes in reverse order to give a retrograde inversion.

5) These four different tone rows can be transposed — each one can start on any of the 12 different notes. This gives you 48 different tone rows to use in your composition (see below).

6) As it uses all the notes of a chromatic scale, this music is not written in any key — it's atonal.

Use the Tone Rows as the Building Blocks of the Piece

1) Pick any tone row — the notes can be played in the bass line or melody and in any octave.

2) Once a row has been started, you have to use all the notes in it (i.e. you can't just use half a row). However, rows can be passed between parts and can overlap.

3) Notes can be combined to make motifs — memorable bits of melody that reappear through the piece.

4) Groups of notes can be piled up to make chords. Notes that were next to each other in the original rows would be played all at once by different instruments. This is called verticalisation — notes that were written out horizontally in the rows are written out vertically in the score.

5) The prime order could be designed to create decent-sounding chords with triads, or to create cluster chords with notes really close together.

6) Serialist music is quite complicated to write, so most pieces are only for small groups of instruments.

'Moses und Aron' by Schoenberg and Alban Berg's Violin Concerto are good examples of serialist pieces.

cluster chord

This is an example of verticalisation.

Not to be confused with cerealism — eating your breakfast in order...

Although this page is all about ordering the notes, serialism can order other elements too — such as metres, dynamics or rhythms. Total serialism, which came a bit later, is when every aspect of a piece is ordered.

British Music — Arnold and Britten

There have been lots of <u>British classical composers</u> from 1910 to today — but the ones you need to know about for this AoS are <u>Malcolm Arnold</u>, <u>Benjamin Britten</u>, <u>Peter Maxwell Davies</u> and <u>John Tavener</u>.

Malcolm Arnold was a Trumpet Player and Composer

1) <u>Sir Malcolm Arnold</u> was born in Northampton in <u>1921</u>. He played <u>principal trumpet</u> for the <u>London Philharmonic Orchestra</u> before focusing on <u>composition</u>. He <u>died</u> in <u>2006</u>.

2) He composed a <u>wide variety</u> of music — including <u>symphonies</u>, <u>ballets</u>, <u>overtures</u>, <u>concertos</u>, <u>operas</u>, <u>choral music</u> and <u>film music</u> (he won an <u>Academy Award</u> for the 1957 film *The Bridge on the River Kwai*). He also wrote music specifically for <u>wind bands</u> and <u>brass bands</u>.

3) Arnold lived in <u>Cornwall</u> for a number of years, which <u>inspired</u> some of his compositions — such as *Four Cornish Dances* (he also wrote <u>suites</u> of <u>English</u>, <u>Irish</u>, <u>Welsh</u> and <u>Scottish</u> dances). He composed '<u>The Padstow Lifeboat</u>' (a <u>brass band march</u>) to celebrate the <u>launch</u> of a new lifeboat.

4) The *Tam O'Shanter Overture* is based on a <u>poem</u> by <u>Robert Burns</u> (it's a piece of <u>programme music</u> — see p.99). It has <u>Scottish</u> elements — for example, the clarinets imitate bagpipes. The <u>drunken Tam</u> is represented by a <u>trombone</u> and <u>bassoons</u>, giving the overture a <u>light-hearted</u>, <u>comedic</u> feel.

5) Arnold's music was quite <u>conservative</u> compared to other composers of the time — he was influenced by <u>late Romantic/early 20th century</u> composers such as <u>Berlioz</u>, <u>Sibelius</u>, <u>Mahler</u> and <u>Bartók</u> (see p.158), rather than <u>atonal</u> and <u>experimental</u> styles. His love of <u>jazz</u> also influenced his work.

Arnold Wrote Concertos For a Wide Range of Instruments

1) As well as writing concertos for more <u>traditional</u> instruments (such as <u>cello</u>, <u>piano</u>, <u>flute</u> and <u>horn</u>), some of Arnold's concertos were written for instruments <u>not</u> usually featured in concertos — including <u>guitar</u>, <u>recorder</u> (recorder concertos were more common in the <u>Baroque</u> era) and <u>harmonica</u>.

2) Many of his concertos were written for <u>specific performers</u> — for example, the <u>Harmonica Concerto</u> was written for <u>Larry Adler</u>, and <u>Clarinet Concerto No.2</u> was commissioned by <u>Benny Goodman</u>:

> <u>Clarinet Concerto No.2</u> has both <u>typical</u> and <u>non-typical</u> features of a concerto. It has the traditional <u>three-movement</u>, <u>fast-slow-fast structure</u> (the movements are marked <u>Allegro vivace</u>, <u>Lento</u> and <u>Allegro non troppo</u>). However, the concerto is <u>unusual</u> in that it has many <u>jazz influences</u> (see p.131-132), as <u>Goodman</u> was a jazz musician. Arnold uses <u>dissonance</u> frequently, and the <u>third movement</u> is a <u>ragtime</u> piece (it's called the <u>Pre-Goodman Rag</u>). The <u>cadenza</u> is marked with the instruction 'as jazzy and way out as you please'.

Benjamin Britten Wrote Both Vocal and Orchestral Music

1) <u>Benjamin Britten</u> was born in Lowestoft, Suffolk in <u>1913</u>. He started composing at a <u>young age</u>, and continued until his death in <u>1976</u>.

There's more on Britten on the next page.

2) Britten wrote a lot of <u>orchestral</u> music — including the *Simple Symphony* (its movements have the light-hearted titles '<u>Boisterous Bourrée</u>', '<u>Playful Pizzicato</u>', '<u>Sentimental Saraband</u>' and '<u>Frolicsome Finale</u>'). *The Young Person's Guide to the Orchestra* is <u>variations</u> and a <u>fugue</u> (see p.82) on a theme by <u>Purcell</u>, and is often used to <u>teach children</u> about the <u>instruments</u> of the orchestra.

3) He is also well known for his <u>vocal music</u> — he wrote a number of <u>operas</u> and <u>song cycles</u> (see p.102). The <u>sizes</u> of the operas vary — some are written for <u>large companies</u>, while others are written for <u>chamber ensembles</u>. Perhaps his most <u>famous</u> choral work is the *War Requiem* (see next page).

I'm going to call my composition 'Morbid Minuet'...

Have a listen to *The Tam O'Shanter Overture* — the poem that it's based on tells the story of Tam, who's making his way home from the pub when he comes across the devil and some dancing witches. When the witches notice him, they chase him until he escapes on his horse, Meg.

British Music — Britten and Maxwell Davies

You're part-way through the section on music from Britain — and coincidentally, part-way through the section on music by Britten as well. It's time to have a look at a couple of his pieces in a bit more detail.

Peter Grimes is an Opera by Britten

1) *Peter Grimes* was first performed in 1945. Britten composed the music, and Montagu Slater wrote the libretto (based on a poem written by George Crabbe in 1810). It tells the story of the title character, a fisherman who is shunned by the people of his town after the suspicious deaths of his two apprentices.

2) Britten later arranged the music used in between the acts into a suite called *Four Sea Interludes*: 'Dawn', 'Sunday Morning', 'Moonlight' and 'Storm'. All four interludes are very descriptive (for example, Britten uses horns playing in thirds to imitate church bells in 'Sunday Morning', and frantic low brass and strings to represent the fury of the storm in the fourth movement). All four movements have a sense of doom to reflect the overall mood of the opera.

War Requiem Was First Performed in 1962

1) A requiem is a mass for the dead (see p.103). Britten wrote his *War Requiem* for the opening of the new Coventry Cathedral (the old one was destroyed by a bomb in World War II).

2) He used Latin words from the Requiem Mass alongside war poems by Wilfred Owen (who was writing about World War I). Owen's poems, such as 'Anthem for Doomed Youth' and 'Futility', highlight the hopelessness of war.

3) Britten varies the instrumentation throughout — a soprano soloist is accompanied by a chorus and full orchestra, while a boys' choir is accompanied by an organ. A tenor and a baritone soloist (who sing the war poems) are accompanied by a chamber orchestra. These three groups are combined in the final section for maximum impact.

Peter Maxwell Davies Was Influenced by Different Genres

1) Sir Peter Maxwell Davies was born in Salford in 1934. He was knighted in 1987 and was made Master of the Queen's Music in 2004. He continued composing until his death in 2016.

2) Throughout his career, he explored many different styles of music — including medieval and Renaissance techniques (especially the use of plainsong, a monophonic chant) and serialism (he used sequences of both pitch and note length — see p.153). He was also influenced by expressionism:

> Expressionism is an early twentieth century artistic movement that followed Romanticism. Artists believed their works should express their inner feelings. To do this, they moved away from conventional forms which they felt were too restrictive. Expressionist music (such as some of Schoenberg's compositions) is characterised by intense emotions, angular, spiky melodies, dissonance and atonality.

3) He composed a large number of orchestral pieces, including ten symphonies and a number of concertos and string quartets.

There's more on Maxwell Davies on the next page.

4) He also wrote a variety of vocal works, such as the chamber opera *The Lighthouse* and the musical drama *Eight Songs for a Mad King*. This is a piece about the madness of King George III — it's written for a baritone and a chamber orchestra of six musicians (who are on stage with the singer and form part of the action).

I prefer the lesser-known 'Six Songs for a Mad GCSE Student'...

A lot of these pieces are 'programme music' — they 'tell a story'. Have a listen to some of the pieces, such as *Four Sea Interludes*, and see if you can pick out how the composer has portrayed the story using music.

British Music — Maxwell Davies and Tavener

You're nearly done with British composers — just a bit more on Peter Maxwell Davies, then a bit on John Tavener as well (not to be confused with the Renaissance composer John Taverner).

Peter Maxwell Davies Was **Inspired** by the **Orkney Islands**

1) Maxwell Davies moved to the <u>Orkney Islands</u> (off the north-eastern tip of <u>Scotland</u>) in the early 1970s. Many of his compositions from the 1970s onwards have <u>Scottish influences</u> (for example, the orchestral piece *An Orkney Wedding, with Sunrise* has a <u>bagpipe solo</u>).

2) He often had strong <u>political opinions</u> — which led him to write *Farewell to Stromness*:

- *Farewell to Stromness* is from a larger work called *The Yellow Cake Revue*, which Maxwell Davies composed in 1980 to <u>protest</u> against a potential <u>uranium mine</u> on Orkney.
- *The Yellow Cake Revue* is a collection of pieces for <u>piano</u> and <u>voice</u> — *Farewell to Stromness* is a <u>solo piano interlude</u>.

  'Yellowcake' is the powder taken from uranium ore.
- The piece is <u>slow</u> and <u>gentle</u>, with lilting <u>Scottish rhythms</u> that sound a bit like a <u>Scotch snap</u> (see p.17), though they're written differently.
- It starts with a steady <u>ostinato bass line</u> (see p.83) made up of crotchets — this is thought to represent people having to <u>leave their homes</u> after the mine opened.

John Tavener Wrote a Lot of **Religious** and **Vocal Music**

1) <u>Sir John Tavener</u> was born in London in <u>1944</u> and <u>died</u> in <u>2013</u>.

2) He came from a religious family, and much of his music has <u>religious influences</u>. In 1977, he converted to the <u>Russian Orthodox</u> church, which inspired some of his later music.

3) Whilst at school, Tavener sang in <u>choirs</u> — much of his work is <u>vocal music</u>. He achieved early success with *The Whale* — a <u>cantata</u> that tells the story of <u>Jonah and the whale</u>. A cantata is similar to an <u>oratorio</u>, with <u>arias</u> and <u>recitatives</u> (see p.86) but uses words from <u>books</u> or <u>poems</u>.

4) His *Song for Athene*, a piece for <u>SATB choir</u>, was performed at the <u>funeral</u> of <u>Princess Diana</u> in 1997.

5) Some of his choral works are settings of <u>poems</u> by <u>William Blake</u> — including *The Lamb* (see below).

6) He wrote some <u>instrumental</u> music too — such as *The Protecting Veil*, a piece for <u>cello</u> and <u>strings</u>.

The Lamb is Often Sung at **Christmas**

The Lamb is a <u>four-part choral piece</u>, based on the <u>poem</u> of the same name from <u>William Blake's</u> *Songs of Innocence* (a collection of poems). It was written for Tavener's <u>three-year-old nephew</u>.

- The <u>score</u> for *The Lamb* is <u>unusual</u>, as it has <u>no time signature</u> and <u>no bar lines</u> (bars are indicated by <u>dotted lines</u>, like in <u>traditional plainsong</u> (see p.85).
- The piece is <u>slow</u> and <u>gentle</u> — the <u>melody</u> is quite <u>simple</u>, and made up of just a few notes.
- It's written for an <u>SATB choir</u> singing <u>a cappella</u>, which adds to the <u>gentle</u>, <u>simple</u> feel. It is <u>quiet</u> throughout (the dynamics range from **pp** to **mp**).
- Tavener creates <u>contrast</u> by varying the <u>texture</u> of the voices — at the beginning, the voices are in <u>unison</u>, then the second part enters in <u>contrary motion</u> (where one part goes <u>up</u> as the other goes <u>down</u>). Finally, all four parts sing in <u>parallel harmony</u> (see p.45).
- In the section in contrary motion, the second part is singing an <u>inversion</u> of the first part (see p.83). This creates <u>dissonance</u>.

Say Farewell to the British composers...

There's a lot of detail about different pieces on the British music pages. Write down the names of the pieces, then shut the book and note down as much info about them as you can...

Kodály and Bartók

Kodály and Bartók were Hungarian composers. They lived around the same time and they were both interested in folk music, but their music is quite different. You need to know about their orchestral music.

Kodály and Bartók Collected Folk Tunes

Kodály was interested in music education — he created a method for learning music.

1) Zoltán Kodály lived from 1882-1967 and Béla Bartók lived from 1881-1945.

2) Like many early 20th century composers, Kodály and Bartók continued the Romantic trend of expressing their national identity by using folk music in their work. Kodály encouraged Bartók's interest in the genre, and together they collected lots of Eastern European folk tunes.

3) They helped establish ethnomusicology — the study of music from different cultures.

4) Bartók is known for his *Concerto for Orchestra*, *Divertimento* and *Piano Concerto No.3*.

5) Kodály also wrote a *Concerto for Orchestra*. His other well-known works include *Psalmus Hungaricus* (a work for tenor solo, choir and orchestra), the *Háry János Suite* and his *Symphony in C*.

Kodály Mixed Hungarian Folk With Western Classical Music

1) Elements of Hungarian folk music can be seen in much of Kodály's work.

> Hungarian folk melodies are often based on pentatonic scales (see p.27). The texture tends to be homophonic, with a clear melody above an accompaniment. The music often contains contrasting slow and fast sections. Dotted rhythms are a distinctive feature.

2) Kodály also took inspiration from Debussy's impressionist music, and introduced Bartók to it.

> Like impressionist art, impressionist music creates an overall impression or mood, rather than focusing on details. Impressionist composers created different timbres or 'colours' by experimenting with new playing techniques and using contrasting combinations of instruments. They moved away from large-scale pieces (such as symphonies) towards smaller works. The tonality tended to be ambiguous, with dissonant harmonies and unusual extended chords.

Kodály was more influenced by the impressionist use of different timbres than the harmony — his music tends to be tonal. Bartók was more experimental with tonality (see next page).

Kodály's Háry János Suite has Elements of Hungarian Folk

The **Háry János Suite** is a set of six orchestral pieces from Kodály's comic opera of the same name.

- A large percussion section is used — including a celesta (which sounds a bit like a glockenspiel), tubular bells and a cimbalom. The cimbalom is a Hungarian instrument that's played by hitting its horizontal strings with sticks. The use of contrasting percussion creates lots of 'colour' in the piece — an impressionist feature.

- The dramatic crescendo to a chord at the start of the first movement represents a sneeze — this refers to the Hungarian belief that a story beginning with a sneeze shouldn't be taken seriously.

- The fifth movement ('Intermezzo') involves fast, virtuosic cimbalom playing, a rich string sound, variations in tempo, and syncopation — these are all typical of Hungarian folk music.

Kodály's **Dances of Galánta** includes lots of elements of folk music.

- *Dances of Galánta* is based on a Hungarian style called 'verbunkos' — this started out in the 18th and 19th centuries as dance music used by the army to encourage people to join up.

- The piece is in rondo form (see p.93), with a slow andante maestoso section returning in between faster sections. This slow-fast format is also a feature of the verbunkos style.

- The clarinet has an important part — it has a cadenza in the first movement. It's imitating a type of woodwind instrument called a tárogató, which is often used in Hungarian folk music.

Kodály and Bartók

Like Kodály, Bartók included elements of folk music in much of his work, but he also tried out new ideas.

Bartók's Music Was More Experimental Than Kodály's

1) In the twentieth century, some composers moved away from traditional forms of harmony and structure.

- Composers in the late Romantic period often used so many chromatic notes that the music began to lose the character of the main key. A lot of early twentieth century music was atonal (p.26).
- Classical forms (see p.91-93) relied on fixed keys to create contrast between different sections. Now fixed keys were gone, traditional structures were used less frequently.

2) Bartók experimented with these ideas. He often didn't use key signatures — he used accidentals (see p.11) instead. Sometimes he made up his own key signatures, e.g. one with a C♯ but no F♯.

3) Some of his pieces frequently change time signature, and use unusual time signatures such as $\frac{4+2+3}{8}$.

4) Like other modern composers, he experimented with using instruments in new ways. A type of pizzicato, where the string is lifted vertically and released to give a snapping sound, is named after him. You can hear it in the third movement of his *Divertimento for Strings*.

5) Bartók shared Kodály's interest in Eastern European folk music, but he also took inspiration from further afield — his *String Quartet No. 2* was influenced by folk music from North Africa.

Bartók's Concerto for Orchestra Mixes Old and New

The 1943 work **Concerto for Orchestra** was one of the last pieces Bartók wrote. Each section of the orchestra is given a chance to shine — hence the name. It has many of the features described above.

- Although *Concerto for Orchestra* has a non-standard five-movement structure, the first and last movements make use of sonata form (see p.92), used in classical concertos.
- It has simple, folk-like melodies. An oboe tune in the fourth movement is based on just 4 notes.
- The time signature often changes — the start of the fourth movement switches between $\frac{2}{4}$ and $\frac{5}{8}$.
- The tonality is ambiguous — there's no key signature in the first movement. There's lots of dissonance — near the start, the cellos and double basses play a C♯ against a C♮ in the violas.
- The timpani have a chromatic line, requiring them to retune quickly to be able to play the notes.

Some of Bartók's music was more influenced by folk music than by 20th century classical music. His **Romanian Folk Dances for Orchestra** are a good example of this.

- Each movement is based on a Romanian folk tune. The melodies are clear, with a simple accompaniment and harmony. The music is much more tonal than *Concerto for Orchestra*.
- In the second movement, the tempo changes frequently — a feature of Hungarian folk music.

Bartók's **Divertimento** for string orchestra has elements of Baroque, Classical and folk music.

- It features five soloists along with a string orchestra — like a Baroque concerto grosso (see p.81).
- It uses Classical structures — sonata form in the first movement and rondo form in the third.
- Despite this, it has a modern feel. The first movement features loud, dissonant chords, and frequently switches between $\frac{6}{8}$ and $\frac{9}{8}$. The syncopated rhythms are a folk influence.
- The second movement is sombre. The timbre is varied using mutes and harmonics (see p.64).
- In the third movement, the solo first violin plays a folk-influenced cadenza (see p.57).

'Kodály' is pronounced 'cod-eye'. 'Bartók' is pronounced... 'Bartok'.

Have a listen to Bartók's and Kodály's music to see if you can hear the differences and similarities.

Minimalism

Minimalist music is music that changes a <u>small subtle bit</u> at a time. It's all about slow, gradual changes.

Minimalism Builds Music out of Repeated Patterns

1) Minimalism is a <u>Western art music</u> style that developed during the <u>1960s</u> and <u>1970s</u>.

2) It was a <u>reaction</u> against twentieth century styles such as <u>expressionism</u> (see p.155) and <u>serialism</u> (see p.153) which were <u>atonal</u>, <u>dissonant</u> and <u>complex</u>. <u>Minimalism</u> was a return to more <u>basic concepts</u> — minimalist composers constructed their music from <u>simple</u> note or rhythm <u>patterns</u>, known as <u>cells</u>.

3) The cells are continuously <u>repeated</u>, with occasional <u>slight</u> changes. They're <u>layered</u> on top of each other, so although the individual cells tend to be <u>short</u> and <u>simple</u>, the music can sound <u>complicated</u>.

4) There's often <u>no clear melody</u>. Harmony is created by <u>layering</u> patterns on top of each other. It develops <u>gradually</u> — there are no sudden changes.

5) In contrast to the atonality of serialism, minimalism is usually <u>diatonic</u>. <u>Broken chords</u> are often used to form cells. <u>Common chords</u> (chords shared between <u>multiple keys</u>) are also used.

6) <u>Rhythm</u> is important — some minimalist pieces are <u>purely rhythmic</u>, e.g. *Clapping Music* (see p.162).

Minimalism Uses Musical Ideas from All Over the World

Minimalist composers often borrowed ideas from <u>other countries</u> and <u>cultures</u>.

Minimalism is Often Used in Film Music

1) The short <u>cells</u> of music used in minimalism can work well as <u>leitmotifs</u> in films (see p.121).

2) Minimalism works well as a way of gradually <u>developing</u> a film's atmosphere <u>over time</u>.

3) <u>Film music</u> often involves <u>repetition</u> (a feature of minimalism) — a gradual <u>crescendo</u> through a repeated bit of music is a great way of <u>increasing tension</u>.

4) Even film music that <u>doesn't</u> 'sound minimalist' can have <u>minimalist elements</u>. For example, the '<u>Chariots of Fire</u>' theme features a <u>constant pulse</u> throughout to represent the characters <u>running</u>.

- <u>Michael Nyman</u> and <u>Philip Glass</u> are <u>minimalist composers</u> who have written lots of <u>film scores</u>.
- Philip Glass composed for the film *The Hours*. The film is set in <u>three different time periods</u>, but Glass's music gives it a sense of <u>whole</u> using <u>repetition</u> and <u>layering</u>.

Minimalism

Minimalist composers use different techniques to bring about gradual changes in their music.

The Cells Change Gradually

There are different ways of changing the cell patterns, as well as the way they fit together. These changes can happen every time the patterns are repeated, or after the same pattern has been repeated a few times.

Gradually adding or taking away notes

The pattern is changed by adding a single note — this is called additive melody.
Another similar idea is to replace one note with a rest, or one rest with a note.

Gradually changing the notes of the pattern

This technique's called metamorphosis — another word for 'changing'.
Small changes to one note, or one bit of the rhythm, are made to the pattern.

The changes often go full circle — the pattern ends up the same or nearly the same as it was at the start.

Adding or removing notes or rests

Two or more performers start with the same pattern.
A note or rest is added or taken away from one of the parts.
They move gradually out of sync and then gradually back in. This is known as phase shifting.

Layering patterns of different lengths together

Cells of different lengths, e.g. a 4-beat cell and a 5-beat cell, are played at the same time.
This has a similar effect to phase-shifting — the patterns move apart then come back together.

4-beat cell

5-beat cell

Music Technology Plays a Big Part in Minimalism

1) Minimalist composers often use music technology to create continuously repeating cells called loops.

2) Composers used to create loops by recording music (or other sounds) onto tape, carefully cutting the bit of tape that contained the music they needed, and sticking the ends together to create a physical loop that could be played continuously. Modern sequencers (p.72) make this process much easier.

3) The different loops are recorded, one on top of another, using multi-track recording (see p.72). This helps create the layered sound of minimalism.

4) The layers can be edited to achieve different effects. For example, two identical loops can be played at the same time but at two slightly different speeds — this effect is another form of phase-shifting.

5) Live performances of minimalist music are often accompanied by recorded backing tracks (p.162).

Riley, Reich and Adams

Terry Riley, Steve Reich and John Adams have all used minimalism in their work.

Riley's In C was One of the First Minimalist Pieces

1) Terry Riley was born in 1935 in the USA — he is one of the founders of minimalism.
2) His influences include jazz (p.131-132) and Indian classical music
   — he studied in India with the singer Pran Nath.
3) Riley's work In C is one of the best-known early minimalist pieces. His other famous works include
   A Rainbow in Curved Air, Uncle Jard and Salome Dances for Peace (a set of five string quartets).

Riley's Compositions Are Quite Varied

- In C can be played by any combination of instruments and/or voices.
- It's made up of 53 cells. The cells are numbered and should be played in order, but each performer can choose how many times they repeat each cell. Some cells are only one quaver in length, but others are much longer. The layering of the cells creates polyrhythm (see p.14).
- Constant C quavers keep the piece together and give it a strong, driving rhythm.
- To finish, all the performers repeat the 53rd pattern together, then each stops when they're ready.

- A Rainbow in Curved Air is different from In C. Terry Riley performed it by recording each track and then layering them over each other. It has three movements.
- The piece is based on repeated cells of music, but also has more 'traditional' melodic lines.
- It uses a variety of instruments to explore different timbres and textures — it features an electric organ, electric harpsichord, a tambourine and a doumbek (a goblet-shaped drum).

- Uncle Jard shows the influences of jazz, blues and Indian classical music on Riley's work.
- In the first movement, influences from Indian music are seen in the modal tonality, singing style and drones (played by saxophones). A harpsichord imitates a sitar (an Indian string instrument).
- In the second movement, syncopated and swung rhythms played on the saxophone and piano create a jazz feel. Riley sings blues-style lyrics over the top (see p.130).
- Salome Dances for Peace has these influences, as well as elements of Western classical music.
- It's more melodic than Riley's early music, but still has minimalist features. It has repeated cells of music which are layered over each other, e.g. in the Ceremonial Night Race section.

Reich was Influenced by Riley

1) Steve Reich is an American composer who was born in 1936.
2) He did a degree in Philosophy, then studied composition with the experimental composer Luciano Berio. He tried writing serial music (see p.153), but preferred composing tonal pieces.
3) Reich began writing minimalist music, and was influenced by Terry Riley's compositions.
4) His works are also influenced by jazz, music from sub-Saharan Africa (especially drumming — see p.133), Balinese gamelan (tuned percussion music from Indonesia) and Middle Eastern singing.
5) Some of his best-known works are Clapping Music, Electric Counterpoint and Different Trains.

You could try composing a minimalist piece...

...and impress the examiners with something different. However, though minimalist music is repetitive, it's not easy to write — all the cells have to work together and the piece needs shape.

Riley, Reich and Adams

Let's have a look at some of Reich's music in a bit more detail.

Reich Wrote a Piece Based Only on Rhythm

1) Reich's _Clapping Music_ is written for two performers who clap throughout the piece.
   - It's made up of one rhythm. The first player claps this rhythm throughout the piece. The second player claps the same rhythm, but after twelve repetitions they shift so they're one quaver behind.
   - This happens every twelve repetitions until the players end up in sync again. This is a good example of phase-shifting.

2) _Electric Counterpoint_ is for a solo guitarist accompanied by a 14-piece guitar ensemble.
   - It has three movements. For live performances, the solo guitarist often plays along with a recording of the ensemble parts made before the performance.
   - The movements don't have titles — they're just marked ♩ = 192, ♩ = 96 and ♩ = 192. People tend to call them 'Fast', 'Slow' and 'Fast'. The middle movement's half the speed of the others, so there's a constant pulse. There should be no breaks between the movements.
   - It's made up of short cells that are repeated lots of times.
   - Because the guitars all have a similar sound, the timbre (see p.74) doesn't really change. This means the parts all blend together.

   Different Trains is one of Reich's best-known works. It was written as a reaction to the Holocaust. It uses samples of people talking about train journeys, then imitates their voices with instruments.

John Adams Uses Minimalist Elements

1) John Adams was also born in the USA, in 1947. He is a composer and conductor.

2) Adams' work is influenced by minimalism, but elements of pop and jazz are also incorporated into his compositions. Some of his pieces are more recognisably minimalist than others.

3) His orchestral works include _Harmonielehre_, _Shaker Loops_ and _Short Ride in a Fast Machine_.

4) Adams has also written a number of operas. Some of these deal with political issues — _Nixon in China_ is about the US President Richard Nixon's visit to China in 1972 and _Doctor Atomic_ is about the construction of the first atomic bomb.

Adams Uses Music to Paint a Picture

- _Shaker Loops_ was originally written as a string quartet called _Wavemaker_. It features lots of tremolo, which represents ripples on water.

- Adams rewrote it and changed it into a string septet (though it can also be played by a string orchestra). The shaking action used to create tremolo inspired the name _Shaker Loops_.

- It features lots of repetition of short cells of music, and it's tonal.

- It becomes rhythmically complex as different instruments enter, adding more layers.

- _Short Ride in a Fast Machine_ was inspired by a ride Adams had in a sports car.

- The woodblock plays crotchets throughout almost the whole piece — a constant pulse is often a feature of minimalist pieces. The rest of the orchestra is forced to keep up, creating a sense of the tension involved in travelling at high speed. When the pulse stops, the orchestra feels freer.

- The brass play a key role, with some fanfare-like sections. The strings are also important, and combine with a variety of percussion and woodwind to create a number of different timbres. The orchestra is large — it features thirteen different types of percussion.

- Although it has repeated cells, the piece changes quite rapidly. It lasts less than five minutes.

Warm-up and Exam Questions

Well, that was a whistle-stop tour through twentieth century styles of music. Try these warm-up questions to get yourself in the zone, and then have a go at the exam-style questions.

Warm-up Questions

1) Where is the ballet *Rodeo* set?

2) Give one feature of a waltz.

3) What is the main time signature used in 'Hoe-Down'?

4) What is a tone row?

5) Name two musical genres which influence Malcom Arnold's music.

6) For which occasion was Britten's *War Requiem* written?

7) Describe two features of expressionism.

8) Name a piece by John Tavener.

9) Describe three features of Hungarian folk music.

10) Give two ways in which Bartók was experimental in his composing.

11) In minimalist music, what are cells?

12) Give two ways in which cells can be varied to create gradual change in a minimalist piece.

13) Name two pieces by Terry Riley.

14) Which composition by Steve Reich is based only on rhythm?

15) Which technique creates the 'shaking' in *Shaker Loops*?

Exam Questions

Have a go at these exam-style questions.

Track 37 is an excerpt from 'Hoe-Down' by Aaron Copland.

Play the excerpt **four** times. Leave a short pause between each playing.

a) What are the violins playing in the first section of the excerpt?
Circle the correct answer.

the melody   **offbeat chords**   **constant quavers**   **downbeat crotchets**

[1 mark]

b) What effect is created by the percussion in the first section of the excerpt?

....

[1 mark]

Exam Questions

c)   Name **two** percussion instruments that play in the excerpt.

....

....

[2 marks]

d)   Explain how contrast between the first and second sections of the excerpt is achieved.
You might want to mention the following musical features:
 •   Instrumentation
 •   Rhythm
 •   Texture

....

....

....

....

....

....

....

....

....

....

[8 marks]

e)   What is the tonality of the second section?

....

[1 mark]

f)   The melody in the second section is based on a folk tune.
Describe **two** elements which give a folk-like sound to this section.

....

....

[2 marks]

Exam Questions

Track 38 is an excerpt from 'Sunday Morning' by Benjamin Britten.
Play the excerpt **four** times. Leave a short pause between each playing.

(Track 38)

a) List **three** differences between the horn and the string parts at the start of this excerpt.

....

....

....
(3 marks)

b) Circle the word that best describes the harmony provided by the horns.

dissonance   **unison**   **consonance**   **suspension**
(1 mark)

c) About halfway through the excerpt, the violins and woodwind play a descending scale. What type of scale is it?

....
(1 mark)

d) After this scale, the mood of the excerpt changes.
Describe **three** ways in which this change of mood is achieved.

....

....

....

....
(3 marks)

Revision Summary for Section Nine

This section contains lots of detail about many different composers, their pieces and the different styles of music they used. You need to make sure you've got it all clear in your head, so have a go at these summary questions. If there are any questions you can't answer the first time round, read through the section again and have another go. Keep doing this until you can answer every question correctly.

1) Give two ways in which Aaron Copland created an American feel in his music.

2) Who is the main character in *Rodeo*?

3) What string technique is used at the start of 'Saturday Night Waltz'?

4) What is the texture of 'Saturday Night Waltz' like?

5) Describe the instrumentation in 'Saturday Night Waltz'.

6) Describe the dynamics in 'Saturday Night Waltz'.

7) Name the Irish folk tune used in 'Hoe-Down'.

8) i) What is the overall form of 'Hoe-Down'?
   ii) Write out the full structure of 'Hoe-Down'.

9) Describe two features of the 'Bonaparte's Retreat' section of 'Hoe-Down'.

10) Give two ways in which a tone row can be rearranged.

11) Describe the tonality of serialist music.

12) What is verticalisation?

13) Name one feature of Malcom Arnold's Clarinet Concerto No. 2 that is typical of a concerto.

14) Name the opera by Benjamin Britten that is about a fisherman.

15) The lyrics for Britten's *War Requiem* come from two sources. What are they?

16) Give three details about the instrumentation in *War Requiem*.

17) Why did Peter Maxwell Davies write *The Yellowcake Revue*?

18) In *The Yellowcake Revue*, what does the bass line represent?

19) What is a cantata?

20) How does John Tavener create contrast in *The Lamb*?

21) Give three features of impressionist music.

22) What is the name of the Hungarian instrument used in the *Háry János Suite*?

23) What does the crescendo at the start of Zoltán Kodály's *Háry János Suite* represent?

24) Describe the form of *Dances of Galánta*.

25) Describe the unusual type of pizzicato used in Béla Bartók's *Divertimento for Strings*.

26) Describe the tonality in Bartók's *Concerto for Orchestra*.

27) In what way is Bartók's *Divertimento for Strings* similar to a concerto grosso?

28) What tonality do minimalist pieces tend to have?

29) i) Where does gamelan music come from?
   ii) Which feature of gamelan is used in minimalist music?

30) How many cells is Terry Riley's *In C* made up of?

31) Describe two elements of Indian classical music used in the first movement of Riley's *Uncle Jard*.

32) Name two musical genres which influenced Steve Reich's music.

33) For which instrument is Reich's *Electric Counterpoint* written?

34) Name an opera written by John Adams.

35) How is the idea of travelling at high speed created in Adams' *Short Ride in a Fast Machine*?

General Certificate of Secondary Education

GCSE
Music

Listening
and Contextual
Understanding Exam

Surname	
Other names	

Time allowed: 1 hour 30 minutes

Instructions
- Write in black ink or ballpoint pen.
- Answer the questions in the spaces provided.
- Answer **all 8** questions in Section A.
- In Section B, answer **Question 9** and **one** of Questions 10-12.
- Give all the information you are asked for, and write neatly.
- Do all rough work in this book. Cross through any work you do not want marked.

Information
- The marks are shown by each question.
- The maximum mark for this paper is 96.
- There are 68 marks available in Section A and 28 marks available in Section B.
- For each question in Section A, you will need to play one or more tracks from the CD. You will be told how many times to play each track.
- You do **not** need to listen to any tracks for Section B.
- Read through the question before you play the track(s).
- Leave a gap between each playing to give yourself time to write.

Instructions for playing the CD:
- There are 8 questions in Section A, covered on the CD by tracks 39-48.

Question No.	1	2	3	4	5	6	7	8
CD Track No.	39, 40	41	42	43	44	45, 46	47	48

- Leave 3 minutes at the start to read through the exam.
- Play the CD, one track at a time, stopping the CD after each track.
- Each question will tell you how many times the track should be repeated.
- Allow a short pause between each playing for writing time.
  After the final playing of each track, allow some time for writing.

Section A: Listening

60 minutes

68 marks

Answer **all** the questions in Section A

1   Area of Study 1: Western classical tradition 1650-1910   9 marks

For this question, there are two excerpts, track 39 and track 40.

Play each track **three** times.

Track 39

a) What type of vocal ensemble is performing this piece? Circle the correct answer.

    Male voice choir   SATB choir   Octet   SSA choir

(1 mark)

b) i)   Suggest a suitable occasion for the performance of this piece.

    ....

(1 mark)

   ii)   Identify **two** features of the excerpt that make it suitable for this occasion.

    ....

    ....

(2 marks)

c) What is the cadence heard at the end of this excerpt?

    ....

(1 mark)

Track 40

d) What instrument is playing at the start of the excerpt?

    ....

(1 mark)

e) This excerpt is from a concerto. What is the name of the part
of the concerto heard in the first section of the excerpt?

    ....

(1 mark)

f) i) To which period of Western classical music history does this piece belong?

....

(1 mark)

ii) Give **one** reason for your answer to part i).

....

....

(1 mark)

2   Area of Study 2: Popular music   9 marks
    Play the track **four** times.

(Track 41)

a) i)   What is the tonality at the start of this excerpt (the 'la la la' section)?
        Circle the correct answer.

        major   minor   pentatonic   atonal

                                                                        (1 mark)

   ii) The bars are numbered from the start of the excerpt, which is in $\frac{4}{4}$.
        The first section of this excerpt is based around two main chords.
        Write X in the bars which use the first chord,
        and Y in the bars which use the second chord.

1	2	3	4

5	6	7	8

                                                                        (4 marks)

b) Name **two** electronic effects heard in the vocal part of this excerpt.

   ....

   ....
                                                                        (2 marks)

c) This song features hooks. Identify **one** of these hooks and explain
   what is meant by a hook.

   ....

   ....
                                                                        (2 marks)

3   Area of Study 3: Traditional music   8 marks
Play the track **four** times.

(Track 42)

a) What type of bass line is used in this excerpt?

....

(1 mark)

b) The tonic chord of this piece is D major. Which chord is heard in bar 5?

....

(1 mark)

c) In which bar of this excerpt does the vocalist first say "yeah"?

....

(1 mark)

d) Which vocal technique can be heard when the word 'low' is sung in the third line?
Circle the correct answer.

       falsetto   portamento   belting   scat

(1 mark)

e) i)   To which genre of music does this excerpt belong?

....

(1 mark)

ii)   Identify **three** features of the excerpt that are typical of this genre.

....

....

....

(3 marks)

Turn over

4 Area of Study 4: Western classical tradition since 1910   7 marks
Play the track **four** times.

(**Track 43**)

a) Suggest a suitable tempo for this excerpt.

....
(1 mark)

b) Suggest a suitable composer for this piece.

....
(1 mark)

This is the melody of the first eight bars of the excerpt.

c) Add phrase marks to the excerpt.

(2 marks)

d) In the first seven bars, on which beat of the bar can pizzicato be heard?

....
(1 mark)

e) Circle the word that best describes the texture of the excerpt.

   antiphonal   contrapuntal   homophonic   heterophonic
(1 mark)

f) What family of instruments is playing in this excerpt?

....
(1 mark)

5 Area of Study 1: Western classical tradition 1650-1910   9 marks
Play the track **four** times.

Track 44

a) Which period of Western classical music history does this piece come from?

....

(1 mark)

b) Fill in the missing notes in bars 2-3 on the score below,
   using the rhythm given above the stave.

(6 marks)

c) Describe the tonality of this excerpt.

....

....

(2 marks)

6 Area of Study 2: Popular music   11 marks

For this question, there are two excerpts, track 45 and track 46.

Play each track **three** times.

Track 45

a) After the opening section, the main theme is heard. What is the interval between the triplet and the minim at the start of this theme? Circle the correct answer.

    octave   perfect fifth   perfect fourth   major sixth

(1 mark)

b) i)   Which instrument plays the main theme the first time it is heard?

    ....

(1 mark)

   ii)   Name a percussion instrument heard in this excerpt.

    ....

(1 mark)

c) Circle two words that describe the string melody when they have the tune.

    staccato   legato   conjunct   disjunct   sforzando

(2 marks)

Track 46

d) This music is for a game in which the player has to carry out a heroic quest to save the world. Describe **two** features of this excerpt that make it suitable for this purpose.

    ....

    ....

(2 marks)

e) The bars are numbered from the start of the excerpt. The excerpt is in $\frac{4}{4}$ time. Read each statement below and put letters in the appropriate boxes to show where each feature is heard.

- Write the letter A in the bar in which triplets are first heard.
- Write the letter B in the bar in which a flute is heard.
- Write the letter C in the bar in which the main theme begins.
- Write the letter D in the two bars where the melody has the same rhythm as in bars 11 and 12.

1	2	3	4	5	6	7	8

9	10	11	12	13	14	15	16

(4 marks)

Turn over

7   Area of Study 3: Traditional music   7 marks
        Play the track **four** times.

(Track 47)

a) From which region of the world does this style of music originate?
   Circle the correct answer.

   Latin America   Africa   Middle East   Caribbean

(1 mark)

b) Which of these rhythms shows the main beat or pulse in the first half of this excerpt?
   Tick the box next to the correct answer.

(1 mark)

c) About halfway through the excerpt, the music changes.
   Describe the rhythmic differences between the two sections.

   ....

   ....

   ....

   ....

(3 marks)

d) The title of this piece is 'Carnivale'. Identify two features of this excerpt
   that make it suitable for a carnival.

   ....

   ....

   ....

(2 marks)

8   Area of Study 4: Western classical tradition since 1910   8 marks
Play the track **four** times.

(Track 48)

a) Suggest a suitable dynamic marking for this excerpt.

....
(1 mark)

b) Describe the rhythm at the beginning of the excerpt.

....
(1 mark)

c) i)   To which genre of 20th century classical music does this piece belong?

....
(1 mark)

ii)   Describe the features of this excerpt that are typical of this genre.

....

....

....

....

....

....

....

....

....
(5 marks)

Section B: Contextual Understanding

30 minutes
28 marks
Answer **Question 9**

9   Area of Study 1: Western classical tradition 1650-1910
     This question is about the second movement of Haydn's Symphony No. 101.

a) Explain why this symphony is known as the 'Clock' symphony.

....

....

....

(2 marks)

b) Describe **two** features of the second movement of this symphony
   that are typical of a Classical symphony.

....

....

(2 marks)

c) Identify the two main keys used in this movement,
   and describe the relationship between them.

....

....

(2 marks)

d) Explain how Haydn varies the first theme (first heard in bars 2-10)
   throughout this movement.

....

....

....

....

....

....

....Turn over...

....

....

....

....

(8 marks)

180

Answer **one** of Questions 10-12

10   Area of Study 2: Popular music

a) i)   *Sgt. Pepper's Lonely Hearts Club Band* is an example of a concept album.
Explain what is meant by a concept album.

....

....
(1 mark)

ii)   Identify **two** features of 'With A Little Help From My Friends'
that show that it forms part of a concept album.

....

....

....
(2 marks)

b) i)   Name **two** Indian instruments that are played in 'Within You Without You'.

....

....
(2 marks)

ii)   Name **one** Western instrument that is played in 'Within You Without You'.

....
(1 mark)

c)   'Lucy In The Sky With Diamonds' is an example of psychedelia.
Explain how The Beatles have created a surreal atmosphere in this song.

....

....

....

....

....

....

....

....

....

....

....

(8 marks)

11 Area of Study 3: Traditional music

a) Describe **two** ways in which 'Migra' is made to sound like a protest.

....

....

(2 marks)

b) Identify **two** genres which influenced 'Love of my Life'.

....

....

(2 marks)

c) Describe **two** features used to make the second half
   of 'Love of my Life' sound lively and upbeat.

....

....

(2 marks)

d) 'Smooth' is a fusion of rock and Latin American music.
   Identify features from both genres which are present in 'Smooth'.

....

....

....

....

....

....

....

....

....

....

....

(8 marks)

12   Area of Study 4: Western classical tradition since 1910

a) Describe **one** feature of 'Saturday Night Waltz' that is **not** typical of a waltz.

....

....

(1 mark)

b) *Rodeo* is a ballet set on a ranch. Identify **two** features of
'Hoe-Down' which give an impression of this setting.

....

....

....

(2 marks)

c) Describe the differences in instrumentation
between 'Hoe-Down' and 'Saturday Night Waltz'.

....

....

....

....

(3 marks)

d) Explain how Copland creates a gentle, subdued mood in 'Saturday Night Waltz'.
You may wish to refer to tempo, dynamics, texture and any other musical features.

....

....

....

....

....

....

....

....

....

....

....

(8 marks)

END OF TEST

Answers

Section Two — Reading and Writing Music

Page 15 (Warm-up Questions)

1)

2) A sharp sign raises the pitch of the note (and other notes of the same pitch later in the bar) by one semitone.
A flat sign lowers the pitch of the note (and other notes of the same pitch later in the bar) by one semitone.
A natural sign cancels out a flat or sharp sign in the key signature or earlier on in the bar.

3)

4) Three beats

5) In simple time, the main beats are divided into 2, 4, 8, etc. but in compound time the beats are divided into 3, 6, 9, etc.

6) Regular, irregular and free

Page 15 (Exam Question)

Track 1

a)

(1 mark for each correct note or correct interval between two adjacent notes, up to 8 marks)

b) *(1 mark)*

c) *(1 mark)*

d)

(up to 3 marks, one for each different feature identified)

Page 21 (Warm-up Questions)

1) (semibreve)

2)

3) Dotted crotchet, one and a half beats
Quaver, half a beat
Dotted minim, three beats

4) A tie joins two or more notes of the same pitch together. A slur joins two or more notes of different pitch together.

5) Presto, allegro, moderato, andante, largo

Pages 21-22 (Exam Question)

Track 2

a) dotted notes *(1 mark)*

b) allegro *(1 mark)*

c) forte *(1 mark)*

d) energico *(1 mark)*

Section Three — Keys, Scales and Chords

Page 31 (Practice Questions)

Track 10 a) natural minor b) melodic minor
c) whole tone d) major

Track 11 Pentatonic (major isn't wrong, but pentatonic is more accurate)

Track 12 a) unison b) perfect 5th c) major 3rd
d) minor 3rd e) major 7th f) perfect 4th
g) minor 6th h) augmented 4th/ diminished 5th

Track 13 a) minor 2nd b) major 3rd c) perfect 4th
d) octave e) major 6th f) perfect 5th
g) minor 7th h) major 2nd

Page 32 (Warm-up Questions)

1) Eight

2) They tell you what sharps or flats to play.

3) They are relative scales – they have the same notes/ same key signature.

4) Natural, harmonic and melodic

5) Major pentatonic

6) It includes every white and black note on a keyboard.

7) A harmonic interval.

8) Diminished 7th

Pages 32-33 (Exam Question)

Track 14

a) i) Four *(1 mark)*
ii) Perfect fourth *(1 mark)*
iii) Minor third/augmented second *(1 mark)*

b) C♯ minor *(1 mark)*

c) Tenuto — played full length or longer *(1 mark)*

Page 40 (Practice Questions)

Track 17 a) major b) minor c) major
d) augmented e) minor f) diminished
g) diminished h) minor

Track 18 a) root   b) 2nd   c) root
          d) 2nd   e) 1st   f) 2nd
          g) root   h) root

Pages 49-50 (Practice Questions)

Track 21 a) perfect   b) plagal   c) interrupted
          d) imperfect   e) interrupted   f) perfect
          g) imperfect   h) perfect

Track 22 a)
          b) first inversion
          c) plagal

Track 23 a)
          b) homophonic
          c) perfect
          d) A

Track 24 a)
          b) F sharp
          c) interrupted

Track 25 a)
          b) (see above)
          c) Relative minor

Track 26 a)
          b) E flat major
          c) G minor
          d) pivot chord
          e) V, III

Page 51 (Warm-up Questions)

1) e.g. piano, guitar
2) I, IV and V or tonic, subdominant, dominant
3) First inversion
4) Block chords, rhythmic chords, broken / arpeggiated chords
5) Diatonic
6) Any three of the following: auxiliary notes, passing notes, appoggiaturas, suspensions, trills or other sensible answer.
7) In the middle of a piece, or at the end of any phrase except the last phrase.
8) Contrapuntal

Pages 51-52 (Exam Question)

Track 27
    a) Piano *(1 mark)*
    b) Alberti bass / broken chords / arpeggios *(1 mark)*
    c) Imperfect *(1 mark)*
    d) G major *(1 mark)*
    e) Accidental *(1 mark)*
    f) Staccato *(1 mark)*
    g) Homophonic *(1 mark)*

Section Four — Structure and Form

Page 59 (Warm-up Questions)

1) *Conjunct* — melodies move mainly by step. Notes are a major 2nd (a tone) or a semitone apart.
    Disjunct — melodies have a lot of jumps. Notes are more than a major 2nd apart.
    Triadic — melodies made up of the three notes in a triad.
    Scalic — melody moves up and down the notes of a scale.
2) A form where each verse has different music.
3) A repeated bass part, usually four or eight bars long that is played by the left hand on the piano or harpsichord, or by cello and double bass in an orchestra.

Pages 59-60 (Exam Questions)

Track 28
    a) i) G major *(1 mark)*
       ii) Minor third *(1 mark)*
    b) Call and response/question and answer *(1 mark)*
    c) A *(1 mark)*

Track 29
    a) Baroque period *(1 mark)*
    b) Oboe, bassoon, violin, viola, harpsichord. *(1 mark for each instrument, up to 2 marks)*
    c) i)

    (1 mark for each correct note or correct interval between two adjacent notes, up to 7 marks)
       ii) Conjunct *(1 mark)*
    d) Basso continuo *(1 mark)*
    e) Bassoon / Harpsichord *(1 mark)*

Section Five — Instruments

Page 76 (Warm-up Questions)

1) E.g. slide — trombone
   Single reed — clarinet or saxophone
   Double reed — oboe or bassoon
   Pizzicato — violin, viola, cello, double bass
   Wooden bars — xylophone

2) *Tremolo* — trembling sound on string instrument (fast, short, light strokes with the bow). Guitars can also produce this type of sound.
   Con sordino — 'with mute', mute placed on the bridge of string instruments to make them sound further away. Brass instruments can also be muted.
   Tenor — higher male voice.
   Falsetto — someone with a lower voice singing much higher than their normal range.

3) Acoustic guitar — e.g. played by strumming or plucking six or twelve strings.
   Electric guitar — e.g. needs an amplifier and loudspeaker to be heard.
   Bass guitar — e.g. has only four strings, is pitched lower than electric and acoustic guitar, needs amplification.

4) Baroque

5) A military band is a marching wind band, with woodwind, brass and percussion. A brass band has brass and percussion. A jazz band can include woodwind, brass, percussion and any other instruments too, and sounds quite different.

6) Piano trio — piano, violin, cello.
   Clarinet quintet — clarinet, first violin, second violin, viola, cello.

7) MIDI — musical instrument digital interface
   Sampler — record, process and play back samples of music
   Remix — mixing together samples of pop or dance music to a fast drumbeat, often speeded up
   Sequencer — computer program that records and replays many tracks of music together

Pages 76-78 (Exam Question)

Tracks 30 and 31

   a) Flute *(1 mark)*

   b) Piano *(1 mark)*

   c) Shape B *(1 mark)*

   d) The left hand of the piano has chords, the right hand melody imitates the flute part. One follows the other around. / The melodies interweave in a two-part texture at a similar pitch. / The parts are contrapuntal.
      (1 mark for each sensible comment up to a maximum of 2 marks)

   e) Flute, clarinet *(1 mark for each)*

   f) Strings *(1 mark)*

   g) Chromatic *(1 mark)*

   h) Shape C *(1 mark)*

   i) Crescendo *(1 mark)*

Section Six
— Western Classical Tradition 1650-1910

Page 104 (Warm-up Questions)

1) There were sudden changes in dynamics (no crescendos or diminuendos).

2) a) A small group of solo instruments.

   b) A larger group of accompanying instruments (often a string orchestra).

3) A set of variations played over a repeated bass part (basso ostinato).

4) A note that clashes with a chord, but which is followed by a note belonging to the chord (usually a tone or semitone away from the first note).

5) Treble, countertenor (or alto), tenor, bass

6) A solo vocal piece, backed by an orchestra — it's used to show the thoughts and emotions of the main characters.

7) Handel

8) E.g. clarinet

9) Three movements — first movement in sonata form (quick), second movement in ternary or variation form (slow), third movement in rondo, variation or sonata form (quick).

10) Exposition, Development and Recapitulation.

11) Clock Symphony

12) E.g. Mozart, Beethoven.

13) Approximately 1820-1910

14) In an undertone.

15) A song for one singer and a piano.

16) E.g. *Introit, Dies Irae, Pie Jesu*

Pages 104-107 (Exam Questions)

Track 32

   a) Acciaccatura *(1 mark)*

   b) Violin, flute *(1 mark for each, up to a maximum of 2 marks)*

   c) Andante (allow largo, larghetto, adagio) *(1 mark)*

   d) Any two of:
      - Simple, clear, balanced phrases
      - Diatonic harmony/major or minor tonality
      - Homophonic texture (melody with accompaniment)
      - Typical Classical orchestra — dominated by the string section
      - Second movement of a symphony (i.e. a slow tempo)

- Clear pulse
- Consistent tempo
(1 mark for each, up to a maximum of 2 marks)

e) Any of:
- The first section is major (G major), while the second section is minor (G minor) OR it modulates from major to minor OR it modulates to the tonic minor.
- Dynamics change from piano to forte.
- The first section is generally legato, while the second section is staccato.
- There are similar rhythmic features (double dotted rhythms) in both sections.
- Higher instruments have the melody in the first section, lower instruments have the melody at the start of the second section.
- The 'ticking' motif continues throughout (but is much less prominent in the second section).
- The tempo is similar in both sections.
- Fuller accompaniment in second section so thicker texture (with imitation/antiphony).
(Award 1 mark for a correct statement about one section of the excerpt, and award a further mark for a correct comparison with the other section of the excerpt, up to a maximum of 4 marks.)

f) Antiphony *(1 mark)*

Track 33

a) i) Requiem *(1 mark)*

ii) Day of wrath *(1 mark)*

b) The excerpt opens with homophonic chords. — T
The bass drum plays on the off-beats. — T
The choir sing in unison. — F
The strings play ascending runs between the choral sections. — F
(1 mark for each, up to a maximum of 4 marks)

c) Any three of:
- When the orchestra is playing alone, the music is mainly homophonic (playing in chords).
- The sections with choir and orchestra are more polyphonic (the choir are singing overlapping parts, while the brass play fanfare-like melodies underneath).
- The texture is rich and thick throughout.
(1 mark for each, up to a maximum of 3 marks)

d) Quick/lively and agitated *(1 mark)*

e) i) Romantic period *(1 mark)*

ii) Any four of:
Instrumentation:
- The music uses a full choir, with a lot of singers — this has a dramatic impact, which was typical of Romantic music.
- The choir is accompanied by a large orchestra, with prominent brass and percussion playing accented notes. This is typical of Romantic music — the development of new instruments meant that composers could write for large orchestras, and composers used these to add drama.

Dynamics:
- Dynamics are generally loud throughout, with crescendos to increase impact — the use of very loud dynamics (even up to *ffff*) to add drama was common in Romantic music.
Harmony:
- This piece involves lots of dissonance/clashing chords and complex harmonies. This was typical of Romantic music — complex harmonies allowed composers to show emotions like pain (which is appropriate for a piece entitled Day of Wrath).
Pitch:
- There is a range of pitch — the female voices in the choir sing in a very high range, while the male voices, brass and lower strings are much lower. Romantic composers used a large range of pitch to add drama and emotion to their works. In the instrumental parts, this was often made possible by developments in instruments.
Tempo:
- The music is quick — it feels frantic and desperate, which adds drama.
Mood:
- This piece is very dramatic and emotional and has a big impact — this is a key feature of Romantic music.
(Award 1 mark for a correct feature that is typical of Romantic music, and award a further mark for a suitable explanation of the use of that feature, up to a maximum of 8 marks.)

Section Seven — Popular Music

Page 125 (Warm-up Questions)

1) Singing without accompaniment (i.e. no instrumental backing).

2) E.g. Michael Jackson

3) 1950s

4) An album with a theme linking all the tracks.

5) E.g. hard rock — loud and aggressive, dominated by distorted electric guitar.
Glam rock — theatrical and glitzy, with costumes and make up. It has a rock 'n' roll feel with catchy hooks.
Heavy metal — harder and more distorted than hard rock, with longer guitar solos.
Progressive rock — experimental and complicated, albums often had a theme.

6) John Lennon, Paul McCartney, George Harrison, Ringo Starr

7) A sound created on some Indian string instruments when the string is stretched or a finger is slid along it.

8) John Lennon

9) Automatic double tracking

10) E.g. it helps them engage with their fans.

11) E.g. 'Someone Like You' by Adele
'Sing' by Ed Sheeran

12) A lighter, more modern version of opera.

13) 4 sections of 8 bars. Sections 1, 2 and 4 use the main theme, section 3 has a contrasting theme.

14) Solo character song, duet, action song, chorus number

15) A phrase of music that represents a character, place or emotion.

16) E.g. to link parts of the film together.

17) To create the mood of a specific time or place.

18) Digital audio workstation software, such as Logic Pro or Cubase.

Pages 125-127 (Exam Questions)

Track 34

a) Clarinet *(1 mark)*

b) The trumpets play with a mute *(1 mark)*. This makes them quieter and alters the tone *(1 mark)*.

c) Perfect fourth *(1 mark)*

d) Any three of:
   - It starts off quiet/*p*/*pp*.
   - There's a crescendo on the word 'shows'.
   - This is followed by a louder section.
   - There's a diminuendo before the next section.
   (1 mark for each, up to a maximum of 3 marks)

e) Tenor *(1 mark)*

f) Any eight of:
   Rhythm:
   - Syncopation and cross-rhythms make Tony sound eager and give a sense of anticipation.
   - Driving rhythm from instruments in most of the excerpt sounds like it's moving towards something.
   - Trumpets blasts in 'miracle' and 'cannon ball' bits add to excitement.
   Tempo:
   - It has a quick, lively tempo (allow allegro/presto) which shows his excitement.
   Tonality:
   - It is in a major key, which shows he is looking forward to the future.
   Melody:
   - There are quaver rests in the melody, giving it a breathless, agitated feeling, showing that Tony is impatient for something to happen.
   - The long note on 'me' sounds triumphant.
   Lyrics:
   - The lyrics reflect his excitement — he's looking forward to a 'miracle'.
   - The language is positive — e.g. 'gleam', 'bright as a rose' which show his anticipation for the future.
   (1 mark for each, up to a maximum of 8 marks)

a) Major *(1 mark)*

b) Perfect *(1 mark)*

c) Any two of:
   - Overdubbing
   - Use of multitrack/4-track recording
   - DI techniques
   - Double tracking
   - ADT (automatic double tracking)
   - Panning
   (1 mark for each, up to a maximum of 2 marks)

d) IV and I *(1 mark)*

e) The lead vocalist sings alone for the first verse *(1 mark)*. The backing vocals come in on the third line of the first chorus, singing in harmony *(1 mark)*. In the second verse, they sing in call and response with the lead vocalist/the lead vocalist sings a question (the call) and the backing vocals answer (the response) *(1 mark)*.

Section Eight — Traditional Music

Page 146 (Warm-up Questions)

1) African slaves in America.

2) Syncopation is when the accent is shifted from a strong beat onto a normally weaker beat.

3) I I I I IV IV I I V IV I I (V)

4) E.g. trumpets, trombones, saxophones, piano.

5) Improvised singing with nonsense words and syllables.

6) A West African instrument with 21 strings.

7) Any interval smaller than a semitone.

8) 2/4 or 4/4

9) Jamaica

10) When two or more styles of music are combined to create a new style.

11) - R'n'B
    - Mento
    - Calypso

12) Upstroke

13) Brazil

14) Bo Diddley beat

15) e.g. Love of my Life

16) Pentatonic

17) An Irish framed drum.

Pages 146-148 (Exam Questions)

Track 35

a) Riff *(1 mark)*

b) The hi-hat cymbals play on the beat in the 'bass guitar' section. — F *(1 mark)*
   An echo effect is used on the whispering in the 'bass guitar' section. — T *(1 mark)*

The bass guitar line changes when the electric guitar solo starts. — F *(1 mark)*
The rhythm guitar plays during Carlos Santana's guitar solo. — T *(1 mark)*

c) Any six of:
- Carlos Santana uses a long decay to sustain notes.
- Pitch bend gives variety to the sustained notes.
- He uses hammer-on/pull-off to play fast scalic passages.
- He uses picking to play longer notes.
- Vibrato makes the sound richer.
- Different levels of distortion create different timbres throughout the solo.
- He slides/glissandos to some notes.
- He uses a wah-wah effect.
(1 mark for each, up to a maximum of 6 marks)

d) Call and response *(1 mark)*

e) Chorus *(1 mark)*

Track 36

a) Percussion *(1 mark)*

b)

(1 mark)

c) Singing in unison *(1 mark)*

d) (Sub-Saharan) Africa *(1 mark)*

e) Cross-rhythm *(1 mark)*

Section Nine — Western Classical Tradition since 1910

Page 163 (Warm-up Questions)

1) In the Wild West/on a ranch

2) Any one of:
- 3/4 time
- oom-pah-pah rhythm
- slow tempo

3) 2/4

4) The twelve chromatic notes in an octave arranged in any order.

5) Any two of:
- jazz
- classical music from the late Romantic period
- early twentieth century classical music
- British folk music

6) The opening of the new cathedral in Coventry.

7) Any two of:
- intense emotions
- angular/spiky melodies
- dissonance
- atonality
- unconventional forms

8) Any piece by Tavener, e.g.:
- Jonah and the Whale
- Song for Athene
- The Lamb
- The Protecting Veil

9) Any three of:
- pentatonic scales
- slow and fast sections
- dotted rhythms
- homophonic texture
- instruments such as the cimbalom and tárogató
- syncopation

10) Any two of:
- no clear key signature
- unusual time signatures
- new instrumental techniques

11) Short, repeated note or rhythm patterns

12) Any two of:
- additive melody
- metamorphosis
- phase shifting
- layering

13) Any two pieces by Riley, e.g.:
- In C
- Uncle Jard
- A Rainbow in Curved Air
- Salome Dances for Peace

14) Clapping Music

15) Tremolo

Pages 163-165 (Exam Questions)

Track 37

a) Offbeat chords *(1 mark)*

b) The woodblock sounds like horses trotting/ horses' hooves. *(1 mark)*

c) Any two of:
- cymbal
- xylophone
- woodblock
- piano
(1 mark for each, up to a maximum of 2 marks)

d) Any of:
Instrumentation:
- In the first section, only the strings, piano and woodblock play.
- In the second section, the whole orchestra plays.
Rhythm:
- In the first section, strong offbeat chords are played.
- Despite the offbeat chords in the first section, the rhythm is clear/the section is quite rhythmic.
- In the second section, there is a strong downbeat.
- The second section also features some syncopation in the accompaniment.
- The second section melody has triplet flourishes.
Texture:
- The first section is an accompaniment section without a clear melody.

- The second section sounds almost monophonic at the beginning, with nearly all of the orchestra playing the tune and only a few instruments accompanying.
- Throughout the second section, multiple instruments play the melody.
- The second section becomes more homophonic after the start.

Tempo:
- The tempo in the first section is slower than in the second.

Dynamics:
- The first section is quite quiet (*mp/mf*).
- Most of the second section is louder (*f*).

Articulation:
- The first section is mostly staccato.
- The second section is less staccato/more legato.

(Award 1 mark for a correct statement about one section of the excerpt, and award a further mark for a correct comparison with the other section of the excerpt, up to a maximum of 8 marks.)

e) Major *(1 mark)*

f) Any two of:
- It has a clear melody.
- There are repetitive phrases.
- The strings play a prominent role.
- The accompaniment is simple.
- The harmony is simple.
(1 mark for each, up to a maximum of 2 marks)

Track 38

a) Any three of:
- The horns play legato, the strings play pizzicato/staccato.
- The horns play long notes, the strings play short notes.
- The horn melody is conjunct/moves in steps, while the string melody is disjunct/moves in leaps.
- The horns use a small range of notes, while the strings use a large range.
- The horn part is an ostinato pattern/is repetitive, while the string part is more varied.
- The horn notes are all the same length, whereas the string rhythms are more complex.
(1 mark for each, up to a maximum of 3 marks)

b) Dissonance *(1 mark)*

c) Chromatic *(1 mark)*

d) Any three of:
- The dynamics are quieter.
- The music is more tonal/less atonal/less dissonant.
- The strings play a legato melody (they played staccato before).
- The string melody is more conjunct.
- The strings play longer notes.
- The woodwind add light-hearted/bird-like flourishes above the melody.
- The horns are no longer playing.
(1 mark for each, up to a maximum of 3 marks)

Page 167-185 — Practice Exam

Pages 168-177 — Section A

1 *Track 39*

a) SATB choir *(1 mark)*

b) i) Coronation/any other celebratory occasion *(1 mark)*

ii) Any two of:
- It's in a major key so it sounds happy.
- The trumpet fanfare sounds celebratory.
- The fast tempo (allegro) makes it sound joyful and upbeat.
- The word 'rejoice' is repeated.
- The timpani make the piece sound grand.

c) Perfect *(1 mark)*

Track 40

d) Flute *(1 mark)*

e) Cadenza *(1 mark)*

f) i) Classical *(1 mark)*

ii) Any one of:
- The concerto is a common Classical form.
- There is a complicated cadenza for the soloist to show off their skills.
- The soloist is accompanied by a standard Classical orchestra.
- The phrases in the orchestral section are balanced.
- The harmonies are simple.
- The texture is homophonic.
(1 mark)

2 *Track 41*

a) i) Minor *(1 mark)*

ii)

1	2	3	4
X	X	Y	Y

5	6	7	8
X	X	Y	Y

(1 mark for each pair of bars (1-2, 3-4, 5-6 and 7-8), up to a maximum of 4 marks)

b) Any two of:
- doubling
- echo
- vocoder
(1 mark for each, up to a maximum of 2 marks)

c) 'La la la' or 'Can't get you out of my head' *(1 mark)*
A catchy bit of tune or lyrics that is memorable/gets stuck in your head. *(1 mark)*

3 *Track 42*

a) Walking bass *(1 mark)*

b) Any of: G major/IV/subdominant. *(1 mark)*

c) Bar 2 *(1 mark)*

d) Portamento *(1 mark)*

e) i) blues

 ii) Any three of:
- 12-bar blues
- blue notes
- swung rhythms
- syncopated rhythms
- sad/mournful lyrics (e.g. rain, trouble, poor)
- the verse is 12 bars long
- the lyrics are 3 lines long with the first line repeated
- guitars
- improvised riffing
(1 mark for each, up to a maximum of 3 marks)

4 *Track 43*

a) Moderato (allow andante/quite slow/ adagio/larghetto) *(1 mark)*

b) Bartók (allow Kodály) *(1 mark)*

c)

(1 mark for each phrase mark, up to a maximum of 2 marks)

d) The first beat *(1 mark)*

e) Homophonic *(1 mark)*

f) Strings *(1 mark)*

5 *Track 44*

a) The Romantic period *(1 mark)*

b)

(1 mark for each correct note or correct interval between two adjacent notes, up to 6 marks)

c) Begins major *(1 mark)*
 Modulates to minor *(1 mark)*

6 *Track 45*

a) Perfect fourth *(1 mark)*

b) i) Trumpet *(1 mark)*

 ii) Any one of:
- cymbals
- timpani
- triangle
- glockenspiel
- piano
(1 mark)

c) Legato *(1 mark)*
 Conjunct *(1 mark)*

Track 46

d) Any two of:
- It opens with a fanfare, which makes it sound heroic.
- It's in a major key, which gives a positive feel to the music and represents the heroism of the player's quest.
- The main theme is smooth but also has leaps, representing the highs and lows of the quest.
(1 mark for each, up to a maximum of 2 marks)

e)

1	2	3	4	5	6	7	8
A							B

9	10	11	12	13	14	15	16
C						D	D

(1 mark each for writing A, B and C in the correct positions, and 1 mark for writing D in both correct bars, up to a maximum of 4 marks)

7 *Track 47*

a) Caribbean *(1 mark)*

b) The second option is correct. *(1 mark)*

c) Any three of:
- In the first half, the rhythm follows a 3-3-2 pattern.
- In the second half, it has a steady 4-beat pattern.
- The first half has syncopated rhythms.
- The second half has little syncopation/mainly on-beat rhythms.
- The first half has longer notes (crotchets and dotted crotchets).
- The second half mainly has running quavers.
(1 mark for each, up to a maximum of 3 marks)

d) Any two of:
- It's in a major key which sounds happy — this makes it suitable for a carnival.
- It has a bright, lively tempo so sounds fun.
- It's easy to dance to, which is suitable for a carnival.
(1 mark for each, up to a maximum of 2 marks)

8 *Track 48*

a) pianissimo/piano/mezzopiano/quiet *(1 mark)*

b) Any one of:
- Regular, quick rhythm
- Constant/repeated quavers (allow semiquavers)
(1 mark)

c) i) Minimalism *(1 mark)*

 ii) Any five of:
- Constant pulse/driving rhythm
- Repetitive cell structure/short repeated phrases/ ostinatos
- No clear melody
- Gradual build up to complex texture
- Gradual build up to complex rhythm
- Notes gradually added/gradual changes in phrases

- Not atonal/music is modal (accept tonal)
- Diatonic/no dissonance
- No sudden changes in dynamics
(1 mark for each, up to a maximum of 5 marks)

Pages 178-185 — Section B

9 a) There is 'ticking' in the second movement (which continues throughout most of the movement).
(1 mark)
The ticking is created by quavers/quavers alternating between two notes/pizzicato or staccato quavers. *(1 mark)*

b) Any two of:
- It's a slow movement (andante), which is typical of the second movement of a symphony.
- The key of the symphony is D major, but the second movement is in a related key (the subdominant).
- There are modulations within the movement.
- There are two main themes with variations.
- It's written for a fairly large orchestra.
- The orchestra is string-dominated, but with independent woodwind parts.
(1 mark for each, up to a maximum of 2 marks)

c) G major and G minor *(1 mark)*

Tonic and tonic minor *(1 mark)*

d) Any eight of:
- Haydn varies the theme by playing it on different instruments — e.g. the first time it's heard, it's played by the first violins, whereas the second time the melody is heard, the violin part is doubled by the flutes.
- He also changes the accompaniment — e.g. at first, the bassoons, second violins, cellos and double basses play the ticking, but at other points, the flutes and bassoons play the ticking.
- He changes the role of the accompaniment too — sometimes they just play ticking, sometimes they play chords or sextuplets.
- These changes in instrumentation (both in the melody and accompaniment) create different timbres and textures throughout the movement (e.g. added viola chords make the texture thicker).
- For part of the movement, he creates antiphony between the first and second violins, which varies the texture even more.
- The melody itself is varied on different occasions — e.g. by extending it by a bar or adding extra notes/ornamentation/sextuplets.
- The theme is sometimes played in a different key (at first, it's in G major, but one version is in E♭ major, an unrelated key).
- The dynamics change — it's generally quiet (either *p* or *pp*), but towards the end it is played *f*.
- At some points, only a small part of the theme is played, to create a variation on the theme.
(1 mark for each, up to a maximum of 8 marks)

10 a) i) An album with a theme that links all the tracks.
(1 mark)
ii) Any two of:
- crossfade from previous track
- introduction of fictional performer/Billy Shears (the concept is that it's a concert by a fictional band)
- audience noises (applause, crowd noise)
(1 mark for each, up to a maximum of 2 marks)

b) i) Any two of:
- sitar
- tambura
- tabla
- dilruba (accept esraj)
- swarmandal/Indian harp
(1 mark for each, up to a maximum of 2 marks)
ii) Any one of:
- (acoustic) guitar
- violin
- cello
(1 mark)

c) Any eight of:
- Surreal lyrics (e.g. 'marmalade skies') make it sound weird. The images created by these lyrics are psychedelic.
- Electronic effects make it sound surreal.
- Panning is used at the beginning to unbalance the listener.
- A Lowrey organ creates an unusual sound.
- Electronic effects (different playback speeds and ADT) make the vocals in the verse sound weird and unearthly.
- Close-miking gives the instruments an intense sound.
- Distortion on the guitar adds to the surreal feeling.
- Unusual instruments (such as the tambura)/ unusual combinations of instruments create an unexpected sound.
- There are noticeable differences between the verses and choruses — the verses are in 3/4, and the choruses are in a faster 4/4 and in a different key.
- The choruses are more typical of rock/pop, whereas the verses are more surreal. The change between the sections has the effect of lurching between different realities.
(1 mark for each, up to a maximum of 8 marks)

11 a) Any two of:
- Two voices singing in unison make it sound like a chant.
- The repetition of lyrics also gives a chant-like feel.
- The lyrics have a political subject — the US immigration authorities.
(1 mark for each, up to a maximum of 2 marks)
b) Any two of:
- Western classical music
- Hip-hop/rap
- Latin American music
(1 mark for each, up to a maximum of 2 marks)

c) Any two of:
  - faster tempo
  - dance feel
  - more instruments enter
  - syncopation
  (1 mark for each, up to a maximum of 2 marks)

d) Any of:
  Rock elements:
  - It has electric and bass guitars, drum kit, piano and vocals, which is a standard rock line up.
  - Smooth is in 4/4, as most rock songs are.
  - Smooth is strophic, which rock songs often are.
  - It has catchy riffs — a rock influence.
  - Technological effects are used, particularly on the guitar — rock music often uses different effects.
  - There's a prominent guitar solo, which is common in rock music.
  Latin American elements:
  - There's Latin percussion such as guiro, timbales and congas.
  - Trumpets and trombones are a salsa (jazz) influence.
  - It has lots of syncopation.
  - Although the lyrics are mostly in English, there are some Spanish words.
  - The bass line is similar to a tango bass line — it often moves between the tonic and the dominant.
  - There's a break a bit like a salsa-break, when the line 'Or else forget about it' is sung without any accompaniment.
  (1 mark for each, up to a maximum of 8 marks. If only one genre has been referred to, award no more than 6 marks.)

12 a) Any one of:
  - It doesn't have the typical oom-pah-pah rhythm/ doesn't have a strong downbeat and weak offbeats.
  - There is syncopation.
  (1 mark)

b) Any two of:
  - The woodblock sounds like horses trotting.
  - A hoe-down is a dance used to celebrate the end of hay-making or other farmwork.
  - American folk melodies are used.
  (1 mark for each, up to a maximum of 2 marks)

c) - The woodwind and brass sections in 'Saturday Night Waltz' are reduced (e.g. only one flute, bassoon and oboe/no tuba and only one trombone), while there are full woodwind and brass sections in 'Hoe-Down'.
  - There's no percussion in 'Saturday Night Waltz', while there is a large percussion section in Hoe-Down (timpani, xylophone, snare drum, woodblock, bass drum and cymbals).

- In 'Saturday Night Waltz', the melody line is often played by one instrument or section (e.g. the main melody is introduced by the oboe before being played by the first violins), while in 'Hoe-Down', the melody is passed around the strings, brass and woodwind.
(1 mark for each, up to a maximum of 3 marks)

d) Any eight of:
  Tempo:
  - 'Saturday Night Waltz' has a slow tempo, which gives it a subdued feel.
  - The tempo is faster for a few bars at the start of the E major section, which emphasises the more subdued mood when the slower section B starts.
  Dynamics:
  - After a loud, dramatic beginning, the dynamics in 'Saturday Night Waltz' are fairly quiet throughout — never more than *mf*.
  Tonality:
  - It is quite diatonic — there is no dissonance to create tension.
  - The E major section is brighter, creating contrast with the E flat sections and making them seem more subdued.
  - The tonality at the start is ambiguous, which makes the diatonic sections seem more reassuring and gentle — there's no tension or confusion about the key.
  Instrumentation:
  - 'Saturday Night Waltz' uses a reduced woodwind and brass section, which creates a thinner texture and a softer sound.
  - The melody lines are often played by only one instrument (or one section), giving a quiet, soft sound.
  - There is no percussion, so there are no percussive, harder sounds.
  - The flute adds soft ornamentation on top of the melody.
  Texture:
  - The accompaniment is often quite simple, with a thin texture.
  - It's homophonic — there's no polyphony to generate excitement or tension.
  Articulation:
  - 'Saturday Night Waltz' is legato throughout, adding to its gentle mood.
  (1 mark for each, up to a maximum of 8 marks)

Index and Glossary

Index and Glossary

Index and Glossary

Index and Glossary

H

habanera A 19th century Cuban dance with a distinctive dotted rhythm. **141**

hammer-on A guitar technique that allows you to play notes quickly and in a **legato** style. **65**

Handel 80, 81, 87

harmonic A technique on stringed instruments (including guitars) that produces a high, ringing note. **64**

harmonic interval The difference between two notes played at the same time. **28**

harmonic minor scale 8-note scale using notes from the **minor key** except for the seventh note, which is sharpened by one **semitone. 25**

harmonic progression A series of chords. Another name for a **chord progression. 36**

harpsichord A keyboard instrument shaped like a small grand piano. It was popular in the **Baroque** period. **57, 66, 80, 89**

Haydn 81, 88-91, 94-96

heavy metal A type of **rock music** that uses a lot of **distortion. 113**

hemiola When the music feels like it's in triple time when it's actually written in duple time, or vice versa. **14**

heterophonic In heterophonic music all the parts have different versions of the tune. **45**

hip-hop Popular music with African-American and Caribbean influences. It features rapping, **DJing** and **beatboxing. 141**

Hoe-Down 150, 152

home key The key that a piece of music starts and ends in. **44**

homophonic Where the tune is accompanied by chords, keeping to roughly the same rhythm. **45, 47, 88, 90**

hook A catchy tune used in pop music and musicals. **110, 111, 113, 118, 120**

I

imitation A phrase is repeated with little variation. Could be one instrument or voice, or two or more imitating each other. **46, 83, 87**

imperfect cadence A **cadence** that usually moves from chord I, II or IV to chord V. **42, 43**

impressionism Late 19th and early 20th century music that focuses on the mood of music. **157**

improvisation Music that's made up on the spot by a performer, often based on a given chord progression or set of notes. It's used a lot in jazz. **91, 109-111, 131, 132, 134-137, 139, 143**

incidental music Music written to be performed as part of a play. **119**

Indian classical music 114, 115, 159, 161

instrumental section 111

interrupted cadence A **cadence** that moves from chord V to any chord except chord I. **42, 43**

interval The gap in pitch between two notes, played one after another or at the same time in a chord. **28, 29**

inversion (chord) Using a chord in a position other than its **root position. 37, 38**

J

jazz Music with lots of **syncopation**, **improvisation** and quirky harmonisation. Influenced many different musical styles, such as **hip-hop** and **salsa. 69, 111, 119, 131, 132, 137-139, 143, 154, 161, 162**

Jenkins, Karl 103

K

key signature Sharps or flats just before the **time signature**, to tell you which key the music's in. **11, 24-26, 44**

Kodály 157, 158

L

larghetto 60-66 beats a minute. Broad and slow, but less so than **largo. 18**

largo 40-60 beats a minute. Broad and slow. **18**

Latin ballad 141

layering Using technology to record several parts separately and layer them one on top of another. **46, 109**

ledger lines Extra lines added above or below the stave, to write high or low notes. **16**

legato Play smoothly. **19**

leitmotif A phrase or piece of music that represents a person, place, time or emotion in film music or musicals. **121, 123**

libretto The words of an **opera. 86, 155**

Lied A **Romantic** song for one singer and piano. The lyrics are often in German. **102**

Liszt 99, 100

Logic Pro 124

loop Section of music repeated over and over. **46, 75, 160**

Love of my Life 143

Lucy in the Sky With Diamonds 116

M

major key A **key** using notes from a **major scale. 24, 26, 90**

major scale Series of eight notes. The **intervals** between them are: **tone**, tone, **semitone**, tone, tone, tone, semitone. **24**

major triad A **triad** with an **interval** of four **semitones** between the bottom and middle notes, and three semitones between the middle and top notes. **35**

male voice choir A **choir** made up of two groups of **tenors** as well as **baritones** and **basses. 68**

mambo A break between choruses in salsa music. **139**

mass Piece of music sung as part of the Catholic church service. **85, 103**

Maxwell Davies 155, 156

mbalax A fusion of **sabar**, **pop** and Afro-Caribbean music. **138**

melismatic A single syllable of text is sung over a succession of notes. The opposite of **syllabic. 87, 109, 117**

melodic interval The difference in pitch between two notes played one after another in a tune. **28**

melodic inversion Version of a tune where the intervals between notes are the same but in the opposite direction (e.g. up instead of down). **83**

melodic minor scale A **minor scale**. Like the **natural minor** but with the 6th and 7th notes raised a **semitone** going up and reverting back to the natural minor coming down. Used for composing melodies in **minor keys. 25**

Mendelssohn 86, 100

mento Type of Jamaican folk music. **136**

Index and Glossary

Index and Glossary

Index and Glossary

Acknowledgements

The publisher would like to thank the following copyright holders for permission to reproduce material:

Track 1	*Caro Nome*, from *Rigoletto*, by Verdi. Performed by the Slovak Philharmonic Orchestra. Licensed courtesy of Naxos Rights US Inc.
Track 2	*Oboe Concerto No. 3 in G minor*, HWV 287, by Handel. Performed by the City of London Sinfonia. Licensed courtesy of Naxos Rights US Inc.
Tracks 3-13	Composed and performed by Sam Norman. © 2010 Coordination Group Publications Ltd.
Track 14	*Prelude in C♯ Minor*, Op.3, No.2, by Rachmaninov. Performed by Idil Biret. Licensed courtesy of Naxos Rights US Inc.
Tracks 15-26	Composed and performed by Sam Norman. © 2010 Coordination Group Publications Ltd.
Track 27	*Sonatina 3*, Op.36, *un poco adagio*, by Clementi. Performed by Sam Norman. © 2010 Coordination Group Publications Ltd.
Track 28	*St Louis Blues #2*, by WC Handy. Performed by Louis Armstrong. Licensed courtesy of Naxos Rights US Inc.
Track 29	*Courante*, from *Suite No. 1 in C major, BWV 1066*, by J.S. Bach. Performed by the Cologne Chamber Orchestra. Licensed courtesy of Naxos Rights US Inc.
Track 30	*Le Merle Noir*, by Messiaen. Performed by Patrick Gallois & Lydia Wong. Licensed courtesy of Naxos Rights US Inc.
Track 31	*Flight of the Bumble Bee*, by Rimsky-Korsakov. Performed by the CSR Symphony Orchestra. Licensed courtesy of Naxos Rights US Inc.
Track 32	*Symphony No. 101 in D Major,* Hob.I:101, "The Clock", 2nd movement: *Andante*, by Haydn. Performed by the Capella Istropolitana. Licensed courtesy of Naxos Rights US Inc.
Track 33	*Dies irae, dies illa*, from *Messa da Requiem*, by Verdi. Performed by the Hungarian State Opera Chorus and the Hungarian State Opera Orchestra Licensed courtesy of Naxos Rights US Inc.
Track 34	*Something's Coming*, from *West Side Story* Tenor: José Carreras Conductor: Leonard Bernstein ISRC: DE-F05-84-30602 Music by Leonard Bernstein Lyrics by Stephen Sondheim Published by: G. Schirmer, Inc. Original Catalog No: 415254 Produced by Hanno Rinke Recording Producer: John McClure Balance Engineer: Karl-August Naegler Recorded by Jobst Eberhardt Recorded by Wolf-Dieter Karwatky Editor: Jobst Eberhardt (P) 1985 Deutsche Grammophon GmbH, Berlin Licensed courtesy of Universal Music Group Limited.
Track 35	*Migra*, written by Carlos Santana, Tony Lindsay and Rachid Taha. © 1999 Divine Revelation Music (ASCAP) and Stellabella Music (BMI) admin. by Wixen Music UK Ltd. All rights reserved. Used by permission.
Track 36	*Gin-Go-Lo-Ba*, from *Drums of Passion*, by Olatunji. Licensed courtesy of Sony/ATV Music Publishing.

Acknowledgements

Track 37
Hoe Down, from *Rodeo*, by Copland.
Performed by Detroit Symphony Orchestra.
Licensed courtesy of Naxos Rights US Inc.

Track 38
Sunday Morning, from *4 Sea Interludes*, Op.33a, No.2, by Britten.
Performed by the London Symphony Orchestra.
Licensed courtesy of Naxos Rights US Inc.

Track 39
The King Shall Rejoice, HWV 260, by Handel.
Performed by the Thomas Tallis Chamber Choir and the Royal Academy Consort.
Licensed courtesy of Naxos Rights US Inc.

Track 40
Flute Concerto No.2 in D Major, K. 314, 1st movement: *Allegro aperto*, by Mozart.
Performed by Herbert Weissberg and the Capella Istropolitana.
Licensed courtesy of Naxos Rights US Inc.

Track 41
Kylie Minogue
Can't Get You Out Of My Head
(Davis / Dennis)
Published by EMI Music Publishing Ltd. / Universal/MCA Music Ltd.
(P) 2001 Parlophone Records Ltd. A Warner Music Group Company.
GBAYE0100913
Licensed Courtesy of Warner Music UK Ltd.

Track 42
Backwater Blues
Artist: Leadbelly
ISRC: US-CA2-89-00492
Music by Bessie Smith
Published by: Ludlow Music, Inc.
Recording Credits: (From the LP "CLASSICS IN JAZZ" H-369) 1953 (From the LP "LEADBELLY" ST-1821)
1963 (From the CD and Cassette "HUDDIE LEDBETTER'S BEST" C2-92075 & C4-92075) 1989
Recording Mix Date: 11 Oct 1944
Recording Mastering Location: Master date MMAS SD 8/6/1.
Recording Mastering Date: 17 May 1989
(P) 1944 Capitol Records Inc.
Licensed courtesy of Universal Music Group Limited.

Track 43
Buciumeana, from *Roman nepi tancok* (Romanian Folk Dances), Sz.56, by Bartók.
Performed by Virtuosi di Kuhmo.
Licensed courtesy of Naxos Rights US Inc.

Track 44
Prelude in Db Major, Op. 28, No. 15, "Raindrop", by Chopin.
Performed by Idil Biret.
Licensed courtesy of Naxos Rights US Inc.

Track 45
Main Title Theme, from *Star Wars: Episode IV — A New Hope*, by John Williams.
Performed by the Richard Hayman Orchestra.
Licensed courtesy of Naxos Rights US Inc.

Track 46
Main Theme, from *Final Fantasy*, by Nobuo Uematsu.
Performed by the London Philharmonic Orchestra.
Licensed courtesy of X5 Music Group.

Track 47
Carnivale, performed by the United States Navy Steel Band.
Licensed courtesy of Naxos Rights US Inc.

Track 48
Phrygian Gates, by John Adams.
Performed by Ralph van Raat.
Licensed courtesy of Naxos Rights US Inc.

Every effort has been made to locate copyright holders and obtain permission to reproduce copyright material.
For material where it has been difficult to trace the originator of the work, we would be grateful for information.
If any copyright holder would like us to make an amendment to the acknowledgements, please notify us
and we will gladly update the book at the next reprint.